Women
on High

To Fran,

Happy reading & hiking!

Robert A____

Women on High

Pioneers of Mountaineering

Rebecca A. Brown

Foreword by Arlene Blum

Appalachian Mountain Club Books
Boston, Massachusetts

Front Cover Photographs: Fanny Bullock Workman,
courtesy of the Appalachian Mountain Club Archives
Cover Design: Mac & Dent
Book Design: Kristin Camp
Interior images courtesy of The Alpine Club and
Appalachian Mountain Club Archives
Map Design: Carol Bast Tyler

Distributed by The Globe Pequot Press, Inc., Guilford, CT.

LIBRARY OF CONGRESS CATALOGING-IN-PUBLICATION DATA

Brown, Rebecca A., 1959-
Women on high : pioneers of mountaineering / by Rebecca A. Brown.
p. cm.
ISBN 1-929173-13-X (alk. paper)
1. Mountaineers—Biography. 2. Women mountaineers—Biography.
3. Mountaineering—History. I. Title.
GV199.9 .B76 2002
796.52'2'0922—dc21
2002009654

The paper used in this publication meets the minimum requirements of
the American National Standard for Information Sciences—Permanence
Paper for Printed Library materials, ANSI Z39.48–1984.

Printed on recycled paper using soy-content inks.

Printed in the United States of America

10 9 8 7 6 5 4 3 2 1   02 03 04 05 06

In Memory of Carmela Brown

1904–2002

Not to flinch when the way is hard,
not to dread the unknown.
DORA KEEN

Contents

THE HIGH MOUNTAINEERS

AFTERWORD

Foreword

In Victorian times, when mountains were considered mysterious, fearful places and women frail creatures in need of protection, a band of courageous female pioneers took to the heights, breaking the rigid rules of Victorian society and achieving remarkable physical feats and unprecedented personal fulfillment. Lacking sophisticated maps and the high-tech clothing and gear of today, these women overcame enormous obstacles from the society of the day—and the mountains themselves—to reach their lofty goals.

The question "Why do you climb?" is still posed endlessly to climbers. But imagine the incredulity with which this question was asked—and with which the answers to it were received—in an era when the "proper" role of a woman was thought to include little beyond bearing children and deferring to a husband. So what were the motivations of these women swaddled in long skirts and bound in corsets? What was it that caused them to defy convention?

Women on High documents how these undaunted women found challenge, adventure—not to mention escape—amidst the mountains of the world. Their achievements, significant even by today's standards, become amazing when the equipment and societal expectations of their time are considered.

When I began leading expeditions in the late 1960s, I had never heard the stories of most of these women. Indeed, only thirty-some

years ago, I also was told women lacked the physical and psychological stamina necessary to climb the world's highest mountains.
Nonetheless, in 1970 I organized the first all-woman ascent of Denali
(20,300') in Alaska; in 1976 attempted an ascent of Mount Everest,
in 1978 led the first American ascent of Annapurna I (26,320') with
a women's team, and in 1980 led an international women's team in
making the first ascent of Bhrigupanth (22,300') in the Indian
Himalaya. If leading expeditions was challenging in the 1970s, one
can only imagine the obstacles these women must have faced in the
1800s and early 1900s. If I had known years ago the extraordinary
climbing stories Rebecca Brown shares here, I have little doubt they
would have provided me with role models, support, inspiration, and
encouragement that would have made my own ascents easier.

Times are different now. Running through the Berkeley hills in
California or bouldering at our local rocks, I encounter large numbers of strong, lycra-clad women athletes. Society now imposes few
limits on women's achievements in the outdoors. I expect these
young women would be astonished to know that beginning nearly
150 years ago, other women, limited by society's perception of womanhood and clad in as much as twenty-one pounds of wool and felt,
pioneered difficult routes up mountains all over the world.

With her detailed research and keen sense of story, Rebecca
Brown has done us all a great service by bringing to life the compelling stories of these women. From the Alps to the White
Mountains, from the Andes to the Himalayas, these climbers took
the stage of adventure, overcame grave hardships and, with inspiring
energy and perseverance, reached the highest of heights.

Brown's research delivers new information about the "Sisters in
Mont Blanc," two intriguing Frenchwomen from very different social
and economic backgrounds, who lay early claim to the legendary
mountain. Maria Paradis, a poor, young woman who ran a souvenir
stand at the foot of Mont Blanc, decided to attempt climbing the
mountain as means of generating publicity and, thus, more business
for her shop. In 1808 she succeeded in reaching the summit and has
gone down in history as the first woman climber to reach the mountain's top. In contrast, the aristocratic Henriette d'Angeville con-

summated a long-term love affair with the mountain when in 1838 she became the second woman to reach the summit.

A succession of strong and determined woman clambered after them in the Alps, pioneering winter climbing and eventually guideless and manless climbing. Jane Freshfield wrote a book about her Alpine exploits, but authorship on its title page is listed only as "By a Lady"—for while a proper lady of that era might be forgiven climbing mountains, she would never draw attention to herself as the author of a book! Englishwoman Lucy Walker amazed the Alpine world by climbing the Matterhorn, and American Meta Brevoort reached the summit just a few days later. Elizabeth Le Blond, who as a young woman was sent to the Alps for her health, wrote *The High Alps in Winter*, which prescribed winter mountaineering as a cure for consumption and other ills. Considered a fragile invalid before she began climbing, Le Blond ultimately was considered one of the premier climbers of her day and went on to found the Ladies Alpine Club in the early 1920s.

In addition to the restrictive social expectations women climbers endured, they also had to contend with the constraints of the awkward—and often dangerous—clothing that impeded their climbing, whether yards of skirts, poorly designed boots, or corsets. Often women wore climbing knickers or bloomers beneath their long skirts or, upon reaching difficult section of an ascent, hitched up their skirts with a system of rings and ties. Some even took off their skirts and hid them beneath nearby rocks, climbing in pants or bloomers.

Brown's account of the achievements and competition for the world altitude record for women between Annie Smith Peck and Fanny Bullock Workman is unforgettable. While Annie Peck climbed Huascaran in Peru and Fanny Workman Pinnacle Peak in what is today Pakistan; both made claim to the record. Fanny, who was much wealthier than Annie, sent a French surveying team to Peru to evaluate Annie's claims, who found that Huascaran was only 21,800 feet high rather than Annie's estimate of 24,000 feet. After an acrimonious correspondence in the pages of *Scientific American* magazine, the Academy of Sciences in London determined that, indeed, Fanny had climbed higher than Annie.

Although they disagreed about which of them had climbed higher, these two formidable women did agree on the importance of women's suffrage. In 1911, on the 21,000-foot high summit of Nevada Coropuna in Peru, Annie unfurled a yellow banner stating, "Votes for Women." Similarly, Fanny was photographed at 21,000 feet on the Siachen Glacier in the Indian Himalaya reading a newspaper with the same headline, "Votes for Women."

Both women were conscious of being role models for female mountaineers as well. Annie wrote that she climbed to increase scientific knowledge, promote friendly relations with South America, and to inspire women. The Singer Sewing Machine Company even included a postcard of Annie in full mountaineering outfit with their new machines in the late 1890s. Fanny offered her experiences at high altitude "For the benefit of women who may not yet have ascended to altitudes above 16,000 feet but are thinking of attempting to do so."

Dora Keen, a wealthy young woman from Philadelphia, organized and led the arduous first ascent of 16,000-foot high Mount Blackburn in Alaska and ended up marrying her climbing companion George Handy. The book concludes with the story of Miriam O'Brien Underhill, another American woman, who pioneered manless climbing in the Alps and made numerous challenging ascents in Europe and North America from the 1930s to the 1960s.

To a large extent, the women portrayed in this book were climbing mountains not to make a statement about women, but for the sheer joy and the challenge of the ascent itself. In so doing, they expanded their horizons and enriched their lives, while broadening the possibilities for women everywhere. They are role models for any of us who want to live lives of challenge and adventure.

Thanks to Rebecca Brown for her scholarship and insight and for the fascinating stories she has unearthed and made available to all of us. They provide entertainment and inspiration to anyone—woman or man—who loves the mountains.

Arlene Blum
arlene@arleneblum.com

Acknowledgments

MANY PEOPLE MADE this book possible. For indulging my search for small historic details, providing unflagging encouragement, reading drafts and sharing ideas, and for helping in many other ways, I am grateful to a wonderful group of individuals.

In the long research process, Ellen Morrow and other staff members of the Littleton Public Library, the Boston University Medical School, the Alpine Club, and the Royal Geographical Society were of tremendous assistance. John Gerber of the Appalachian Mountain Club library graciously lent his time from the outset through final fact checking. Peter Rowan and June Hammond Rowan kindly shared correspondence from early White Mountain women. The Nancy FitzGerald Vaughan Fund provided needed assistance for research.

Ellen Gainor, Jane Roy Brown, and Gale Lawrence gave invaluable insight and feedback as friends, authors, and editors. As a friend and reader, Edith Tucker offered enthusiastic support throughout the entire project. I am grateful to Tim McCarthy for giving me the opportunity to start a career in journalism and then encouraging my writing outside the newspaper, and on this book. The good wishes from many others were always heartening during this work.

The editors of AMC Outdoors first raised the idea of investigating the lives of the Appalachian Mountain Club's earliest female members, and the idea for this book grew from a feature story for that magazine. I want to thank them for their continued encouragement for this project. Publisher Beth Krusi of AMC Books championed the book from the beginning and saw it through with clear vision. Blake Maher's gentle but incisive editorial guidance pulled the manuscript together, and Belinda Desher and Laurie O'Reilly brought the book to reality. It was a pleasure working with the small, dedicated, energetic AMC staff.

Finally, I am most grateful to family and friends. For their help in innumerable ways, I thank Elsie and Thom Brown, Barbara and Carl Belz, Nancy and Carl Martland, Rufus Perkins, Terri McNamara, and most of all, my husband, Harry Reid, whose good cheer, equanimity, flexibility, and belief in the final outcome truly made this possible. I thank him with all my heart.

SECTION ONE

Sisters in Mont Blanc

A lady climbs Mont Blanc. (ALPINE CLUB LIBRARY COLLECTION)

Chapter 1

Maria Paradis

(1778–1839)

I could not breathe, I could not speak.

Mont Blanc, French Alps
July 14, 1808

Maria Paradis would not, could not, take another step.* "Non, non, non," she muttered, and pitched forward into the snow. The young men dragged her to her feet for the umpteenth time that day. "Courage! Courage! You'll make it!" they urged. Propping her between them, they lurched on, slowly gaining on the towering white mass above them, the summit of Mont Blanc.

Stiff with cold, desperately tired, thirsty, and nauseous, Maria feared her heart would burst at any moment. Her ice-encrusted smock felt as heavy as chain mail. The men's voices sounded far away. But a persistent rasping filled her ears. Dimly, she realized it was her own breathing—panting like a chicken in the heat, she'd later say.

The procession came to yet another crevasse. Maria opened her eyes and squinted into the deep blue-green depths of this great glacial chasm.

---

* Based on accounts of Paradis' climb by Mrs. Aubrey Le Blond, *True Tales of Mountain Adventure*, and Henriette d'Angeville, *My Ascent of Mont Blanc*.

"Throw me in and go on yourselves!" she pleaded. But her friends just laughed. "You've made it this far. We're almost there. You will get to the summit!"

WHY WOULD MARIA PARADIS, a poor, thirty-year-old maid-servant living in the little French village of Chamonix two centuries ago, want to climb to the top of Europe's highest mountain?[1] Why would anyone? Most people considered mountains mysterious, frightening places. Certainly Maria knew people who still believed mountains harbored dragons, witches, and evil spirits; it's possible she feared this herself.

It turns out that Maria's motivations were entirely modern. She calculated the publicity would serve her well, and it did. Her summit experience was inauspicious—"They seized hold of me, they dragged me, they pushed me, they carried me, and at last we arrived," she recalled. "Once at the summit, I could see nothing clearly, I could not breathe, I could not speak."[2] Nonetheless, travelers sought her out to see for themselves the first woman in recorded history who'd achieved such a remarkable feat, and left her a few coins for the pleasure. "I have made a very nice profit of it, and that was what I reckoned when I made the ascent," she acknowledged years later.[3]

Maria Paradis shattered expectations of what women could do by entering—and surviving in—a world still largely unknown and mis-understood, and for this effort alone she deserves a place in history. But despite this accomplishment she should not be considered the world's first female mountaineer, especially since there's no evidence that after Mont Blanc she ever set foot on a mountain again. So what, then, makes a mountaineer? A. F. Mummery, one of the first great British alpinists of the nineteenth century, answered that a mountaineer is "any man who is skilled in the art of making his way with facility in mountain countries."[4] His contemporaries also considered a true mountaineer one who climbed year after year; simply making a few ascents was not enough. Today we think of mountaineers as pursuing peaks above snow line that require special skills in negotiating glaciers and rock. The nineteenth-century idea was somewhat broader, particularly in the northeastern United States, where the highest peaks reach but 6,000 feet and are snow-covered only in the coldest months. Then, as now, special gear or technical proficiency is not needed for climbing them. Today we call those who scale such mountains hikers, but in the nineteenth century they called themselves trampers and, more important, considered themselves mountaineers.

Leaving conveniences of using the male pronoun aside, it's natural to assume that Mummery had only *men* in mind when he stated his definition. After all, he was writing in England in 1894. How many women mountaineers could there have been? The fact is, there were quite a few, if one considers that the total number of mountaineers—male and female—was quite small (and still is). It was a heavily male dominated world, yet that small circle contained women of exceeding skill—including Mummery's own wife.

In the hundred years following Maria Paradis' painful, faltering ascent of Mont Blanc, women began climbing mountains in Europe and the United States and practicing the art of mountaineering with a vigor and verve that rivaled many of their male counterparts. They started slowly; it was thirty years before another woman ventured up Mont Blanc, and then two more decades before others began earnestly exploring the high peaks and passes of the Swiss Alps and the mountains of the United States.

But in the first half of the nineteenth century, mountaineering itself was a very new pursuit practiced almost exclusively by an elite group of male European naturalists, scientists, explorers, and their local guides. And even as it became more a sport and less a scientific excursion after about 1855, mountain climbing attracted an unusual and select group of women and men. These individuals possessed tremendous courage, the willingness to take great risks, and the ability to endure intense physical discomfort. In addition, mountain climbing was expensive and required lots of leisure time and money. In the sport's early years, many in the general public considered it a reckless and unjustifiable waste of time, the practice of rich, thrill-seeking eccentrics.

For men mountain climbing meant a certain amount of breaking with convention, but as the sport grew in popularity it became institutionalized in its own way. By the late 1850s British and European men had their own organization, the Alpine Club, which created an elite and a hierarchy even within the small mountaineering community. In the United States outdoor recreation and mountain climbing became quite popular—some would even say faddish—by the last decades of the 1800s. Unlike their British counterparts, the newly formed American mountaineering clubs quickly included women.

But if mountain climbing was somewhat unconventional for men, it was tremendously so for women. Female pioneers of mountaineering on both sides of the Atlantic faced obstacles substantially more severe than their male counterparts. For one thing, their dress was totally unsuitable for the activity, though an amazing number of women succeeded in spite of it. Voluminous skirts and viselike corsets made walking tedious enough, let alone mountain climbing. By the last years of the century many women solved the dress difficulty by leaving their corsets at home and stashing their skirts under rocks until after the climb. Overcoming other social conventions was not so easy.

Mountaineering was fraught with "unladylike" aspects: It introduced possibilities of inappropriate contact with the opposite sex, and many believed its extreme physicality would injure women's fragile bodies and minds. It also put women into situations where they could be construed as competing with men—and some male climbers, threatened by the suggestion of female competency, wanted to keep the mountains all for themselves. And women's lives, even those of the wealthy, were still extremely circumscribed. Through much of the Victorian era (which officially ended with the death of Queen Victoria in 1901) women occupied a pedestal from which they were viewed as exemplifying true femininity. In addition to moral goodness, this meant exhibiting frailty in mind and body. Particularly for women who did not have to labor on the family farm or toil in a factory, the proper place was in the home as wife and mother—not crossing a glacier or scrambling up a cliff.

But even in the midst of the age's stifling conventions, underlying socioeconomic and technological conditions were changing.

And nontraditional as women's mountaineering was, its inspiration is found in the crosscurrents of the very Victorian culture it defied. These factors also gave rise to general public interest in mountains and recreational mountaineering. They included the changing nature of work in the Industrial Age, which meant that for the first time, a large class of people had the wealth and time to devote to leisure. Improved transportation systems allowed the English to reach the Alps and Americans to travel to the mountains of New England and, by the end of the century, even to the West Coast with increasing ease. At the same time, long-standing beliefs in feminine frailty gradually weakened as medical thinking evolved and the emerging women's rights movement began influencing popular thought. "Physical education" and organized sports began to assume an important place in the training of young upper-class men, and eventually young women. And the mountains, once feared as the abode of demons, attracted a new, more adventurous public that looked to nature and wilderness for a physical and spiritual escape from the increasingly urban landscape.[5]

For women, climbing mountains was a way of finding meaning and enjoying a freedom of physical expression largely denied in other spheres of life. Men, too, enjoyed the departure from life's everyday concerns that mountaineering allowed. But for women, it also meant something more. It rekindled and satisfied the yearning for adventure that often flickered and died away as girls matured into the confining roles of adulthood. A turn-of-the-twentieth-century University of Chicago sociologist recognized this possible motivation. He attributed the "emergence of the adventuress and the sporting-woman" to Victorian society's insistence on female passivity. "Human nature was made for action," Prof. William Thomas asserted. He decried the modern woman's condition of "constraint and unrest," in which many intelligent, energetic, and well-bred individuals led lives with "no more serious occupations than to play the house-cat."[6] No wonder, he concluded, that women craved stimulation. Some found it in adventure (while others, he warned, found it in crime).

The number of women mountaineers in the nineteenth and early twentieth centuries may surprise many. And the number may have been far greater, for we only know about the ones who left some kind of record behind. Naturally enough, these are the ones whose achievements earned great notoriety, or who wrote about their adventures for publication. Today some may be familiar with a figure like Englishwoman Lucy Walker, who claimed one of her sport's greatest prizes by making the first female ascent of the Matterhorn. But other women with equally compelling stories have drifted off into the twilight of history. Their adventures deserve telling.

Some of these mid- to late-nineteenth-century women left fairly clear accounts of their climbs; others appeared briefly on the mountain stage and then disappeared, with even basic details of their births, deaths, and lives outside mountaineering rather obscure. Sometimes we are not even sure of their given names, but know them only through the names of their husbands. Some of the most gifted climbers left no written record of their own, so we have to rely on the impressions of those who knew them to get a sense of their spirit and motivation. Others left much clearer self-portraits. Many of these early mountaineers gave scant nod to the unconventionality of their sport, preferring, perhaps, to let their actions speak for themselves. Others acknowledged the iconoclasm of their endeavors, and spoke to some of the challenges they faced as women.

As the nineteenth century progressed, and then in the years before World War I, a growing number of women began climbing mountains and extensively chronicling their adventures. The three whose stories I chose to tell are Americans—Annie Smith Peck, Fanny Bullock Workman, and Dora Keen—who left a wealth of information about themselves. They were all from the Northeast— Peck and Workman from New England. They all completed their mountaineering careers before the war; they all cut their climbing teeth in the Alps; and each made pioneering expeditions to remote corners of the world. All three were intrepid, bold, colorful characters who were acutely aware—and proud—of their roles as women in a male-dominated domain.

In telling the stories of the early mountaineers I rely as much as possible on their own words and have also drawn on biographical and historical sources. In writing about them I express how the women acted, what they felt, and attribute motivation only when they made it clear themselves through their own writing. In introductions to the chapters, however, I use my own imagination and intuition about a climber's character to begin her story, though still basing the circumstances on historical records.

In 1808, when Maria Paradis contemplated climbing Mont Blanc, it's unlikely that many of her contemporaries, the ordinary peasants and workingmen and -women of Chamonix, would ever have considered such a venture. At nearly 16,000 feet Mont Blanc loomed over the village, the most massive peak in a forbidding mountain landscape. It was a perilous place, its steep, glaciated slopes rent with bottomless crevasses known to open up without warning and swallow men whole. It unleashed crashing avalanches, and its lightning and thunderstorms were legendary. "But what a terrible sight it was!" exclaimed one observer. "Seen from near and from far below, it stands alone, like a huge white monk swathed in an icy cope and cowl, dead and yet standing. . . . Its wide snow cap looks like a cemetery."[7]

The idea of climbing Mont Blanc, or any other mountain, for reasons other than the utmost necessity was still quite new, and for most people seemed unfathomable. For hundreds, if not thousands of years prior, when mountains were climbed at all it was for motives far from those of sport or recreation. Ordinary travelers went out of their way to avoid the peaks, not scale them. But throughout history a few men did brave the heights for purposes of conquest or religious conviction, and sometimes both. Moses, for instance, sought divine inspiration on top of Mount Sinai. In the second century B.C. the Carthaginian warrior Hannibal invaded Italy by crossing the Alps with a herd of elephants. Centuries later medieval monks and priests proved uncommonly avid climbers. The crosses, statues, and shrines they constructed still stand on some Alpine peaks. One of the earliest climbing feats involving specialized equipment was in 1492. King Charles VIII of France ordered his chamberlain to scale Mont Aiguille, near Grenoble. Until then these sheer rock buttresses were considered impregnable—and remain a challenging climb to this day. The chamberlain and his aides attacked the cliffs with ropes, ladders, and even iron claws on their hands. Once on top, they erected three crosses and said Mass. So difficult was this climb that it was not repeated until 1834.[8]

In the Enlightenment of the eighteenth century, hunger for scientific knowledge of the natural world grew, and among the educated, mountains started being viewed as places for exploration and discovery. Geographers, geologists, and other natural scientists became fascinated with the topography, climate, glacier movement, and additional aspects of mountain environments. To guide them to the heights—and also lug their equipment and provisions—they enlisted chamois hunters, shepherds, crystal collectors, and other locals who knew the mountains and were adept at Alpine travel. Explorers started writing about their journeys and offering advice on crossing glaciers and surviving in extreme cold. Some of these hardy souls even slept overnight on the snow and ice—defying another long-held belief that such behavior would be fatal.

As the highest of the Alps, Mont Blanc was the special object of many of these science-minded adventurers. By the mid–eighteenth century a growing number had designs on being the first to climb it. Some managed to attain considerable height, but no one made the top. To bolster efforts, in 1760 a wealthy Swiss naturalist promised to reward the first man on the summit. Many historians date the origin of serious mountaineering to this challenge and see in it the impetus that moved climbing from a strictly utilitarian pursuit bent on acquiring scientific knowledge to one that might be done for sport. And yet it took another quarter century and several attempts before the prize was claimed (the contents of the reward seem lost to time). A Chamonix guide named Jacques Balmat, along with a local doctor, finally made the summit in August 1786. "Since the conquest of Mont Aiguille nearly 300 years previously," wrote eminent Alpine historian W. A. B. Coolidge, "no more plucky feat of climbing has been performed, for in 1786 the glaciers were still regarded with awe. And it required enormous courage to venture one's life in these trackless deserts of ice, seamed everywhere with yawning chasms, ready to engulf the unwary visitor."[9]

Two decades later Jacques Balmat accompanied Maria Paradis on her historic ascent. It seems that some of his sons, who'd followed him in the nascent profession of guiding, may have instigated this groundbreaking escapade. As Paradis related the story, these young men were friends of hers, and they considered her strong, a good walker, and a "stout-hearted wench" who'd benefit from the notoriety. "Visitors will want to meet you, and they'll pay good money too, and that will help you," they told her. Being very poor, with her own son to feed, the idea had some appeal—but she didn't think she could make it. The guides assured her safety and promised they'd carry her to the top if need be. "And then all the world will know a woman went up," they pressed. She agreed to go.[10]

While Paradis achieved what she wanted from her climb, her ascent was roundly criticized in later years as a publicity stunt. One British Alpine historian labeled her self-promotional purposes "sordid," while a Canadian commentator labeled her motivations "mercenary" and dismissed her as being "hauled up like a sack of potatoes" to boot. Even contemporary adventurer and writer Dervla Murphy has asserted that her climb "hardly counted." Henriette d'Angeville, the next woman to climb Mont Blanc, sniped that in contrast to Paradis, she was the first female on the summit "capable of remembering her impressions."[11]

But the fact remains that Paradis succeeded in her goal. Hers may not have been the most auspicious start for women climbers, but it was the first step. The next step, and arguably the expedition that truly started women's mountaineering, came in 1838 with Henriette d'Angeville's ascent of Mont Blanc. Like Paradis, she was French, and she too took some barbs for her supposed motivations in climbing. D'Angeville is often overlooked today, perhaps because some interpretations of her achievement—as will become clear—have not been kind. But unlike Paradis, she was not a one-mountain wonder. She climbed Alpine peaks before and after Mont Blanc, and she planned, organized, and paid for the entire Mont Blanc expedition herself. She is the first woman ever to have undertaken this kind of initiative.

Henriette d'Angeville and her guides on the summit of Mount Blanc.
(ALPINE CLUB LIBRARY COLLECTION)

Chapter 2

Henriette d'Angeville

(1794–1871)

Follow your path with confidence.

Mont Blanc
September 4, 1838

The guides looked down at Henriette d'Angeville curled in the snow, fur cloak pulled tight around her, fast asleep without a care in the world.* They knew she was proud, rich, and uncommonly determined, but what they didn't know was whether she could go any farther. At more than 15,000 feet, they all felt the toll of climbing in frightening cold and thin air. They glanced at each other, unsure what to do. None of them had ever taken a lady up Mont Blanc, and very few had expected her to get this close to the summit in the first place.

Should they let her rest and then point her in what seemed the most reasonable direction: downhill? Or should they keep moving higher? This noble lady had performed valiantly so far. If she couldn't make it the rest of the way, more than one guide thought, it wouldn't be the worst thing. They could all just turn around, go back to camp, and at least enjoy hot food, drink, and some much needed rest. But others resisted giving up.

---

* Based on Henriette d'Angeville, *My Ascent of Mont Blanc*.

After all, she'd hired them to do a job. As long as she was willing, they'd keep driving toward the top. But doing that meant keeping her conscious.

"We've got to wake her up!" one exclaimed.

"Maybe she's already dead," another offered.

"It's impossible!" grumbled head guide Joseph-Marie Couttet. "This is the last lady I take up Mont Blanc."

That remark penetrated Henriette's torpor. She groaned, rolled over, sat up, and shook her head. The brim of her oversized hat flopped emphatically.

"If I die before reaching the summit," she exclaimed, "promise me you'll carry my body to the top and leave it there!"

The men couldn't help but smile. She was nothing if not courageous—more so than most of the gentlemen they'd guided up.

"Have no fear," Couttet sighed. "You will reach it—dead or alive."

But Henriette's eyelids were already fluttering. She toppled over, asleep once again. Couttet swore under his breath. He called her name, but she didn't flinch.

One of the younger guides stepped forward. "Should we carry her? I can do it; I'm still strong enough." Kneeling by her, he asked loudly, "Mademoiselle, do you want to be carried?"

Henriette jerked her head up. "I will not be carried!" She got to her knees, clutched her alpenstock, and planted it before her. With two men at her elbows, she staggered to her feet. The gleam returned to her eyes as she faced up the snowy slope. "I intend to make the whole journey on my own two feet. Truly there would not be much merit in going up Mont Blanc on someone else's back!"

THREE DECADES STOOD between the Mont Blanc ascents by Maria Paradis and Henriette d'Angeville's. During that time the popularity of mountain landscapes grew tremendously. Inspired partly by growing interest in natural history, partly by Romantic notions of the redemptive value of unspoiled nature, and partly because the Napoleonic Wars ended in 1815, ordinary tourists began traveling to the Alps to admire such wonders as the Mer de Glace, the spectacular glacial ice flow near Chamonix. "Walking" or "pedestrian tours" started becoming popular summertime activities, particularly among the British. Tourists trekked from village to village, enjoying the spectacular Alpine scenery, breathing in the crisp, clean air, and relishing the time away from their increasingly squalid cities.

While most of these visitors contented themselves with appreciating mountains from afar, some ventured off the beaten path and explored the higher terrain. A few were women, but they have left only the sketchiest details of their adventures. The mother-daughter team of Mrs. and Miss Campbell is a case in point. They were British, but not much else is known about them, including their full names. What we do know is that they were among the earliest women to make an Alpine traverse, meaning they went up one side of a mountain and down another. In 1822 they crossed the Col du Géant, a rugged 11,000-foot pass in the Mont Blanc range. It was a long, arduous climb during which the guides lost their way, forcing the group to spend the night in an unplanned bivouac, staying warm as best they could without proper clothing, equipment, or shelter. The Campbells remained unfazed, and despite the befuddled guides found a route down the next day. Encountering them on his way up Mont Blanc, another climber noted, "These ladies have shown how female intrepidity may finally surmount danger, where even the experience of guides may fail."[1] To the Campbells, then, goes the distinction of being the first women we know of who demonstrated Mummery's criterion of "facility" in the Alps.

When Henriette d'Angeville announced her intention to climb Mont Blanc, women were not unknown in the mountains, but few, if any, possessed her ambition. Keep in mind that at this time only a small number of men climbed, though they practiced the art with increasing vigor. In the first decades of the 1800s men reached the summits of some important peaks in the Swiss Alps, including the Jungfrau (13,670 feet), several in the cluster of summits that make up Monte Rosa (the second highest mountain in Europe, its summits ranging from just less than 14,000 feet to more than 15,000), and the Finsteraarhorn, at 14,026 feet the highest peak in the Bernese Oberland. The joy of discovery, the desire to survey uncharted

Romancing the Mountains

What was it about mountains that so inspired people 150 years ago? Although most didn't share Henriette d'Angeville's obsession with climbing to the top of one of the world's greatest peaks, many did express a fervent love of mountains and nature in general.

In both the United States and Europe this interest in nature and natural landscapes may be interpreted as a response to the rise of the Industrial Age. Cities were getting crowded and increasingly dirty; new market-driven economies made some rich and left others destitute. Many people began searching for a truer, healthier, purer sense of the world. Their critique of industrial growth and rampant materialism found expression in artistic Romanticism. Late-eighteenth-century and early-nineteenth-century writers, poets, and artists flocked to the Alps and to the mountains of New York and New England to paint and contemplate. Their sometimes mystical reveries inspired others to look to nature to recall an earlier golden age of virtue and innocence.[1]

In Europe the theme of seeking the sublime in mountain landscapes was associated with poets and aesthetes, including Samuel Coleridge, Percy Bysshe Shelley, and John Ruskin. In the United States nature writers such as Henry David Thoreau and John Muir sought spirituality and a greater sense of self in wilderness. In 1867, while walking a thousand miles from Indiana to the Gulf Coast, Muir wrote: "You cannot feel yourself out of doors; plain, sky, and mountains ray beauty which you feel. You bathe in these spirit beams, turning round and round, as if warming by a camp-fire. Presently you lose consciousness of your own separate existence: you blend with the landscape, and become part and parcel of nature."[2]

At the same time, many feared that spirituality was losing ground to modern advances. In the United States, Appalachian Mountain Club president Charles Fay struck this theme when he complained that he lived in "an age when the struggle for life has become so bitter, when the ideals of the past are losing their hold, when religion . . . is becoming generation by generation a less potent influence." In such a time, he asserted, people needed to look for something more, "something tangible, which by its inherent majesty may speak for the superhuman—of power in comparison with which man's is weakness."[3] Fay—and many others —found it in the mountains.

Women, as much as men, suffered the pressures of the changing society and were swayed by Romantic ideas of nature. Jane Freshfield, an Englishwoman who walked through the Swiss Alps in the late 1850s, expressed the Romantic vision by suggesting that being in the mountains could put one closer to God. "When listening to the 'voice of the mountains,' speaking in the thunders of the rolling avalanche, or the rushing of the mighty winds, surrounded by wondrous combinations of grandeur and beauty, we realise something of the vastness of an Almighty power."[4] Others noted the "mystical attractions of mountaineering" and the "religious fervour" of its first devotees.[5]

On her first attempt at mountaineering in the Alps a few decades later, Englishwoman Helen Hamilton reflected this enduring theme. "We plodded on again, up and up, until at last all sounds were left behind. We were in a region of peace, so all-embracing, so unearthly, that it seemed we had been admitted, however unworthy, into a sanctuary whose existence we had not so much as suspected."[6]

terrain, the quest for scientific insight, and a growing competitiveness to first conquer a major peak drove these early climbers. Some felt so deep a dedication to mountains and climbing that it defined their lives. But few possessed d'Angeville's passion for scaling a single mountain. Indeed, no one embodied the Romantic obsession with mountains more than she.

Her affair with Mont Blanc was by no means an easy one. She yearned for the mountain as any expectant lover; when she caught sight of it, distant, icy, and unattainable from her Geneva home, she suffered all the anguish of the unrequited: "My heart beat furiously, my breathing was impeded, and deep sighs burst from my breast."[2] For more than a decade she only watched from afar, resigning herself to walking up lesser peaks, waiting for the moment when she might consummate her passion. "It seemed to me that I was in exile in Geneva and that my real country was on that snowy, golden peak that crowned the mountains," she opined. "I was late for my wedding, for my marriage . . . for the delicious hour when I could lie on his summit. Oh! When will it come!"[3]

What accounted for her peculiarly personal relationship with Mont Blanc? Some interpreters focus on her character as a supposedly repressed, forty-four-year-old spinster. French Alpine historian Claire Engel called her "bold" and "haughty," a "romantic woman longing for glory and excitement: a thwarted maiden lady in her forties . . . who loved Mont Blanc because she had nothing else to love." Engel further suggested that d'Angeville possessed a "morbid passion for self-advertisement." Her rather outrageous climbing costume, Engel speculated, was a response to the notoriety—some would say outrage—inspired by the novelist George Sand, who in the late 1830s flaunted men's clothing on the streets of Chamonix. D'Angeville's Mont Blanc outfit included voluminous checkered wool trousers, unusual attire indeed for a woman. But the effect was anything but masculine. With pants and matching tunic cinched at the waist with a wide belt, accessorized with a luxurious black boa and a plumed beret, she cut quite an alluring figure for a mountaineer.[4]

D'Angeville's background may lend different insight. She was born to an old aristocratic family at the height of French revolution-

ary terror and endured a sad and violent childhood. She lost her
father for a time to prison, and her grandfather forever to the guillo-
tine. She settled in Geneva sometime after her father's death in
1827, and there continued a lifelong enjoyment of vigorous walking
among the hills. She didn't detail her personal disappointments as an
adult, but she made it clear that by standing on France's highest summit she hoped to vanquish some lasting sense of hurt:

> It was not the puny fame of being the first woman to venture on
> such a journey that filled me with the exhilaration such projects
> always call forth; rather, it was the awareness of the spiritual well-
> being that would follow. This one memory would counterbalance
> many others less welcome. Happy a thousand times those who are
> not impelled to flee the disillusion of life's trivial round and to seek
> refuge in fantasy![5]

Whatever her psychological baggage, d'Angeville possessed
remarkable curiosity, immense energy, perseverance, and flair. She
considered it sign of character, if not an outright duty, to follow
through on one's convictions, no matter how unconventional or
unpopular. Her sense of adventure went beyond mountains; days
after her success on Mont Blanc, she expressed her desire to fly in a
balloon and explore the ocean in a diving bell.[6] To friends who persisted in asking why she pursued such extraordinary interests, she
gave an eloquent and simple explanation: "Because that is where I
find my particular pleasure and happiness. The soul has needs, as
does the body, peculiar to the needs of each individual. And a desire
to subordinate these needs to the general rule is as unreasonable as
an attempt to bring up the weak on precepts laid down for the strong,
or vice versa."[7]

In August 1838 she decided the time had come for her attempt
on Mont Blanc. She'd climbed some minor mountains near
Chamonix that summer and noted with some pride that she suffered
none of the fatigue afflicting other travelers. Brimming with confidence, she returned to Geneva and boldly announced her plans. Her
friends thought her mad. Though male climbers attempted Mont

Blanc with growing regularity, the mountain still held its grand and terrifying mystique. Even a guidebook written more than a decade later read, "The ascent of Mont Blanc is attempted by few; those who are impelled by curiosity alone are hardly justified in risking the lives of the guides. It is a somewhat remarkable fact that a large proportion of those who have made the ascent have been persons of unsound mind. Those who have succeeded have, for the most part, advised no one to attempt it."[8]

Friends and strangers alike besieged her with questions. Why Mont Blanc? Why not travel to some safer place, like other tourists? She patiently explained why the ordinary cultured places were not for her: "I am among those who prefer the grandeur of natural landscapes to the sweetest or most charming views imaginable . . . and that is why I chose Mont Blanc." Besides, she added, a woman's perspective might prove of interest, for "women sometimes see and feel things very differently than men." She also reminded questioners that the only previous woman on the summit had been incapable of remembering her impressions.[9]

But her reasoning failed to convince many. "In a city of twenty-five thousand [Geneva]," she wrote, "I was supported by exactly three." She didn't name these three, but she also counted a brother and a female friend for a total of five allies.[10] Her personal physician tried to talk her out of the adventure, but gave up and simply suggested how she might equip herself for the cold. Others warned she'd suffocate, bleed from her eyes, nose, and ears, or simply perish in a storm. But she shrugged off the "general outcry of amazement and disapproval." Residents of Geneva, she decided, "are particularly prone to a general conformity of manners and behaviour, and are uncommonly surprised by any action that deviates from the ordinary patterns of life."[11]

In the weeks before the ascent she scurried around the city assembling gear and setting her affairs in order. The preliminaries included putting together her remarkable outfit. Flamboyant, yes, but the costume was not assembled simply for show. It represented her best assessment of how she might protect herself from a harsh and unrelenting Alpine environment, while maintaining a modicum

The Dress Question:
"It Is Time We Should Reform"

Henriette d'Angeville gave a tremendous amount of
thought to how she should outfit her Mont Blanc expedition. Even today, with the advantages of featherweight
titanium gear and high-tech fabrics, most of us still feel we
carry too much when we climb mountains or hike long
distances. It's hard to conceive of carrying the weighty
equipment that was considered cutting edge a century ago.
Harder still is imagining climbing in a long skirt and a
corset.

Corsets—which exerted as much as 70 pounds of pressure on women's midsections to achieve a wasplike figure—
made breathing difficult and damaged internal organs.
Heavy, voluminous skirts made even nonathletic movement awkward. For these reasons, many nineteenth-century
women began viewing dress as a metaphor for how they
approached their lives. Though it symbolized true womanhood and femininity, they considered it a yoke dragging
them down with literal and figurative weight.

Women began asking themselves whether they should
dress for practicality and mobility, or in the conventional
styles that reinforced their confining lives and subjugation
to men as the "weaker sex." Particularly in the United
States, where the dress reform movement took hold in the
second half of the nineteenth century, appropriate dress
became seen as a key to enjoyment and health in all circles of life, including outdoor recreation.

As the wife of one of the founders of the Boston-based
Appalachian Mountain Club and an experienced mountain walker herself, Mrs. W. G. Nowell (we don't know
her given name) knew the subject of dress well. Ladies
tended to climb slowly, she said, "not always from physical

weakness, but from skirt entanglements." Sometimes the wearers became so entangled in brush and rocks that "jack knives had to be brought out to cut them adrift," leaving them looking "as if they had just come out of a London rag fair."[1]

But bruised vanity paled in comparison to the potential for serious injuries caused by long skirts when they snagged and sent women sprawling—sometimes during rock climbs and on other tough terrain. Dragging hems also dislodged stones and sent debris raining down on others. And then there was the weight. Dry, the full complement of a long two-layered skirt, plus knickers or bloomers underneath (the typical costume until well into the 1900s), weighed at least 10 to 15 pounds. Wet, all that wool flannel and stout cloth could easily double in weight. Frozen, it must have felt like a sheet of armor.

If women were to enjoy wilderness on an equal footing with men, Mrs. Nowell argued, they had to change their outfit. She fired off a salvo in the very first issue of the AMC's journal, *Appalachia*, in 1877: "Our dress has done all the mischief. For years it had kept us away from the glory of the woods and the mountain heights. It is time we should reform."[2]

———

of femininity. She listed her clothing as follows: a man's shirt; English flannel "to be worn next to the skin"; Scotch plaid, fleece-lined trousers and jacket with "six layers of wool to protect the chest and back"; a leather belt "arranged to sit rather low on the waist"; a Scotch plaid bonnet, trimmed with black fur and affixed with a green veil; a large straw hat "with a green lining and four strings to hold it firmly in place"; a black velvet mask; a black boa; plaid coat; a fur-lined pelisse, or cloak; and two pairs of nailed boots, one large enough to accommodate layers of silk and wool stockings. The costume, minus the pelisse and plaid coat and counting only one pair of boots, weighed 14 pounds. Fully appareled, she wore 21 pounds of clothing. (In comparison, a climber today layered in today's lightweight "technical" fabrics and synthetic or goose down insulation might wear 8 pounds on her back and feet.)

D'Angeville's list may sound excessive, but men, too, piled on the clothes. From the advanced perspective of 1892, one mountaineering historian remarked that it "excites the wonder of a modern climber [to consider] the enormous load of clothing carried by his predecessors."[12] For instance, an English climber who braved Mont Blanc the year before d'Angeville reported he "had on a good pair of lamb's wool stockings, two pairs of gaiters, two pairs of cloth trousers, two shirts, two waistcoats, a shooting coat, and over all, a blue woolen smock frock, a nightcap, three handkerchiefs round my neck, two pairs of woolen gloves, and a straw hat, from which hung a green hood. For my eyes, a pair of spectacles, and a green gauze veil."[13]

In a flat straw basket Henriette carried a few personal items, including those suggested by her doctor. Among them were "an enormous fan in case I had to be given air, [and] a small one, to fan myself"; cucumber face cream; "a friction brush in case of numbness"; a rubber pillow; a "first-class" telescope; a thermometer; a spirit kettle, tea, and alcohol; a flask of lemonade and one of almond milk; a looking glass "to examine the skin and see what ravages the mountain air has wrought"; a notebook and pencils; and a folding pocketknife.

Perhaps the most important part of her preparation was hiring guides, the men on whom the success of her venture—and her life— would ultimately depend. She selected as leader Joseph-Marie Couttet, at forty-five a year older than she and the veteran of nine Mont Blanc ascents. She described him as short, witty, and intelligent. She commissioned five others, the youngest of whom was thirty-nine; all had climbed Mont Blanc at least once. The guides secured six porters.

By the time Henriette arrived in Chamonix, the town was abuzz with news of her plans. If anything, residents there were even more incredulous than in Geneva. "The natives of the valley regard Mont

Blanc with such awe that they did not credit that a woman conspiring to conquer it could be in full possession of her senses," she observed mildly. Bets flew back and forth: would she turn back at the first deep crevasse, or die in an avalanche? This flurry of commerce surrounding her mortality took her aback, but she kept a confident public face. Even when two guides backed out because of "sinister forebodings," she simply replaced them and went on with her work. As she saw it, she'd scrutinized all aspects of the plan, especially the dangers, and made her decision. Once one's mind is made up, she advised, "everything but the advantages should be forgotten and one should remain fixed in one's intentions, unmoved by the praise or blame of the world. Otherwise life would be frittered away in every kind of uncertainty and doubt." Privately, however, she calculated that if an avalanche buried her guides, it would create six widows and twenty-seven orphans.

In the meantime she attended to the all-important provisions. Couttet warned that on no account should the men go hungry on the three-day, two-night expedition. His food list for the twelve men illustrates just how arduous an undertaking it was, and why Henriette commented that "luggage becomes a real burden" on Mont Blanc expeditions:

> 2 legs of mutton
> 2 sides of veal
> 24 fowls
> 6 large loaves
> 18 bottles of St. Jean [wine]
> 1 bottle of brandy
> 1 bottle of vinegar
> 1 bottle of fern-syrup
> 12 lemons
> 3 lbs sugar
> 3 lbs chocolate
> 3 lbs prunes
> 1 cask of *vin ordinaire* for the porters

To this she added her own rather spare requirements: lemonade, a pot of chicken broth, a flask of barley water, and white wine.

When the morning of departure arrived, the crowds astounded her. People gathered on every balcony and jammed the hotel court-yard. Soldiers fired off honorary rounds. While the guides appeared composed, Henriette described herself as "filled with uncontrollable joy." She checked her pulse. Sixty-four, four beats higher than usual. Someone remembered one more detail: the pigeon, taken so climbers could send it flying back with a message when they reached the top. Finally the clock struck six, and it was time to go. Henriette's maid burst into tears. The soldiers saluted and the crowd cheered.

D'Angeville's nervous excitement followed her onto the mountain. "I did not walk," she reported. "I flew." Her years of tramping among the mountains paid off. She felt surefooted and strong, "reminiscent of my prime." When the party reached the first crevasse, she agreed to tie a rope around her waist, a precaution against falling into the deep fissure. Then she jumped while one guide held the rope and another assisted her with a long stick for her to hold. But as she watched the men leap across unaided, she asked that she take the same course next time. She proudly noted the guides' decision: "She goes as well as we do and fears nothing. We'll not interfere."

The group camped high on the mountain at granite buttresses called the Grand Mulets. D'Angeville approved of her tent, constructed of brown canvas and "elegantly appointed with two candles impaled on sticks." Even at 10,000 feet there came a social call. Henriette received a card from a Polish nobleman, also intent on the summit, who was camped nearby. While she received him, an English party joined the throng. This group included another female—a canine named Diane. This dog, d'Angeville reported, scored a major "first" by climbing and descending the mountain on her own four feet. (This record was evidently forgotten, for years later another dog claimed a "first" on Mont Blanc.) After sumptuous suppers, guides from all three groups traded stories and songs as the day faded into night.

Henriette enjoyed the festivities, but when the camps quieted down and the others went to sleep she remained wide-eyed. She tossed and turned in her sheepskin bed, bothered by aching limbs and cold feet. Finally she got up and pulled back the tent flap. A magical world greeted her. The far summits glistened in the moon-light, and nearby ice formations assumed fantastic, sparkling shapes. Spellbound, she jotted down a few notes. "Nothing spoke of the earth as we know it," she wrote. "I felt I had been transported into a new world, that the great mystery of creation would be revealed to me on this mountainside, and that my proximity to the heavens would expose me to divine inspiration."

Indeed, as she sat there contemplating time and space, she did imagine a voice from the sky. It told her: *Do what is right, and follow your path with confidence.* At that moment an avalanche crashed down a distant slope.

Finally it was 2:00 A.M., time to rise. She had twelve cooked prunes and a cup of soup, all she'd eat for the next sixteen hours. As the other two parties prepared to leave, Henriette pressed Couttet to get ahead of them. No, he counseled, she'd already proved her courage; better to let the others break trail. She started climbing quickly nevertheless, and the guides urged moderation. "Slowly," they advised. "Walk as if you did not want to reach the top."

The rising sun illuminated a spectacular landscape. Granite pin-nacles necklaced with rose-tinged snow towered overhead. Far below them stretched the mouths of the great glaciers, the rugged forested foothills, and the green pastures and tiny villages dotting the valleys. The climbers wended their way through huge ice chunks and around crevasses of deep blue depths. In one hand d'Angeville wielded her alpenstock, a stout wooden pole tipped with a curved iron spike. Like a walking stick, it helped her maintain balance, and in case of a fall on a steep slope, she could drive its spike into the snow to stop her sliding. She moved along easily, pleased with how her layers of wool, silk, and flannel kept her warm. But a fresh, cold wind stung her face, and she realized that for all her careful preparations, she'd neglected shaded spectacles. She squinted through watery eyes at the dramatic scenery, so enthralled that she nearly pitched off a snow bridge into a crevasse. "Instead of gazing at dangers far off, look at those beneath your feet," one of the guides implored.

By the time they passed 13,000 feet and reached the final, pre-cipitous granite-and-ice wall guarding Mont Blanc's summit cone, many in the group suffered the effect of the altitude. Exhaustion, migraines, and nausea afflicted several of them. Henriette, however, still felt quite fit. She suggested the most indisposed should wait at the bottom of the wall. These men refused, noting it would not do for their reputations should a woman make the summit while they stayed below.

Ascending the wall was like climbing a very steep ice staircase. Henriette dug in her nailed boots, focusing on each tricky step and trying to ignore the sheer dropoff below. But the altitude, the exer-tion of nearly twelve straight hours of climbing, and the effects of too little sleep started catching up with her. Her pace faltered. She stopped and leaned on her alpenstock, breathing hard. A strange feeling of inertia came over her, and she could hardly keep her eyes open. Through a "lethargic doze," she somehow staggered up the wall and onto the final broad snowfield leading to her goal.[14] There, sur-rounded by such what seemed a snowy blanket, she succumbed to sleep.

Though the guides had to keep prodding her awake, "the thought of giving up never entered my spirit," she later avowed. Refusing to be carried, she did consent to clutching a stick held like a stair railing by two guides, one ahead and one behind her. But shortly before the summit she cast off the stick, and "alone and unaided, took the three steps that lay between me and victory." Gone was her lover's sweetness. Now she viewed her actions with the hard mien of a conquering warrior: "At twenty-five past one, I finally set foot on the summit of Mont Blanc and drove the ferrule of my stick into its flank, as a soldier plants his standard on a captured citadel."

Her fatigue swept away by the thrill of triumph, she marveled at the scene around her. The magnificent view to the ends of the earth surpassed even her wildest fantasies. She scrawled in her book:

> This astonishing sky, the desolation of colossal mountains, the fret-work of clouds and grey peaks, the eternal snows, the solemn

silence of the wastes, the absence of any sound, any living being, any vegetation, and above all of a great city that might recall the world of men: all convinced to conjure up an image of a new world or to transport the spectator to primitive times. There was a moment when I could believe I was witnessing the birth of creation from the lap of chaos.

The guides raised glasses of champagne, then hoisted her onto their shoulders—she was higher than Mont Blanc! they cheered. The pigeon sped off with a parchment declaring success tied to its foot. Henriette took her pulse—108. Her thermometer read eight degrees below zero Centigrade. She wanted to linger, but the guides pointed at clouds massing on the horizon and promising bad weather. As they prepared to start down, she inventoried the condition of her little troupe. Blisters covered several men's faces, and they smiled at her through bleeding lips; one's vision was blurred; migraine racked another. Curious, she withdrew her mirror and faced a monstrous visage: her skin stretched swollen and purple from the roots of her hair to the base of her chin, and crimson streaks filled the whites of her eyes. But that hardly mattered. Aside from this "mask of horror," she felt "physically and morally in the best of health, light of foot and sound in wind and limb."

The way down proved far easier than the ascent. Henriette moved quickly, unhampered by symptoms of altitude sickness. She delighted in learning to glissade down the slopes, leaning with her alpenstock anchored behind her in the softened snow. But during a rest stop she accidentally let go of her alpenstock, and it slipped down the mountain and into a crevasse. She must have looked positively devastated at losing her treasured tool, for one of the porters volunteered to retrieve it. With a rope the other men lowered this brave fellow into the chasm, and when they hauled him out again he proudly returned the stick.

The party made it back to the Grand Mulets in only four hours. With the wind picking up and a storm imminent, they ate a hasty supper and stowed their gear under rocks. The men deemed erecting a tent out of the question in the coming gale, so, like them,

Henriette found a little crevice among the rocks and wedged in, trying to shelter herself as best she could. She pulled on her warmest clothes, wrapped herself in a fur-lined sleeping bag left her by the English party, donned her velvet mask, and tried to sleep. Dawn arrived none too soon. Stiff and sore, but still awash in triumph, she plodded down the rest of the way.

The party was still miles from town when the cannons started signaling victory. The crowds in Chamonix greeted her "like a queen," Henriette giddily noted. "Here's to courage, in whatever dress!" one man bellowed. A young woman ran up and embraced her. "Dear lady," she gushed, "what an heroic exploit! What a glorious day for womanhood!" Despite the cheers, d'Angeville was well aware of the fickleness of public opinion. "Suppose an avalanche had swept me away," she mused to herself. "Those who now heap praises on me would not have shed a tear, and the general opinion would have been summed up in one declaration: 'The foolish woman! Her desire for fame has cost her dear indeed!' "

She basked in glory for the rest of the day. She couldn't hear too many times how anxious crowds kept watch through telescopes for her progress. Later she luxuriated in a hot bath, then held forth at her hotel's evening supper. But she did take the time to send out a special invitation for the next day's celebratory feast. It was to Maria Paradis. Perhaps flush with esprit de corps, perhaps having a new appreciation of what her predecessor had faced, she viewed Paradis with new understanding and respect. Now sixty, white-haired and still petite, Paradis showed up at Henriette's hotel room early the next morning. D'Angeville embraced her, and bestowed a new title on the women she called the "little peasant":

"We are," she declared, "Sisters in Mont Blanc."

After Mont Blanc, Henriette did not rest on her success, but continued climbing for twenty-five years. She scaled twenty-one new peaks, plus Mont Blanc once again. She ascended her last mountain at age sixty-five. "The Oldenhorn is my twenty-first Alpine ascent," she wrote a friend in 1859, "and it will probably be my last, for it is wise at my age to drop the alpenstock before the alpenstock drops me."[15]

The same year as d'Angeville climbed her last mountain, a young Englishwoman named Lucy Walker was just beginning her climbing career. Walker went on to become the first woman to climb the Matterhorn, which, after Mont Blanc, is perhaps the most legendary peak in Alpine history. Because of the Matterhorn, and her long list of other first-class ascents of more than 4,000 meters, Walker is usually remembered as the world's first female mountaineer. Ironically, Walker made her stunning Matterhorn achievement in 1871, the year d'Angeville died. It takes nothing from Walker's well-earned reputation to acknowledge that Henriette d'Angeville, because of her accomplishments, deserves recognition as the true pioneer of women's mountaineering.

Ladies and guides on the Mer de Glace, near Chamonix, France, c. 1886. (ALPINE CLUB LIBRARY COLLECTION)

Chapter 3

Doing the Mountains Jolly

The Titlis, Swiss Alps
June 1859

*Lantern light cast strange shadows as the small group followed the two
guides through the dark farm fields and up steep wooded slopes.* Jane
Freshfield walked along with her husband, her son, and her friend
C____, breathing in the cool, sweet predawn air and wondering what
was in store for them. Her apprehension rose with the sun. When its first
fiery rays struck the snow-flecked mountains ahead of them, Jane thought
their destination looked exceptionally high and very far away. She wondered if she was alone in feeling anxious. She'd spent much of the night
tossing and turning, picturing herself climbing the Titlis. Now the mountain loomed ahead of her.*

*The going proved even more strenuous than she imagined. At the
roughest spots the guides tied ropes between themselves and their clients'
waists in case of a fall. As they moved higher the rock slabs gave way to
snow and then hard-packed snow and ice. On a particularly steep and
icy gully, one of the guides seized his ax and started hacking out steps the
other climbers could follow. The second guide showed them how to plant*

---

* Based on "A Lady" [Jane Freshfield], *Alpine Byways*.

their alpenstocks in the snow on their uphill side, so that if their feet
slipped the stout staff would hold them. Slowly, but with growing confi-
dence, Jane made her way up the slope.

A few minutes later the whole party stood at the top of the gully. Jane
felt quite exhilarated and proud of herself. But then C____ spoke up.

"How are we to get down?" she asked nervously.

The practical Mrs. Freshfield suggested they postpone that issue until
the necessary time came. More immediately, she needed to attend to her
husband, who was looking pale indeed.

A FTER HENRIETTE D'ANGEVILLE'S success on Mont Blanc in
1838, women didn't exactly line up to follow in her footsteps.
Neither did many men. It took nearly two decades for the sport of
mountaineering to come into its own.

By the 1850s a growing group of men, many of them British, were
climbing with intense dedication. Historians call this period, beginning about 1857 with the establishment of the all-male Alpine Club
in London and ending in 1865 with the deaths of four men on the
Matterhorn, the Golden Age of mountaineering. Hotels and inns
catering to Alpine travelers started being built, and the first high-
altitude huts made multiday climbs and mountain traverses more
practical. A new cadre of *mountaineers* devoted whole summers to
exploring peaks, putting up new routes, and sharpening their skills
on known ones. Guiding emerged as a profession with its own set of
standards and expectations. Climbing for recreation, or "healthy and
manly amusement," gained in social respectability, and devotees no
longer felt compelled to couch descriptions of their sport with goals
of scientific advancement.[1] The Alps, a female traveler observed in
1861, had become the "playground of England."[2]

An American visiting Zermatt in 1859 encountered some hearty
young English climbers and observed, "Mountain climbing for them
has become a passion. To get to the top of the highest and most inaccessible mountains, to stand where man has never stood before, to
dare the avalanches, to cross the most frightful of the glaciers, is a
great ambition with them."[3]

During this time the lure of the peaks was not lost on women. Many of them joined organized pedestrian tours, and some struck off on their own. Several climbed significant peaks in the company of their husbands. A few of them wrote of their excursions, adding the first female voices to the emerging genre of mountaineering literature.

One pedestrian tourist who left the beaten track was Mrs. Henry Warwick Cole. From 1850 to 1858 she made three extended trips through the Alps, along the way completely circling Europe's second highest mountain, Monte Rosa (15,203 feet) on the Swiss-Italian border, and climbing some of the minor peaks around it. She described her perambulations in A Lady's Tour Around Monte Rosa, and also encouraged other women to explore the mountains. Her account appears to be the earliest book published by an English-woman on the subject of Alpine excursions. She reported encoun-tering a few other female walkers in her travels, including two English ladies "already past the noon of life" who'd just completed their own circuit of Mont Blanc.[4]

Not all people took their mountain walking as seriously as did Mrs. Cole. Others visited the Alps as part of their European grand tour and, in between socializing, walked up a few lesser peaks and vis-ited some of the celebrated natural sites. A physician and artist known only by the pen name Miss Jemima left a humorous little account of one of these early pedestrian tours. Her diary was discov-ered in a bombed-out London warehouse after World War II and later published as Miss Jemima's Swiss Journal.

In June 1863 Miss Jemima joined sixty-three other ladies and gentlemen on the first tour of the Alps conducted by excursionists Thomas Cook and Son Ltd. of London. Like other English tourists, they traveled by boat to France, then by rail to the Alps. There they encountered others "doing Switzerland jolly," as well as "doing" par-ticular peaks. Early on, Miss Jemima and her cohorts climbed the Montanvert glacier on Mont Blanc. As part of the spectacular Mer de Glace, this was an exceedingly popular tourist destination. They braved "dizzying heights" and "blue and crystal-lined jaws" of "yawning crevasses," Miss Jemima reported.[5] Prompted by their fear-lessness, the group members promptly dubbed themselves the "Junior

United Alpine Club," as distinct from that "other" Alpine Club.

Miss Jemima and her female friends were familiar with the moun-taineering feats of other women, though they made no pretense of following them. Their goals lay elsewhere: "Whilst M. and Mme. Angeville and Mrs. Winkworth* have conquered Mont Blanc and the Jungfrau, the Misses Jemima, Sarah, Eliza and Mary have settled the universally important baggage question and claim to have trav-eled the Alps with less luggage than any previous tourists," Miss Jemima declared.[6] It is interesting that she assumed that Henriette d'Angeville was a "Madame" in the company of a "Monsieur." Certainly that was the expected arrangement, though women moun-taineers sometimes bucked that convention.

Mrs. Jane Freshfield was an intriguing figure who bridged the gap between casual walking tourists such as Miss Jemima and ambitious mountain climbers such as Lucy Walker. In 1859 and 1860 Jane trav-eled through the Swiss Alps with her husband, Henry; son Douglas, who grew up to become president of both the Alpine Club and the Royal Geographic Society; a woman friend simply identified as "C____"; and a guide named Michael Couttet. She wrote about these excursions in *Alpine Byways*, a dainty little volume issued in 1861 under the byline of "A Lady." Mrs. Cole and Mrs. Freshfield knew each other; Jane referred to her predecessor's travels, and inscribed a copy of her book to Mrs. Cole "with kind regards."

The Freshfields liked to get off "the beaten paths," Jane tells us.[7] She and C____ were well aware that few if any women had preceded them. While they occasionally encountered other women in walking parties, their wanderings sometimes took them to villages so remote that no foreign lady travelers had ever been seen before. They always checked the *Livre des Voyageurs* in local inns to see if any women recorded climbing nearby peaks—and usually found none had. Still, Jane assured her readers that her climbs required "only ordinary powers of exertion or endurance." This nod to maintaining feminin-ity and social acceptability reveals the conventional wisdom of her

---

* Mrs. Stephen Winkworth was the first woman to climb the Jungfrau (13,670 feet). She made the ascent with her husband and guides in 1863.

Ladies Unattended

"The chief reason why women so seldom climbed fifty years ago," wrote Ladies Alpine Club president Elizabeth Le Blond in 1932, "was that unless they had the companionship of a father, brother, or sister, it was looked at as most shocking for a 'female' to sleep at a hut or a bivouac."[1]

Le Blond knew this firsthand. One of the premier mountaineers of her time, she "scandalized all London" in the early 1880s, as one horrified relative exclaimed, by staying out overnight with her guides. Such behavior contradicted the Victorian dictate that proper women not go "alone" with men who weren't family members. Le Blond was amply equipped, both financially and with a seemingly bottomless reserve of self-confidence and determination, to ignore protestations over her behavior and do what she wanted. But not everyone desired or was able to defy convention with her apparent ease.

The great English climber Lucy Walker was introduced to mountaineering in 1858 by her father and brother. Lucy developed a close and lasting professional relationship with her guide, but in their twenty-one years together they never climbed unchaperoned; they were always joined by one of the male Walkers. A younger nephew was the constant climbing companion of one of the first notable American alpinists, Marguerite ("Meta") Brevoort. In this case she interested him in trying the sport, and they began climbing together in 1865.

Women climbing together was unusual, but not unheard of, and some female partnerships were quite renowned for their accomplishments. Perhaps the first well-known female duo was the Pigeon sisters, Anna and Ellen. Between 1869 and 1876 these Englishwomen climbed sixty-three peaks and seventy-two passes, and made the first women's traverse of the Matterhorn from Breuil to Zermatt in 1873.[2] They usually hired guides, but also may have struck off on their own. The sisters had the reputation of being very fast climbers; one observer reported, "They simply flew."[3] They demonstrated that climbers need not be burly men, and some even attributed their speed to their petite physiques.

Though expert mountaineers, the Pigeons received a chilly reception from the male establishment embodied by the Alpine Club, apparently because they occasionally eschewed male companionship altogether. In 1892 Ellen wrote of how they were treated. "In days gone by, many A.C. members would not speak to us. . . . Now, people are more accustomed to lady climbers, and even solitary ones. We were the first, I think, to go unattended by a male protector, and we got on very well, but then two together must be pleasanter than one alone, when you must have guides."[4]

By the end of the century the moral tone had loosened somewhat, and women traveling alone did not prove nearly as shocking. But in the decades prior we may wonder how many women's dreams of climbing mountains were never realized for lack of suitable companionship.

———

day—that women must guard against "overtaxing" themselves. Although she took issue with a popular guidebook that declared the Gries on the Italian frontier "not a pass for ladies," she also believed women had limitations. One evening her family arrived at a hotel in the Bernese Alps and found both guests and staff in a state of high anxiety. A mother had allowed her two daughters to join a party going up the Oldenhorn (10,243 feet), and when they hadn't returned by dark, everyone expected the worst. The two girls eventually turned up unharmed, but Jane concluded that the climb "proved too long and fatiguing for ladies to undertake." She was apparently unaware that sixty-five-year-old Henriette d'Angeville had ascended the Oldenhorn just a year or two before.

Jane Freshfield was particularly proud of her family's ascent of the 10,627-foot Titlis, a picturesque peak just south of Lucerne. She was quite sure that she and nearby C____ were among the first few, if not *the* first, women to climb it. Before starting out from the village of Engstlen, she wrote, "The ascent is apparently a rather unusual one for ladies. And even while providing the necessary aid for the enterprise, I suspect that the good folks at Engstlen were somewhat incredulous to its accomplishment."

The Freshfield's Titlis adventure started at 3:00 A.M. when two local guides arrived at their inn. The pair thrilled fifteen-year-old Douglas by carrying rope and a hatchet—a sure sign, his mother noted, "that some real ice climbing might be expected." They were not disappointed. By midmorning they'd already climbed up steep rock slabs and ice-filled gullies. But the effects of altitude and exertion were wearing down Freshfield's husband, Henry. "When we reached deep snow, through which the walking was really fatiguing, his breathing became oppressed and painful," Jane reported. Henry wouldn't consider turning back, and the slope was too steep to stop and rest. So on they continued, creeping up to a narrow rocky ridge. From here the summit seemed just above. "But a deceitful little hollow intervened," Jane reported, and they plunged once more into heavy snow before finally pulling themselves to the bare, rocky crest. Happily, it was calm and sunny, and they basked on the rocks admiring "a scene of wild and striking grandeur." A guide found a tin visitors box tucked into the stone pillar marking the summit. There were no recent entries, "and lady visitors were apparently not numerous," Jane noted. It turns out her party may have just preceded Lucy Walker. Walker scaled the Titlis in July 1859, at the beginning of her first big season of mountaineering.

After enjoying the summit, the issue for the Freshfield party became getting down. When the group reached the steep gully where C____ had questioned the descent, they found that the afternoon

Unfeminine Exploits

Conventional ideas about their bodies and physical and mental capabilities presented some of the foremost obstacles for aspiring nineteenth-century women climbers. In the United States, where mountaineers prided themselves on doing things differently from their European counterparts and women sometimes outnumbered men on excursions of the early outing clubs, women still faced advice like this from one of the first American how-to-camp guides: "There are very few mountains that it is advisable for ladies to try and climb. Where there is a road or the way is open and not too steep, they may attempt it; but to climb over loose rocks and through the scrub-spruce for miles, it is too difficult for them."[1]

Until the late 1800s, "even the mildest female exercise regimens won little public approval," wrote Stephanie Twin, who has analyzed the evolution of women in athletics. "Hard work, ambition, diligence, and perseverance were considered unfeminine and so were women who displayed them." Demanding physicality was seen as a threat to women's health, and especially their reproductive functions. Physicians warned that the strain of too much physical activity on women's frail minds and bodies could harm their nervous systems, in turn jeopardizing their uteruses and leading to "weak and degenerate offspring." Falling—an obvious risk for mountaineer climbers—was considered quite grave, for it could cause "pelvic disturbances" and disrupt menstruation.[2]

While purveyors of conventional wisdom looked askance at hard physical exercise for women, other voices took a different tack. Equal rights activist Elizabeth Cady Stanton was one of the earliest to assert that vigorous activity would help shape stronger and healthier bodies, as well as intelligence and self-reliance. "We cannot say what the woman might be physically, if the girl were allowed all the freedom of the boy, in romping, swimming, climbing and playing ball," she wrote in 1850.[3] Others took up the cause and urged exercise, as well as dress reform, as healthy steps for women.

By the 1890s, especially among the better educated, Victorian womanly virtues were challenged by the "New Woman" who possessed independent spirit and athletic zeal.[4] In the early 1900s, the idea of the New Woman continued gaining strength. Canadian climber Mary Crawford was one of the most adamant advocates of mountaineering for women. In 1909 she addressed the question, "Should women climb mountains?" Her answer echoed the sense of expanding horizons and new choices for women, as well as the influence of Freudian psychology.

> [Mountaineering] is for women one of the new things under the sun and every fresh mountain is a delight. Ennui has no place in the vocabulary of a woman who climbs, the words which rout it are enthusiasm and exhilaration. Diseases of the imagination cannot be discovered anywhere on a mountainside, where Nature asserts herself so grandly to the consciousness and with such insistence that the "ego" and its troubles sinks out of sight.[5]

By 1920 a male writer informed readers that "the feminine mountaineer is by no means a modern phenomenon." Climbing is in fact "eminently suited for women, and they are taking to the sport in increasing numbers," continued Harold Raeburn, whose wife served as president of the Scottish Ladies Alpine Club. He then bestowed on the sport a most unassailable virtue. Alpinism, he confided, is "the secret to eternal youth."[6]

sun had softened the ice and snow. "C____'s previous problem was quickly solved," according to Jane. "The younger guide took her in his charge, and, holding her in a firm grasp, commenced a glissade, which increased to such a velocity that H____ looked on in perfect horror, almost expecting to see them both disappear in a crevasse at the end of their career!" But the guide knew what he was about, and the slide ended uneventfully. Relieved, the Freshfields "all descended merrily"—though not quite so hastily.

Down in the valley, the party expected to meet their horses and baggage brought along from Engstlen by some local men. But no one was there. As they discussed what to do, the sky let loose a tremendous thunderstorm. They all huddled under umbrellas, which they'd carried with them all day. When the storm passed, their guide Couttet went off to find horses. Douglas stayed with his father, now nursing a wrenched knee. Jane and C____ continued alone on the track toward the next village. But as they walked, another storm blew in and thoroughly drenched them, for they'd left their umbrellas behind. By the time they reached their new inn they presented a sorry sight.

"We made our *entré* in somewhat ludicrous plight, with our cloaks over our heads and wet up to our knees," Jane wrote. But their embarrassment quickly evolved into well-deserved pride. "The appearance of such 'unprotected females' evidently created some surprise when we entered the hotel, and said we had come from the Titlis," she observed.

Jane Freshfield allowed her readers just a few other glimpses of the ironic pleasure she took in defying assumptions about her gender. The clearest was an encounter with an old man who loaned her party a horse. As he walked with them, the older man asked Couttet how he liked guiding two ladies. Jane reported the rest of the conversation: " 'Ordinairement ceci va mal, et cela va mal! á fin tout va mal,' "* was his opinion; to which the sententious reply given by our good friend was, 'Mais, avec *mes* dames, tout va bien.'† Certainly a flattering report at the end of a long journey!"

---

* "Usually, this goes badly and that goes badly! In the end everything is bad."
† "But with *my* women, everything is fine."

By the mid-1860s many of the highest peaks in the Alps had been climbed at least once. But the most magnificent peak of all remained untouched: the Matterhorn. For alpinists, making it to the summit of this great lone pyramid rising over Zermatt was like the quest for the Holy Grail. Besides its steepness and great height, the Matterhorn (14,691 feet) is frightening for what mountaineers call exposure. It forces climbers out on rock faces where nothing remains below them but the glacier thousands of feet down. It is also a fickle mountain; clear days can suddenly dissolve into terrific thunder and snowstorms. Despite repeated attempts, the Matterhorn rejected all challengers until the summer of 1865.

On July 14 six well-known English climbers and a Chamonix guide finally made the top. But the mountain did not yield easily. On the descent a rope snapped, and four of the party, including the guide, plunged to their deaths.

"Shall we say that pride goes before a fall?" asked the Alpine historian W. A. B. Coolidge, who first visited Zermatt shortly after the accident. "Or shall we count it simply as a last expiring act of revenge on the part of the Spirit of the Mountains? . . . Never before had so many lives—still less those of three Englishmen—been lost at one time on a high peak, never before had such experienced climbers paid the penalty of a slip, . . . never before had victory in the Alps been so quickly followed by Death. . . . The cause of mountaineering seemed lost for ever, so deep and lasting was the impression made by this terrible event."[8]

For many, this tragedy marked a kind of loss of innocence, and ended the Golden Age of mountaineering for men. Five years after the accident Lucy Walker shocked the world by scaling the mighty Matterhorn. She achieved this just days before the mountain was climbed by Meta Brevoort, an American who had also set her heart on being the first woman on the summit. These two mountaineers inspired many others to follow, and their careers mark the beginning of what might be called the Golden Age for women.

SECTION TWO

The Golden Age

Lucy Walker and family, friends, and guides, 1870. Lucy sits at rear, with Melchior Anderegg to her left. Her brother is in the middle row, second from left; her mother next to him at right; her father is seated in the middle, front. (ALPINE CLUB LIBRARY COLLECTION)

Chapter 4

Lucy Walker

(1836–1917)

A Climbing Girl.

The Matterhorn, Swiss Alps
July 21, 1871

Lucy Walker focused on her toes, making sure her boot tip was wedged in the fracture of rock as firmly as it could be. She took a deep breath and lowered herself, probing with her other foot for a tiny ledge, a ripple—anything on which to get a purchase and continue climbing down. Below her heels stretched half a mile of thin, cold air. She forced herself to focus on the rock, on its texture beneath her callused fingers, on its solidity, on her ability to balance and shift her weight and move her feet and feel instinctively where the next safe step would be.

The rope pulled tight around her waist as she went, and she was thankful for the sensation of security. She never doubted that with her friend and guide Melchior Anderegg holding its other end above her she was in good hands, but it was impossible not to think of the men who'd died here six years before. Maybe they'd clutched this same flake of granite—maybe their boots had scraped the same rough rock. She scolded herself. Never, ever think about falling—her father had told her that on her

*very first climb more than a decade before. "Think it, you'll do it," he'd
admonished.*

*Still, she wondered fleetingly, had they a premonition before one of
them fell, and hurled three others into space?*

By REACHING THE SUMMIT of the Matterhorn on July 21, 1871,* Lucy Walker cemented her place in history as the first great female mountaineer. If she'd waited a day or two, it's possible that Meta Brevoort might hold that distinction, but in truth Walker had an outstanding career even without the Matterhorn. Over twenty-one summers she built a résumé of ascents that reads like an Alpine greatest hits list. Included in her ninety-five peaks and passes are the Eiger, Jungfrau, Monte Rosa, Weisshorn, Finsteraarhorn, Wetterhorn, Mönch, and Mont Blanc—some of the highest, most celebrated peaks in the Alps. She set the standard for female mountaineers after her, for many of her climbs earned her the coveted "first ascent by a lady."

Unfortunately for us, Lucy didn't leave any reminiscences about her experiences, making it impossible to know exactly why she embraced mountain climbing so wholeheartedly and how she felt about her extraordinary accomplishments. Acquaintances described her as the perfect Victorian young lady: unassuming, a charming hostess, a wide reader in several languages, a devoted friend. Even after she earned international notoriety on the Matterhorn, she was still described as modest and self-effacing. Climbing mountains seemed to be her only nonconforming habit; her other pastimes included croquet and needlework.[1] What she lacked in athletic training or background, she made up for with tremendous willpower and drive to succeed. In fact, the timing of her Matterhorn ascent was not accidental. Over the course of her career, as more women followed her into climbing, competition grew among them to reach a

---

* Some sources put the date at July 20. Frederick Gardiner, who was with her on the ascent, stated it as July 21 (*Alpine Journal* 31, 1917, p. 97). It was the nineteenth recorded ascent of the mountain, the tenth from the Zermatt (Swiss) side. The others were from Italy.

summit first. Lucy may well have accelerated her start for the Matterhorn because someone tipped her off that Meta Brevoort was close to launching her own attempt.

Like Jane Freshfield, Lucy Walker lived in a family of climbers. Her father, Frank, was among the first members of the Alpine Club, and younger brother Horace was also an expert climber. From mid-century on, the Walkers left the family lead-dealing business in Liverpool each summer and visited the Alps. Like many others in the mountaineering fraternity, they'd set up housekeeping in a particular mountain district and then make excursions from that home base.[2]

Lucy started climbing in 1858, when the family was in Zermatt. She was twenty-two years old, sturdily built but of ordinary height, her pleasant, round face framed with ringlets of dark hair. Reportedly she started serious mountain walking when one day her father and brother decided to walk up the Théodule Pass, a rugged gap between the Matterhorn and the Monte Rosa, and someone suggested she go with them.[3] Lucy settled the question of proper mountaineering attire for a young woman by sticking with the white print dress she customarily wore. Years later, even after some other women began wearing bloomers and knickers (and men, too, traded their long trousers for less cumbersome knickers), Lucy insisted on climbing in her dress. It turned into something of trademark for her. A rumor that she slipped off the dress in favor of something more snug on her Matterhorn climb was never substantiated.

Lucy climbed the Théodule Pass easily and found the view out across Italy breathtaking. A few days later she joined Frank and Horace on a climb up the Monte Moro, another pass east of Monte Rosa. If the weather was clear, Lucy would have had a magnificent view of the rugged glaciers and icefalls on Monte Rosa's vast eastern face.

Apparently these new perspectives on the world inspired her deeply. The next summer, when her family established its base in the Bernese Oberland, Lucy started climbing in earnest. She first ventured up the Titlis, possibly days after Jane Freshfield and her family. After she had added a few more peaks, her father suggested it was time for her to establish a relationship with a guide. He suggested

The European Solution: "Slipping Off and On"

Meta Brevoort, a great American climber in the Alps in the late 1860s and 1870s, handled many challenges with aplomb. Freezing cold, heat, rain, snowstorms, treacherous crevasses, falling ice—she took them all in stride. But one element of her mountaineering career gave her endless exasperation: her dress.

"My dress plan too has failed," she wrote her sister around 1870. "Descending snow slopes the snow enters between the rings and stuffs up the hem and makes me heavy and wet. I have had to baste up both dress and skirt."[1]

"Slipping off and on" became a strategy some women employed over the next decades. Once out of sight of civilization, they'd slip off their skirts and tuck them in knapsacks or under rocks. Underneath they wore knickers or bloomers. Later, the climb over, they'd slip the skirt back on, for knickers were still considered too risqué for general public observation. Usually this worked well enough, unless a guide forgot to retrieve the skirt, or an avalanche or rock slide happened to obliterate its hiding place.

Such misfortunes were not unheard of. Preeminent mountaineer Elizabeth Le Blond, who employed the "off and on" technique in the 1880s and 1890s, tells us that one day an avalanche "gaily whisked" away her skirt from where she'd left it. Clad in her knickers, she snuck back to the village, then concealed herself behind a tree while her guide went to her hotel to fetch another skirt—he returned with an evening gown instead![2]

The evolution in acceptable outdoor dress from long skirts to bloomers, knickers, trousers, shorts, and finally today's unisex approach was not a steady one. Women constantly experimented with their outfits, trying to find the right combination of utility and femininity. While some defied convention by wearing knickers, others stuck to dresses. Even Le Blond didn't always advocate slipping off one's dress and admitted that the skirt was a "badge of respectability."[3]

In 1892 she and Katherine Richardson, another leading climber of the time, took a conservative tack in the most comprehensive book available on mountain-climbing technique, simply titled *Mountaineering*. Le Blond and Richardson didn't recommend, at least to this audience, that one "slip off" the skirt when climbing. "When climbing, the skirt must, whatever its length, be looped up," they directed. "Therefore it is easy to have a skirt which, in the valleys or towns, does not look conspicuous." They offered that the climber should have "an extra belt of strong ribbon . . . which is then pinned to [the skirt] in fish-wife style. The length is then arranged according to the requirements of the occasion."

The woman climber also had to anticipate periodic returns to civilization if she was out for multiple days. Her climbing skirt could easily be dressed up for the evening with the addition of a dark blue or gray silk blouse, a small dark felt hat, and flat shoes. A pair of kid leather gloves would complete the transformation and "do away with the stamp of the climber."[4]

By the 1930s the skirt as climbing attire finally seemed permanently buried as a relic of the past. As the editor of the Ladies Alpine Club *Yearbook* observed in 1930, "What centuries would seem to stretch between these [current climbing] records and those of the Victorian era! Strolling down the main street of Zermatt last summer, watching not without envy, some of our members setting forth in their trim, practical climbing kit, free and unencumbered, it was difficult to realise how few years ago one had set off down that same street with nether limbs discreetly veiled beneath a skirt both long and wide only to be discarded when well away from the haunts of man."[5]

Melchior Anderegg, a gentlemanly, soft-spoken thirty-two-year-old already considered one of the leading members of his profession. The new pair climbed well together, and along with her father until his death, and then her brother, Melchior was Lucy's constant companion throughout her climbing career. Later in her life, when someone asked Lucy why she never married, she is said to have replied, "I love mountains and Melchior, and Melchior is married."[4]

In the absence of her own words, we can imagine Lucy through the eyes of a male climber who encountered her one stormy day in an Alpine hut and recorded the following:

> We were extremely surprised when, creeping into that dark den we saw a young woman endeavoring to dry her garments soaked with water and crisp with frost in front of a wretched fire. . . . She was coming from the top of Mont Blanc and was going to the top of Monte Rosa; indeed she climbed that peak a few days later. Her name was Miss Walker. A moment later we saw her moving off. She had two guides [the writer probably mistook her father or brother for a guide]. One was going in front of her, the other behind and a thick rope tied round her slender waist bound her to both hardy mountain natives. She was walking quickly, though floundering in the snow and she was soon out of sight behind a thick mist, and sheets of drizzle driven by the blizzard.[5]

Lucy's Matterhorn ascent was considered an exceptional achievement not only for the novelty of her being female, but also because it was done while the memory of sport's first great tragedy was still fresh. Mountaineering historian W. A. B. Coolidge arrived in Zermatt and tried climbing for the first time just three days after the 1865 accident. He described the "palsy" and "public derision" that fell upon the entire sport after the four climbers died coming down the Matterhorn. Alpinists, he wrote, "went about under a sort of dark shade, looked upon with scarcely disguised contempt by the world of ordinary travellers." Six years later, Coolidge climbed the Matterhorn for the first time just a few weeks after the Walkers. He wrote that in that summer of 1871, "it was still considered a remarkable thing that within the same week *two* ascents of the dreaded peak should have been made with complete success." Curiously, in his otherwise exhaustive history of mountaineering, Coolidge doesn't mention Lucy Walker. Perhaps it's because she edged out his aunt for that desired "first." But neither does Coolidge note that his aunt, Meta Brevoort, was among the climbers who scaled the mountain shortly after the Walkers.[6]

In any case, six years after the deaths of the four highly regarded and skilled mountaineers, climbing the Matterhorn remained a daunting challenge. That Lucy's ailing, sixty-five-year-old father, who died within a year, made the ascent with her adds to the story's allure. Brother Horace stayed home, nursing a broken arm. No one on the climb left a record of it, but we can imagine some of what Lucy experienced based on other accounts of the time.[7]

The Matterhorn party, which also included Melchior Anderegg, three other guides, and some young Alpine Club members, would have left Zermatt by midmorning and walked up to the small hut on the peak's northeastern approach, taking the same route as the first successful group in 1865. They would have arrived late in the afternoon, had supper, and tried sleeping for a few restless hours, wrapped in blankets and nestled in straw, before the guides woke them at about 2:30 A.M. They'd sip hot coffee and have a small bite to eat if they had the stomach for it. Lucy reputedly suffered all her life from mild altitude sickness and found champagne and sponge cake helped ward it off.[8] Maybe with her coffee—or champagne—she had a square of cake. As the group started out, the soft glow of candle lanterns would have illuminated the rocky path and cast weird shadows into the blackness. The hard climbing was ahead of them; if Lucy ever did shed her white print dress, she would have done it sometime in the next few hours.

They would advance carefully, steadying themselves with their ice axes or alpenstocks, digging in with their hobnailed boots for footholds on the hard snow and ice-glazed rocks. The climbers, roped together now, would hoist themselves higher and higher on the exposed ridge, gradually leaving the valley behind. Far below, smoke would rise lazily from the breakfast fires in Zermatt kitchens.

At some of the steepest sections they'd grab hold of chains or ropes left by earlier climbers. At last only a final, hazardous rock wall, then a short, steep, snow-covered slope stood between them and their goal. A guide would hack out steps while the climbers ducked the shards of ice spraying down on their heads. At about 8:00 A.M. they would step up to the long, narrow, and rocky summit ridge, and each would touch the stone cairn built by the first climbers six years before.

We can imagine Lucy feeling tremendously satisfied as she gazed down on Zermatt, knowing that a crowd watched though telescopes. Maybe she envisioned them cheering when they saw her and the other tiny figures standing on top. Looking south she could see the quiet pastures of Breuil, the little village tucked into the valleys on the Italian side. With nothing to block her view, she may have admired the full sweep of the mountains to every horizon, across Italy, France, and Switzerland all the way to the Maritime Alps fringing the Mediterranean, 130 miles away.

Lucy may have recalled the words of the celebrated mountaineer Edward Whymper, one of the three surviving climbers from the 1865 ascent. In his book *Scrambles Amongst the Alps*, published that same year Lucy climbed the mountain, Whymper described the view from the summit:

> There were forests black and gloomy, and meadows bright and lively, bounding waterfalls and tranquil lakes; fertile lands and savage wastes; sunny plains and frigid plateaux. There were the most rugged forms and the most graceful outlines—bold, perpendicular cliffs and gentle, undulating slopes; rocky mountains and snowy mountains, somber and solemn or glittering and white, with walls, turrets, pinnacles, pyramids and domes, cones and spires! There was every combination that the world can give, and every contrast that the heart could desire.[9]

We can also imagine that Lucy was a little apprehensive, knowing full well that it was on the descent that the first climbers perished.

After an hour or so on the summit, the group would start their way down. Roped up again, Lucy and the others would pick their way carefully, pausing a moment or two when they passed near where the four pioneers had plunged to their deaths. The snow would be soft now, and they'd test each step before moving on. Perhaps five hours later they'd reach the hut, rest for a while in the afternoon sun, and then head back for Zermatt and the celebration that awaited them.

Lucy Walker's triumph earned her international notoriety and instant recognition both in and outside Alpine circles. A poem in the English magazine *Punch* reflected her celebrity status:

A Climbing Girl

A lady has clomb to the Matterhorn's summit,
Which almost like a monument points to the sky;
Steep not very much less than the string of a plummet
Suspended, which nothing can scale but a fly.

This lady has likewise ascended the Weisshorn,
And, what's a great deal more, descended it too,
Feet foremost; which seeing it might be named Icehorn,
So slippery 'tis, no small thing to do.
No glacier can baffle, no precipice balk her,

No peak rise above her, however sublime.
Give three cheers for intrepid Miss Walker.
I say, my boys, doesn't she know how to climb![10]

In addition to being celebrated, Lucy apparently received some barbs for her climbing exploits. Her friend Frederick Gardiner, an Alpine Club member who was with her on the Matterhorn, recalled that "in those far off mid-Victorian days, when it was considered even 'fast' for a young lady to ride in a hansom, Miss Walker's wonderful feats did not pass without a certain amount of criticism, which her keen sense of humour made her appreciate as much as anyone."[11] A public record of these critical comments is hard to come by; it may well be that many were issued by envious climbers in the male domain of the Alpine Club itself.

Some who knew Lucy related that after she retired from mountain climbing in 1879, she delighted in leading her friends on scenic walks and in reminiscing about her travels. But as one acquaintance noted, if listeners didn't already know about her formidable climbing career, they'd never guess it from talking with her. If the subject came up, she wouldn't mention that she'd actually scaled a particular mountain; she'd merely relate some "quaint occurrence or troublesome experience" that had occurred there. She'd also remark, "when looking at some trimly tweed-clad maiden, how in the early days she climbed in a white print dress, of the difficulty of managing it on the mountains, and of restoring it as nearly as possible to its original shape and colour on her return to civilization."[12]

For reasons that remain unclear, her physicians advised Lucy to stop climbing when she was forty-three. Still, she remained active in mountaineering circles and helped other women get involved, helping found the Ladies Alpine Club in 1907 and serving as its second president. She died in 1917 at the age of eighty-one.

Among those for whom Walker provided inspiration was the American Meta Brevoort, who so desperately wanted to beat Walker to the Matterhorn. By the time Meta began climbing in 1865, Lucy had already completed thirty-two peaks and passes, and her achievements were well known in the tight-knit mountaineering community. Coolidge wrote, "My Aunt (Miss Brevoort) would certainly never have started if Miss Walker had not set the example."[13] The two women met only once: on the day of Walker's greatest triumph—and Brevoort's biggest disappointment.

Meta Brevoort and her climbing party. From left: Christian Almer,
William Coolidge, Brevoort, Tschingel, Ulrich Almer, c. 1874.

Chapter 5

Meta Brevoort

(1825–1876)

We could not give up our summit.

Zermatt
July 21, 1871

In her second-floor room of the Monte Rosa Hotel, Meta Brevoort could hear the hullabaloo coming up from the lobby. Lucy Walker and her party were on their way back from the mountain, and an excited crowd of residents, guides, porters, tourists, and other hangers-on had already gathered to greet them. Meta sat on her bed, chin in hand, peering glumly out the window.

For weeks she'd been obsessed with Lucy Walker. Everywhere Meta went, it seemed, Walker's name was on people's lips. "Do you think she'll do it? Do you think she'll climb the Matterhorn?" Time and again Meta had simply smiled and shook her head; she had no way of knowing Walker's plans, though she had her suspicions. Walker was a tremendous mountain climber, she readily admitted, but this assumption—that an Englishwoman would be the first lady to scale the fearsome Matterhorn— irked her to no end. She determined there was only one thing to do: climb the mountain first herself.

So she'd made her way from the Bernese Alps toward Zermatt as hastily as she could—stopping only to climb the Eiger and the Jungfrau along the way. Now, she thought darkly, she could have saved those beauties for later. For the crushing blow was still fast upon her. She was too late. Walker had beaten her. And everything she'd looked forward to—the thrill, the notoriety, the everlasting record of the women's first ascent—now all that was dashed.

A soft nose nudged her leg. Tschingel, her constant companion and climbing partner, looked up at her with a hound dog's soulful eyes. Meta smiled and stroked the dog's floppy ears. Tschingel suddenly pulled away, a low growl rumbling from deep within her. She sprang for the open window, and Meta grabbed at her collar. The dog stopped with her front paws on the sill, and they both looked outside. Up the street the Walkers approached, surrounded by an admiring throng. The dog's growl erupted into a full-throated howl.

"Oh stop!" Meta scolded. "We must keep our manners."

Pulling the dog away from the window, she closed the sash. Then she took a deep breath and shut her eyes. "You know," she told Tschingel after a few minutes, "just because Lucy Walker's gone up from Zermatt doesn't mean she can go down the other side. That's said to be even tougher."

A knock interrupted her. The door swung open and her nephew Will stepped in, still clad in his heavy boots and tweed climbing trousers and jacket. At least he'd combed his hair, she thought. He wore an expression even more dour than usual. "I'm sorry, Auntie," he said, his words barely audible.

"No matter!" Meta said briskly. "I know where we're going."

"I thought we were going downstairs," Will replied cautiously.

"We're going to Italy, via the Matterhorn."

"A Matterhorn traverse," her nephew mused, a rare smile crossing his bearded face. "Zermatt to Breuil. That's only been done three times. Never by a lady—or a dog," he added quickly, and bent down to scratch Tschingel's ears.

"Shall we then?" Meta asked as she moved toward the door.

"Go to Breuil? Right now?" Will sounded incredulous as he stepped to catch up with her.

"No, dear. We'll go meet Miss Walker—but not a word to anyone *about our traverse. I suppose we've learned that lesson the hard way."*

With Will and the dog beside her, Meta paused at the top of the staircase, brushed a few specks from her long skirt, and gave her jacket a little tug. Then, moving with a grace and assurance that belied her ample frame, she descended the steps to the lobby like a queen to her court. But once at the bottom, she faltered, unsure of the appropriate next move.

From across the room, in the midst of a crowd of guides and other climbers, Meta spotted Lucy Walker. The Englishwoman, like herself, was no lightweight, but she still looked feminine and tidy in her white print dress. Walker turned and caught Meta's eye. Meta watched Walker excuse herself from the men and make her way toward where she stood.

"Miss Brevoort," Lucy Walker said as she approached, extending both her hands. "It is such a pleasure to meet you at last." Looking into Lucy's smiling, open face, Meta felt a strange surge of emotion. Replacing sour jealousy, a warm sense of pride began swelling within her.

"Well done, my dear. Well done," Meta said. "What a joyous day for women."

L IKE LUCY WALKER, Marguerite Claudia "Meta" Brevoort was an adventuresome and bold mountaineer. She was also competitive and innovative. As well-trod regions around Zermatt, Bern, and Chamonix offered fewer and fewer opportunities for first ascents of major peaks, Meta, along with the most dedicated male climbers, turned to more remote, largely unexplored Alpine ranges in a quest for virgin summits. But unlike Walker—and unlike most men—she extended her climbing season into the winter months. She also helped initiate the practice of camping high in the mountains with a minimum of supplies—called bivouacking—which opened up possibilities for reaching distant peaks and multiple summits in a single day. She and her nephew William Coolidge were the first Americans who practiced Alpine mountaineering over many years with expert skill.

Also like Lucy Walker, Meta never married. She almost always climbed with Coolidge, twenty-five years her junior, who came to establish himself as a leading Alpine historian and mountaineer. The third regular member of the Brevoort-Coolidge party was another accomplished female climber—arguably the most unusual of all. She was a dog named Tschingel, who rose from the obscurity of puppy-hood in a small mountain village to amass a résumé of ascents envied by many two-footed climbers.

Meta Brevoort was born in New York in 1825. Her Dutch ances-tors had emigrated to what is now New York City in the 1600s, build-ing their farm in the vicinity of today's Union Square. Her father made his fortune in Hudson Bay fur trading, and her mother came by considerable means through her prosperous Charleston, South Carolina, family. Like children of many other wealthy New Yorkers, Meta, her older sister, and two brothers took their schooling in Europe and spent many summers in Switzerland. Perhaps Meta came by her interest in mountains naturally, for her mother is listed as vis-iting the summit of the Faulhorn (8,803 feet), a small peak in the Swiss Alps, in 1835.[1]

After their schooling, the Brevoort daughters returned to New York while in their twenties. After her sister married Frederick William Coolidge, a member of an old Boston family, Meta periodi-cally lived with them. The family grew to include son Will, and seven years later daughter Lil. As her sister suffered through various ailments, Aunt Meta gradually assumed responsibility for Will's upbringing, and the two formed a very close, lifelong relationship.[2]

Young Will evidenced the same delicate health as his mother. In the winter of 1864–65, when the boy was fourteen, the father packed the whole family off to Europe so mother and son might restore their vigor in the clean country air. From then on, neither Meta nor Will ever lived in the United States again. British writer Ronald Clark, in his biography of Coolidge, suggests that it was then that Meta first started thinking that mountain climbing might provide healthy recreation as well as spiritual uplift for both herself and Will.[3] That summer the family visited Switzerland, and Meta took the opportu-nity to put her ideas into action. Despite reaching Zermatt in July 1865 only three days after the fatal Matterhorn accident, and witnessing the "palsy" Will later described, Meta initiated their

Tschingel, the Climbing Dog

For more than a decade Meta Brevoort and Will Coolidge made an almost inseparable team. Their canine companion made their partnership even more distinctive. Tschingel—named after the first mountain pass she crossed—joined the pair early in their climbing career. In photos she resembles a large beagle, with floppy ears, soulful eyes, and a long nose. Reportedly she stood 1 foot 7 inches high, with a red-brown coat contrasted with a white chest, belly, stockings, and muzzle. Her voice, Coolidge reported, was deep and musical. In the mountains she favored red wine or weak tea, and she responded to German, English, and a Swiss dialect, but never French.[1]

Guide Christian Almer gave Tschingel to Coolidge when the dog was just a few months old. She went on to become an accomplished pathfinder and climber, with sixty-six major climbs and upward of a hundred minor ones over her eleven-year career. The Alpine Club named her an honorary member—"the first lady ever admitted into that exclusive body," Meta proudly noted, though her membership might have been offered as a practical joke.[2]

Tschingel preferred leading the way. Her only flaw as a leader seemed to be the inordinate number of stones she'd dislodge and send flinging down on the heads of her party. She proved adept at avoiding crevasses or sniffing out snow bridges strong enough to hold climbers' weight; occasionally even the guides followed her instincts. When conditions seemed particularly risky she would whine and howl— "rather trying to our nerves but . . . we understood well enough that her instinct was not at fault," Coolidge wrote.[3]

Tschingel didn't seem bothered by altitude, though her nose sometimes burned and peeled in the strong

Alpine sun. Tough as she was, ice occasionally abraded her paws and left them raw and bleeding. Coolidge tried outfitting her with leather booties to protect her pads, but the dog disdained them. Perhaps, like the Swiss guides, she considered extra accoutrements on one's feet—crampons, in the case of humans—a no-no for serious climbers. When tricky conditions called for it, Tschingel would join the rope with the rest of the party. She'd wear it through a loop on her rough "work-a-day collar"—as opposed to her "Sunday" collar, which sported silver clasps engraved with the names of her ascents.[4]

Tschingel punctuated her mountaineering career with several time-outs for motherhood. Despite this rather undeniable sign of her gender, Meta Brevoort often and inexplicably referred to the dog as male sometimes female and occasionally both. "The Hund's health is very satisfactory," Meta wrote her sister from the Dauphiné. "It seems that he is the mother of no less than 34 pups!"[5]

Tschingel's signature ascent was Mont Blanc, which she accomplished in 1875 at the advanced age of ten. Meta reported that a special cannon was fired in Chamonix in honor of the first dog who'd made it to the top completely under her own power. Tschingel "trotted into the village with her head erect and her tail wagging, immensely proud of herself," Meta recalled. "The next day, lying luxuriously on a sofa in the hotel drawing-room she held a kind of state reception which was attended by several hundred persons, including all the guides."[6]

Tschingel's accomplishment was notable indeed, but it may not have been a "first" for a dog. Apparently Diane, the dog Henriette d'Angeville reported as having climbed Mount Blanc in 1838, was either forgotten, or perhaps discredited.

climbing career on some minor peaks. She was forty and Will, fifteen.

As aspiring mountain climbers, Meta and Will must have appeared an unlikely pair. Later, the adult William was described as a "tubby, undersized little man" and was undoubtedly a chubby teenager.[4] Meta was also less than athletic looking. She described herself as slow moving, and her voluminous Victorian attire and ample build no doubt hindered her even further. She constantly fiddled with how she wore her dress, trying to reach a balance between practicality and social acceptability—a problem with which women would continue to struggle for decades. Meta's solution to the dress issue reflects what seems—aside from her choice of hobby—an essentially conservative character. Early in her career she'd begun to shed the formal crinoline petticoat worn underneath her long skirt and stow it in a porter's pack when a climb got rough. Later, she wore knickers underneath, but persisted in wearing a skirt over these. And she never stopped carrying the long wooden alpenstock, that trademark of the early Victorian climbers, even after her companions switched to ice axes.

Despite her build and her cumbersome dress, Meta Brevoort proved a bold and tireless climber. She compiled a long list of peaks, including many first ascents by a woman as well as several first ascents by any person, male or female. She also climbed in style. The end of her introductory season found her celebrating on the summit of Mont Blanc, the first American woman ever on Europe's highest summit. Her party consisted of two guides and one of their wives (Will didn't make this ascent)—perfect for dancing a quadrille. She led the group in a rendition of the "Marseilles," which was banned at the time, and they all hoisted the obligatory champagne.

Meta reveled in "firsts," and the Matterhorn represented the shiniest brass ring in moutaineering. She'd been planning its ascent long before the summer of 1871. In fact, she and Will had already tried climbing it two years before from the Italian side, but bad weather drove them back. Nor was she the only female climber other than Lucy Walker aspiring to that peak. Isabella Straton and Emmeline Lewis-Lloyd, two friends who often climbed together, had their 1869 attempt driven back by falling rocks. When Meta arrived in Zermatt on July 21, she felt confident of her prospects. The weather was promising, and she was climbing well. Over the previous few weeks she and Will had put a new route up the southwest arête of the Eiger, made only the third ascent of the Silberhorn (a mountain Walker never climbed), and climbed the 12,156-foot Jungfrau.

After hearing the crushing news that Lucy Walker had claimed the Matterhorn, Meta surmised that a climber she'd encountered some days before arriving in Zermatt had divulged her plans. This patriotic Brit apparently hastened to let the Walkers know that another woman—and an American at that—figured to climb the Matterhorn first.[5]

Though greatly disappointed, Meta didn't let Walker's success deter her. A few weeks later she climbed up the Matterhorn from Zermatt and descended into Italy, recording the first-ever traverse by a woman, and only the fourth by any party.

A report from the *Alpine Journal* illustrates what an active season the Brevoort-Coolidge partnership enjoyed in 1871. In his dispatches Will included the dog Tschingel like any other member of the team. This is the first time a canine climber appeared in the staid *Journal:*

FÜSSHORN, *August 28.*—Miss Brevoort, Messrs. S. P. Cockerell, and W. A. B. Coolidge, with Tschingel, a dog, effected the first ascent of the highest point of the Füsshorner. . . . [This peak is today known today as the Rothstock.]

EIGER-JOCH, *July 5.*—Miss Brevoort and Mr. W. A. B. Coolidge, under the guidance of Christian and Ulrich Almer, effected from the Little Scheideck the second recorded passage of the Eiger-joch. The ascent of the great wall, which was formed of ice with a thin coating of loose fresh snow, occupied three hours. Owing to very unfavourable weather, no view was obtained, and the party was forced to halt $5\frac{1}{4}$ hours in a tent on the summit of the pass till the violence of the storm subsided sufficiently to allow them to descend to the Mönch-joch hut.

EIGER, *July 14.*—The same party ascended the Eiger by a new route. . . . Tschingel, our dog, accompanied us.*

SILBERHORN AND JUNGFRAU, *July 17–18.*—On July 17, the same party ascended the Silberhorn, and, passing the night in the Silberlücke, the next morning attained the summit of the Jungfrau, which the dog reached also.

MATTERHORN, *September 5.*—The same party, with the addition of Nicholas Knubel, reached the summit of the Matterhorn at 7 A.M. by the Zermatt route, and descended by the Breuil route. This is the first time the feat of crossing the mountain has been accomplished by a lady.†

WEISSHORN, *September 10.*—The same party, starting from a bivouac on the "Kastel," above Randa, made the second recorded ascent of the Weisshorn. . . .

DENT BLANCHE, *September 14.*—. . . the same party . . . bivouacked on the rocks at the foot of the southern arête of the Dent Blanche, and the next morning attained the summit. . . .

BIETSCHHORN, *September 20.*—The same party, starting from a bivouac on the left bank of the Nest glacier, ascended the Bietschhorn by the northern arête, and descended by couloirs and ridges on the western arête. This line of descent is not recommended. It is believed that this is the first time

---

*In his *Alpine Studies* (p. 178), Coolidge informs us that the dog was left behind at the foot of the summit's rocky tower, because the way seemed too steep for her. But she followed the party up anyway, and then led the tricky descent.

† Tschingel did not make this climb and never did climb the Matterhorn. In 1876 Meta and Will considered another ascent so the dog could add this crowning achievement to her list, but she was getting too old. "As for D. P. [Dear Pet], I am sure he couldn't do the Matterhorn even in two days this year," Meta wrote her nephew. "The least bit of a longish walk knocks him up and he is so stiff the next day" (Ronald Clark, *Eccentric in the Alps,* p. 99).

any of the three last-mentioned peaks had been ascended by
a lady.

This last entry, coolly noting the chosen route as "not recommended," only hints at the perils the climbers encountered.
Towering over the Rhône River valley, the 12,907-foot Bietschhorn
is a striking peak, its summit a long, broken ridge capped by three
rock towers. It was first climbed in 1859 and only once more before
the Brevoort-Coolidge ascent, which was chronicled in the *Alpine
Journal*. The story is a classic mountaineering tale set in a sublime
landscape of "wild savage cliffs" and involving numerous perils. The
Alpine Journal published the account under the name W. A. B.
Coolidge, for it did not accept contributions by women. Will, who by
the fall of 1871 was an Alpine Club member, didn't have time to
write up the story himself before returning to his Oxford studies.
Instead, he and Meta decided to put his name on her essay. Brevoort's
writing—which has a flair quite distinct from her nephew's more
pedantic prose—brings her to life as a cool customer in the face of
danger and possessing a fine eye for ironic detail. She also cleverly
disguised and hinted at her authorship by listing the climbing party
as "a lady, myself, the two Almers [guide Christian and his son
Ulrich]" and two others.[6]

Meta and Will had longed to climb the Bietschhorn for several
years, but poor weather and other unspecified obstacles always
deterred them. True to form, foul weather greeted them as they set
off by horse cart on the appointed morning of September 18, 1871.
This was a bad sign for Meta and Will, but not so for guide Christian
Almer. Instead of climbing the mountain, he thought he'd visit a big
cattle fair nearby, "where he hoped to have an opportunity of buying
'the last sweet thing' in the way of cows and pigs—a prospect as
charming to him as a day's shopping in Paris would be to most
ladies," Meta observed. The peak would be there next year, Almer
promised, trying to take the sting out of their disappointment.

But then the rain ceased and the sky brightened. Soon the sun
was "shining out in the most brilliant mood imaginable" and illuminating the grand and alluring white summit of the Bietschhorn.

Instead of viewing cows, the group made haste for the village of Reid, where they would recruit local porters and guides and spend the night. In Reid, they found a small inn run by a proprietor promising a bountiful supper. "Unheard of delicacies were at length spread out before us," Meta reported. "Brains, livers, and the interiors of all sorts of wild animals, culminating in an entire squirrel! which looked in the dish so very like an obese snake, that, the edge of our hunger having by this time been taken off, we could not make up our minds to taste it, although no doubt it was capital," she added diplomatically.

At noon the next day they set off for the base of the mountain. Their party now included a porter looking "like a walking haystack," Meta noted, as he carried a huge bundle of straw for use as bedding. A local guide named Siegen resembled "the conventional stage representation of Mephistopheles," his dark eyes, long hair, and twisted mustache accented by a slouched hat trailing a long bunch of cock's feathers. As tough as this character appeared, she realized he was less than enthusiastic about the venture. "We were much edified," Meta remarked, "when, as he pulled out his handkerchief, two or three sets of [rosary] beads came out with it, which, he laughingly said, were none too many for the Bietschhorn."

Meta's notes from camp that evening captured the aesthetic appeal the mountain held for nineteenth-century climbers and the melodramatic Romantic style of describing them. "On our right were wild savage cliffs, which rose higher and higher behind us, until, far above, we could see the sharp summit of our peak looking down upon them. It seemed almost to beckon us on to attempt it, as it shone out gloriously in the light of the setting sun, the rays of which made the snowy range on the opposite side of the valley glow with new beauty."

They waited for the rising sun to take the edge off the cold before starting out the next morning. Tschingel stayed behind in the tent— "*not* because of any supposed incapacity on his part, as he was perhaps the most accomplished mountaineer of the party," Meta assured her readers, but because the way was loose and rocky, and the fewer stones kicked down, the better.

Two hours of steady climbing took them high up the Nest glacier. They passed the entrance to a small snow cave and awhile later stopped for breakfast near the base of the peak's northern arête. For reasons Meta didn't make clear, Siegen decided at this point to return to their camp. The remaining five carefully climbed the ridge composed of rotten, splitting rock. So far it had been a perfect day. But as they gained on the summit, things began to change. Icy wind whistled about their ears, and clouds rose up from the valleys. As the wind grew in fury, the climbers dropped below the ridge for shelter. But they kept moving higher, laboriously hacking out steps where snow hardened into ice. Another hour passed without reprieve from the howling wind and thickening clouds. It was clear they'd never get a view even if they reached the top. Undaunted, Brevoort declared, "We *could* not give up our summit."

Seven and a half hours after they started, they pulled themselves onto the rocky summit. They stayed only twenty minutes, long enough to wolf down lunch and leave their names in a bottle carefully tucked in a stone cairn. Their situation was not for the faint of heart, but Meta found the scene exhilarating. She wrote:

> We could see nothing beyond the rocks immediately around us, as we were enveloped in clouds, which the wind drove around tumultuously. But, although we regretted the magnificent prospect from the top, we were struck with the grandeur of what we could see—jagged rocks, splintered into every conceivable shape, piled up or strewn out in fantastic confusion. The drifting clouds also enabled us occasionally to form some idea of the startling precipices on all sides.

Picking their way back down the narrow ridge, another sight startled them. It was what today is called a Brocken specter. Their own shadows, cast as huge, rainbow-haloed images, played on the clouds below them. "It was almost unearthly to see these figures of gigantic proportions moving as we moved," Meta recalled.

The descent proved no easier than the climb up. The climbers were still far from their tent when the day—and visibility—began fading. Meanwhile, the temperature had risen, and rocks that once seemed stable under a coating of ice and snow gave way beneath them. According to Meta, "They rolled down if one did but look at them." At one point, without warning an immense fragment broke loose from a ledge where they'd all been standing just moments before and crushed the rope between Christian Almer and the porter. It threw these two off their feet, causing them to drag down Ulrich Almer, the third man on the rope. The three of them executed some "prodigious somersaults" before Meta and William seized the rope, dug their boots, alpenstock, and ax in hard, and stopped them all from hurtling down the slope. It seemed, Meta recalled, "that the whole mountain was coming down around our ears like a card-house."

Well after dark, the group made it back to the base of the arête and the top of the wide, broken Nest glacier. The temperature was dropping, and they were hungry, tired, and still far from safety. To everyone's tremendous relief, Christian Almer found the exact place they'd stopped for breakfast thirteen hours before. They'd left a "precious little barrel of wine" buried in the snow there, "the recovery of which we had been for some time anticipating," Meta noted, "as we had had nothing to drink since quitting the summit."

Now they had only to cross the glacier before reaching their tent. But an easy traverse in the daylight was a much different prospect by night. The elder Almer advanced carefully, sometimes on hands and knees, feeling his way along their earlier steps. Whenever they reached a crevasse, son Ulrich sat down, dug into the snow, and held his father on the rope while he sought a safe crossing in the dark. The going was excruciatingly slow. As the night wore on, the climbers began shaking with cold and exhaustion. Someone thought of the little ice cave they'd passed hours and hours before. That might be their only hope of shelter, and survival. At nearly 11:00 P.M. Christian Almer finally led them, one by one, into the small cavern. Marveling that he'd found the cave they'd passed that morning with hardly a second glance, Meta credited the guide with saving their lives. She was sure they would have frozen if they'd spent the night in the open, exposed to the withering cold.

Huddled inside the icy cave, they had no food, but were too "delighted to be off the ice and able to sit down to complain of anything," said the ever cheerful Meta. Still, they did have a few matches and the wine. The matches they'd light occasionally to check their watches for the interminable passage of time. They handed around the wine, but in the dark it was nearly impossible to keep the "spiteful little cask" from spilling. Christian Almer worried his charges might never wake up if they drifted off to sleep in the deadly cold. So according to Meta, he "would jump up and begin yodeling in the most aggravating manner, or else he would circulate the hateful little cask, addressing us in the liveliest manner, and thus to our disgust effectively rousing us up from our slumbers."

Calm air and new snow greeted them at five o'clock the next morning when they left "the hospitable hole." They followed their previous route, and an hour and a half later reached shouting distance of the tent. Siegen greeted them waving a bottle of champagne. Tschingel, a bit put out from spending the night with this devilish-looking man, howled an uproarious welcome. They rested for a while, and that afternoon walked back to Reid and the inn. "Our host received us with the choicest hospitality in his power," Brevoort concluded: "a dish of brains for dinner."

Two years after their outstanding 1871 season, the quest for unclimbed peaks led Meta and Will to the Dauphiné, a rugged and remote section of the French Alps. Their lodgings were primitive and dirty, the food poor, and the fleas unending. But they found spectacular mountains. Plenty of unexplored peaks beckoned them, and two they scaled are now called Pointe Brevoort and Point Marguerite, both named after Meta.

Around this time Will and Meta also turned to a new area of mountain endeavor: winter climbing. They were among the earliest to take on this extremely challenging, often uncomfortable and risky activity. British author Ronald Clark credits them with helping to popularize, if not initiate, the new sport. As he described the first days of winter climbing, "In the 1870s . . . [winter] mountaineering was considered an eccentricity which was definitely useless, probably dangerous, against the interests of the native Swiss who wished to rest and recuperate during the winter months, and without doubt against the interests of the Alpine Establishment whose members had many other things to do between October and June."[7]

But Meta and Will had the time, financial means, toughness, and competitive drive to pursue this new pastime. Will had only his Oxford studies to keep after, and Meta juggled other obligations back in England to ensure that they could return to the Alps in winter. Meta's disappointment on the Matterhorn may have been part of the impetus for climbing in winter, for then, there were almost unlimited "firsts" to be had. Their long association with guide Christian Almer also favored them, as he agreed to lend his services. But in explaining this new pursuit, Coolidge simply cited their aesthetic curiosity about how the mountain landscape would appear in winter. His account of their first winter excursion, to the Wetterhorn and the Jungfrau in January 1874, is replete with descriptions of the magnificent views, as well as the penetrating cold and the danger of avalanches.[8]

With Almer's guidance, Meta Brevoort and Will Coolidge also popularized the high-mountain bivouac, first in the warmer months, and then in winter. Clark suggested that Almer proposed the idea as a way to catch two peaks in a single day.[9] By camping higher than the highest huts, they'd have a shorter climb to a summit, and could either do another nearby peak or have a longer day in case of unexpected difficulties. By necessity, they also camped out when they visited the lesser-known regions where huts hadn't been built. In winter the huts were closed, though unlocked, and while the climbers would sometimes clear out the snow inside and use them, often they'd simply find shelter on the mountain.

Even today, with all of our highly technical insulated clothing, sleeping bags, and tents, winter mountaineering isn't an easy proposition. It's hard to imagine Meta Brevoort, maybe in a tent but perhaps tucked among some boulders, trying to stay warm under piles of wool blankets and fur wraps, wrestling with her skirts, and wearing frozen, uninsulated boots. But her discomfort must have been compensated for by the astonished reactions from below. Their Wetterhorn and Jungfrau climbs in January 1874—both first winter ascents—were "received in triumph in Grindelwald," Will reported, and both the local papers and the British press hailed their feats.[10]

Two years later the Brevoort-Coolidge team tried the first-ever winter ascent of Mont Blanc. They got higher than any previous winter climbers, but bad weather drove them down below the summit. And once again, another woman beat Meta to a "first." A few weeks later English mountaineer Isabella Straton claimed the first winter ascent of Mont Blanc by anyone, male or female.

At the age of fifty, Meta craved even more exotic locales and bigger challenges than the Alps. In a letter to Will she speculated about making an expedition to Mount Everest. She related to him what she'd learned from an English engineer on leave from government work in India. "He has told me a lot about Mt. Everest," she wrote. "No fear of wild beasts, nor rains at the proper season, nor hostile natives if one could get properly accredited, but the height he thinks would be an insuperable objection."[11] Despite the difficulties, she found the prospects encouraging and thought the Royal Geographic Society in London might assist an expedition. But in the near term she had other goals.

At the top of her list in the summer of 1876 was the Meije, at 13,068 feet, a premier peak in the Dauphiné. Its precipitous walls had preserved it as one of the last great unclaimed peaks in Europe. Like the Bietschhorn, she'd wanted to climb it for years. On one occasion, she and Will thought they *had* reached the summit, only to realize there was another, higher crest. But now, other obstacles would prove equally insurmountable. Her sister had died in early 1875, and apparently the steady flow of funds to which she and her nephew were accustomed began to grow smaller. In addition, someone now had to look after Will's younger sister Lil, and the task fell to Aunt Meta. So while she managed the budget as well as her niece, Will went off to the Dauphiné. She planned to join him if the conditions looked promising, but as the summer wore on these never materialized. Meta winced at the thought of the competition—the growing number of climbers who also wanted to be first on the summit. "Alas! Alas! And to think of all the others who will be coming and the *one* who may succeed," she wrote. "Dear Will, give my love to all my dear old friends [other peaks she'd climbed], and especially to that glorious Meije and ask her to keep herself for me."[12]

But the Meije was not to be hers. That December, when she and Will were back in England and eagerly planning their winter climbs for the new year, Meta became ill. It didn't seem serious at first, but then doctors diagnosed rheumatic fever, and within days Meta Brevoort was dead at the age of fifty-one.

After his aunt's death, some who knew Will described him as going into a bit of a tailspin, for he'd essentially lost both his two best friends and favorite climbing companions: Not only was Meta gone, but his "Dear Pet" was no longer there for him. Suffering from the stiffness of old age and many miles, Tschingel had climbed her last mountain the previous summer. She died three years after Meta, passing away in her sleep.[13]

Nine months after Meta's death, W. A. B. Coolidge, now a Fellow of Oxford's Magdalen College, finally climbed the Meije. It was a bittersweet experience; his aunt was not with him, and on top were two cairns built by others. He wrote about the ascent for the *Alpine Journal*:

> It was a moment of my life which I can never forget. Yet my feelings were very mixed. The pleasure of having attained a long wished-for goal was very great, but at the same time my thoughts recurred involuntarily to my companion on many expeditions to the Dauphiné, one of whose most cherished wishes it had been to stand on this lofty pinnacle, a wish which was doomed to remain for ever unsatisfied.[14]

Coolidge went on climbing, completing well over a thousand ascents. He authored the first definitive history of Alpine mountaineering as well as numerous essays and other mountaineering titles, and edited the *Alpine Journal*. Because of his achievements in winter mountaineering and exploring the Dauphiné, and his contributions to the sport as a historian and through his involvement with the Alpine Club, historians list him as the first American mountaineer to achieve fame in the Alps.[15] This is only partially true.

Coolidge was the first American man to achieve such fame. Though Meta Brevoort's name is usually but a footnote in mountaineering histories, she too deserves her place as one of the sport's important early innovators and pioneers, as well as one of the first two Americans who made mountaineering careers in the Alps.

Meta died long before the establishment of the Ladies Alpine Club, and just as a new generation of female climbers were starting their careers, so she likely never enjoyed the camaraderie of other women. In the quarter century after her death, however, more and more women traced Meta's footsteps on the great peaks of the Alps. They also climbed mountains she never had the chance to attempt in her unexpectedly short career. For them the world of mountaineering was slowly changing; some of these women adopted new styles of clothing more suited for the rigors of climbing; others saw their names printed as authors in the *Alpine Journal*. And unlike Meta, some chose to comment on what it meant to be a woman practicing the unconventional pastime of mountaineering.

Elizabeth Le Blond on a Norwegian peak, 1899. (JOSEF IMBODEN, ALPINE CLUB LIBRARY COLLECTION)

Chapter 6

Elizabeth Le Blond

(1861–1934)

I had to struggle hard for my freedom.

Monte Rosa, on the Italian-Swiss frontier
March 1883

Elizabeth Le Blond watched as the gray-blue wash of predawn gradually lit the eastern sky, making the clouds hanging on the mountains appear even darker as they concealed the contours of the sharp peaks. Only her cashmere face scarf kept her nose and cheeks from freezing entirely. She'd never felt cold this penetrating.* She moved slowly but steadily with the pace of an experienced Alpine climber, focusing on the rhythm of her feet and trusting the guides walking ahead, the soft glow of lantern light illuminating their way. For several hours they'd walked through a world so vast and silent that their party seemed like its own little solar system in the midst of a frozen inky black universe. She and the Italian mountaineer Vittorio Sella at its center, the single-file line of eight guides stretched before and after them, all trudging up the long, steep glacier toward the summit of the Monte Rosa, after Mont Blanc the highest peak in the Alps.

---

* Based on Mrs. Aubrey Le Blond, *The High Alps in Winter*, pp. 157–65.

Elizabeth Le Blond had prepared for the cold. On her feet she wore four pairs of wool socks inside her oversized leather boots, and a double layer of thick wool mittens protected her hands. Underneath her dense tweed outer skirt she wore two more skirts of fine wool flannel, and beneath those tweed knickers and undergarments of soft angora. She used the same dense tweed for her jacket, cut large enough for wearing over multiple layers: a heavy Irish wool sweater, two blouses of English flannel, and a silk and angora camisole. With all this, she felt tolerably warm. Then, too, the adrenaline pumping through her as she headed toward a summit never before climbed in winter was enough to keep her fired up.

The sky brightened into pastel shades of lavender, then salmon and peach. As the bottom of the clouds began glowing orange they started lifting and dispersing from the peaks, and Elizabeth wondered if the wind would lift too. The guide ahead of her extinguished the candle and put down his lantern. It was time for breakfast.

The ten of them huddled close. The guides produced biscuits, squares of chocolate, and cheese. Everything was so hard from the cold it took a few minutes before it could be slowly chewed and finally swallowed. They washed the meal down with weak tea that scarcely hinted at its once boiling state. Sella's Marsala refused to leave its frozen flask. Le Blond's wine still flowed, but the group decided they'd better save it for later. Each time Elizabeth lifted her scarf to take a bite the air stung her cheeks. When she was done she quickly wrapped her face and neck again and pulled her wool helmet tighter on her head. She couldn't remember ever being out in such cold.

As she feared, the rising sun awakened the wind. Within an hour it howled around their ears, and they leaned into it, trying to keep their footing on the ice. The pitch steepened, and the lead guide began hacking out steps the rest could follow. He took off his outer mitt so he could grip his ice ax, and within a few minutes his hand was too cold to continue. Another guide stepped around and took his place. While he worked laboriously, the rest of them stamped their feet and pounded their hands against their thighs to keep their circulation going. Several of the guides started grumbling. Elizabeth heard snatches of conversation, all of it sounding unhappy.

She glanced at Sella, who somehow maintained a tranquil look. She was aware that underneath the swaths of wool around his head was a handsome, sharp-featured man, one of the finest mountaineers around and a famous Alpine photographer. He'd done the Matterhorn in winter, and he'd already tried Monte Rosa once before. When they got down she'd have to ask him how those ascents compared to these conditions. She still felt flattered that he'd suggested joining forces on Monte Rosa, rather than each doing it individually.

Bits of windblown ice sprayed the group like pellets from a shotgun. Sella drew a thermometer from his pocket, and Elizabeth edged next to him to look. She watched the silver mercury pool in the bottom of the thin tube, where it could drop no farther. "The lowest it goes is thirteen below zero Fahrenheit. Must be a little colder," he said without a trace of misgiving.

She hunched her shoulders and squeezed her eyes as another powerful gust rocked them and nearly ripped her scarf away. This is becoming crazy, she thought.

"If we keep on we're all going to freeze!" she yelled over the roar of the gale.

The guides looked her way and she saw their eyes widen.

"Madame's nose! Madame's nose!" one of them cried. He stepped to her and thrust his hand in her face. She instinctively ducked, but he held her shoulder. "No, no," he said, and started rubbing her nose with his coarse, ice-flecked mitten.

Funny, she thought, he's assaulting my nose but I can't feel a thing. "What is it?" she demanded.

"Hold still, Madame. Your nose is white," the guide answered, as the others gathered around.

"Rub, rub hard!" several of them urged.

Finally, he stopped. "Ah, it's beautiful now!"

"Beautiful! What do you mean?" Elizabeth asked, her eyes tearing from the wind and wool.

"Yes," answered the guide, "it's now getting quite black!"

ELIZABETH LE BLOND'S early life gave little hint that she'd become an expert climber, a pioneer of winter mountaineering, a respected Alpine photographer, a prolific author of mountaineering literature, and a founder and first president of the Ladies Alpine Club. Because of her accomplishments, her leadership in the field, and her public persona, when people thought about "lady climbers" in the last two decades of the nineteenth century, it's a good bet they thought of her.

Elizabeth was one of those "characters" of the late Victorian age that upper-class British society seemed to breed. Because of her social standing and wealth, she possessed the ability to follow her own path. But she also possessed tremendous self-confidence, curiosity, and a great sense of adventure that aided her not only in climbing mountains, but in other unusual pursuits during her life as well. Her privileged background also belied her ability and willingness to withstand the physical discomforts of mountaineering. As Alpine historian Claire Engel suggested, "She was a typical Victorian lady with a certain amount of eccentricity toned down by beautiful manners and mental poise, which allowed her to do very daring things in such a way that they seemed quite normal."[1]

Le Blond rode a bicycle through France and Italy before most people had ever seen such a contraption. She was also a superb ice skater and the first woman to insist on taking, and then to pass, the so-called men's test of expertise by the prestigious St. Moritz Skating Club. She loved what today we'd call adventure travel and made long and arduous journeys all over the world in the years just before and after World War I. Her autobiography starts with the statement, "All my life I have been fortunate in meeting interesting people, visiting interesting places, taking part in interesting events and never knowing what it meant to be bored."[2]

Born into the heart of proper English society in 1861, Elizabeth grew up at a family estate in Ireland with frequent visits to London. She was the only child of a family listing aristocratic lineage all over Europe and was eleven when her soldier father died. In 1878 when she entered London society as a delicate and pretty seventeen-year-old she caught the eye of a distinguished man two decades her senior, a soldier like her father. He was Col. Fred Burnaby, a power-fully built, impressively tall British army officer whom Elizabeth con-sidered a "man of the world." They married, and the following year she gave birth to a son, Arthur St. Vincent Burnaby. Later, her grandmother assumed care of the young child while Elizabeth pur-sued her peripatetic interests. On January 17, 1885, Elizabeth was widowed for the first time when Colonel Burnaby died in the Egyptian battle of Abu Klea.[3] After this she lived almost entirely in Switzerland and married twice more, first to D. F. Main, who died in 1892 and whom she did not mention in her autobiography, and then to Aubrey Le Blond, who outlived her. Le Blond was a porcelain expert who eventually donated his collection to the Victoria and Albert Museum. With him she traveled across Asia on the Tran-Siberian Railway in the years before World War I.

Elizabeth climbed and wrote as Mrs. Burnaby and Mrs. Main, but is most commonly remembered as Mrs. Aubrey Le Blond. While none of her three husbands shared her passion for climbing, the lack of familial companions never deterred her from pursuing her inter-ests. She brushed off the presumption that she needed such "protec-tion," much to the consternation of some of her relatives.

Ironically, Elizabeth's path to mountaineering started with her family's concerns for her health. Like many who suffered from con-sumption, or tuberculosis, Elizabeth was sent to Switzerland and France for the restorative powers of clean mountain air. She first traveled there around 1880. Until then the closest she had come to mountains was as a young girl listening to her mother read from *Scrambles Amongst the Alps,* by the British climber Edward Whymper. "As for mountaineering," she admitted, "I knew nothing and cared less." Indeed, when she first saw the Jungfrau, it struck her as "noth-ing more than a far-off vision of glittering snows on which none but the foot of folly could ever wish to tread." Like many others in the aftermath of the Matterhorn disaster and subsequent deaths in the mountains, she condemned the "wickedness" of climbers "who risked their lives 'for nothing.' "[4]

Nonetheless, the Alpine landscape began exercising a profound effect. Elizabeth found walks in the stunning countryside both invigorating and inspiring, and as she grew stronger and climbed higher, the peaks stirred a taste for adventure. Apparently with her son in family care back in England, and her husband off on military maneuvers, in 1881 she and three friends started engaging guides to take them to the ordinary tourist attractions such as the Mer de Glace, the spectacular glacier near Mont Blanc. Then playing to their "youthful vanity and enthusiasm," the guides started urging more ambitious expeditions. Over the next two summers she climbed rocks, crossed glaciers, and otherwise went far beyond ordinary walks. And while young female walking tourists were common enough at that time, those with aspirations for more aggressive climbing finally had a celebrated role model. Years later, Elizabeth acknowledged she owed her start to the example provided by Lucy Walker.

Yet climbing mountains, no matter how propitious for her health, and despite the increasing number of women practicing it, was not met with hearty approval back home. When word of her activity reached relatives, alarm rang through the great halls of the country estates of Elizabeth's extended family. Particularly outrageous was her practice of going off "alone" with her guides and spending nights in Alpine huts and bivouacs. Most offended by this unladylike behavior was her elderly great aunt, who still possessed the early Victorian belief that a young woman must be chaperoned by a family member, preferably male, at all times.[5] Interestingly, Elizabeth's mother intervened for her.

"I owe a supreme debt of gratitude to the mountains for knocking from me the shackles of conventionality," Elizabeth later wrote, "but I had to struggle hard for my freedom. My mother faced the music on my behalf when my grand-aunt, Lady Bentnick, sent out a frantic S.O.S. 'Stop her climbing mountains! She is scandalizing all London and looks like a Red Indian!' "[6] Elizabeth ignored the aunt's directive. She didn't stop climbing, and unlike women who were horrified at the mere thought of losing their fair complexions (and looking like a "Red Indian!"), she considered her sunburned face a badge of courage and adventure earned as a mountaineer.

But Elizabeth didn't completely leave convention behind, either. She always enjoyed the privileges of her class, and as she started her climbing career she took along its actual accoutrements, such as her personal maid. The story of her initial steps on Mont Blanc reveals both her start in mountaineering as well as her dawning realization that some upper-class habits could be a hindrance.[7]

During the summer of 1882 she and her friends flirted with the idea of going up Mont Blanc, but the mountain's size and reputation intimidated them. Their misgivings seemed justified when they met a young woman just down from the Grand Mulets, the dramatic rock buttresses about halfway up. Enthralled by her bravery, they asked her how she felt after such an adventure. She was happy to have climbed that high, she told them, but she'd "never do it again."

"More than ever impressed, we felt sure that the Grand Mulets was not for the likes of us," Elizabeth acknowledged. But their guides had another plan. They suggested a shorter walk about a quarter of the way up the mountain. The four young women were game, so wearing their usual high-buttoned boots and shady hats, they set out, following a rocky path past the treeline and leading between the mountain's great glaciers. They lunched at a little restaurant looking out over the valley. Then, alpenstocks in hand, they trudged up a steep and winding path right to the edge of the glacier.

As they approached the ice, they met climbers coming down with ice axes and rope—and "other thrilling accessories of an expedition to the summit of Mont Blanc," Elizabeth noticed. The guides for this other group asked if the four women were on their way to the Grand Mulets. Their query thrilled Elizabeth with its inference that her group was actually a climbing party. "We hadn't supposed anything of the kind, but at that same moment at least two of us began to suppose very hard indeed," she recalled. Conveniently, their guides "happened" to have ropes, she noted happily, and agreed to lead them "up there." For Elizabeth, at least, any lingering feelings of intimidation vanished in a rush of adrenaline. "By this time 'up there' was the one place in the world we were determined to go," she recalled. Not sharing her determination, however, two others in her group turned back. She and her remaining friend tied in to the rope and were soon clambering up and down among the séracs and crawling over ladders bridging the biggest crevasses. When they reached the hut at the Grand Mulets they assessed their condition. "Our boots were pulp, our stockings wet sponges, our skirts sodden," Elizabeth reported.

But the guides had brought along dry clothes, including enormous felt slippers. Wearing these, the two young women climbed to the top of a rock pinnacle and enjoyed a dramatic sunset. Coming down from their perch flush with the day's accomplishments, they begged their guides to take them the rest of the way to the summit the following day. The guides refused, pointing out the necessity of proper footwear and clothing. The next morning when she reached for her boots, Elizabeth appreciated the wisdom of their advice. She could tell from their shriveled condition the boots would never survive a climb up the rest of the mountain. She also experienced a minor epiphany. For the first time in her life she faced putting on her own boots; she wasn't even sure which shoe went on which foot. Her maid had always seen to such mundane tasks.

Although it probably occurred to Elizabeth that if she was serious about mountain climbing she'd have to go without some of the conveniences of home, for several years afterward she insisted that her maid accompany her on mountain trips. These young women didn't have an easy time following in their mistress's footsteps. On a late-autumn expedition in the Italian Alps, for instance, her maid fainted and suffered frostbitten hands. Like a piece of luggage, she was carried down the mountain on a guide's back.[8] Eventually Elizabeth realized she could do things for herself and dispensed with the maid. She considered this step a form of "independence" and part of breaking the "shackles of conventionality." Besides, she viewed her maids as providing as much frustration as assistance. "One of the species had incessant hysteria whenever I returned late from an expedition," she wrote. Another eloped with a courier.[9]

After returning from her first foray up Mont Blanc, Elizabeth outfitted herself with proper mountaineering apparel and began climbing in earnest. By summer's end she twice reached the summit of Mont Blanc. She also climbed the rugged Grandes Jorasses, the second highest peak in the Mont Blanc massif.

The Grandes Jorasses excursion showed Elizabeth the importance of being prepared for all contingencies in the mountains, for a planned one-day climb lengthened into an overnight ordeal. And the story of this climb demonstrates that even early in her climbing career, she possessed a great deal of physical and mental toughness. After a long and difficult day reaching the summit, she and her two guides were still high on the Grandes Jorasses when darkness fell. They hadn't brought lanterns or extra food, but the guides deemed continuing in the dark too risky. Without any other type of shelter they dug into the snow and spent the night huddled together in their impromptu bivouac, Elizabeth wrapped only in a red Indian shawl.

What must have been an uncomfortable and even nerve-racking experience didn't deter her from her growing passion for climbing mountains. Indeed, several weeks later, after she'd left Chamonix to spend fall and winter in Montreux on Lake Geneva, the mountains kept calling her back. "Six weeks of damp . . . proved too much for me," she wrote, explaining her return to Chamonix, "in spite of kindly warnings against ten feet of snow, starvation, isolation, dullness and many other evils." With a lack of other interesting diversions, she started winter expeditions.[10]

In more than two decades of mountaineering Elizabeth compiled an impressive list of more than one hundred ascents. Her first important contribution, and her true place as a mountaineering pioneer, is in winter mountaineering. In her initial season she racked up several first ascents. One of her failures, in the sense of not making the summit, was her attempt on the Monte Rosa in March 1883. But the venture illustrated both her matter-of-fact approach to the risks of winter mountaineering and her solid reputation. It is reasonable to imagine that Italian mountaineer Vittorio Sella, who'd already established his credentials with his winter ascent of the Matterhorn, would not have consented to share the risks nor the potential rewards of the summit with just anyone.

Elizabeth chronicled her early winter experiences in *The High Alps in Winter; or Mountaineering in Search of Health*. This was the first book by any author devoted entirely to winter climbing. Her expeditions caught the attention of the climbing establishment and she was "electrified," she recalled, when the *Alpine Journal* stated,

"This unparalleled series of ascents executed by a lady will form one of the most brilliant chapters in the history of winter mountaineering."[11] Years later, at the very end of her climbing career, she contributed another chapter in climbing history by making what is regarded as the first "manless" climb. Without men or guides in their party, in 1900 she and her friend Lady Evelyn McDonnell completed a winter traverse of the beautiful, snow- and ice-capped Piz Palü, a 12,800-foot peak on the Swiss-Italian border. This feat, the great twentieth-century British climber Dorothy Pilley later wrote, was "hushed up and regarded as somewhat improper." At that time, two women "alone," facing and beating the odds on a tough winter ascent, seemed a bit more than the still-male-dominated climbing establishment could handle.[12]

Elizabeth made notable ascents in summer as well—one being her Matterhorn traverse of August 1883, an epic lasting forty-three hours.[13] Led by guide Alexander Burgener, she and a porter left Zermatt at 11:00 P.M. and reached the summit the next morning. A glaze of ice—called *verglas*—made the descent on the Italian side extremely treacherous and painstakingly slow. The three climbers spent the day negotiating icy rocks, dodging falling stones, and avoiding avalanches. Nightfall found them still on the mountain, feeling their way down by moonlight. After the moon set, the men slept the few hours until dawn, but Elizabeth stayed awake and moving the entire time in an attempt to stay warm. The next morning they finally reached the Italian village of Breuil and by mules and then on foot made it back to Zermatt that night. Interestingly, this climb with Le Blond was not the first time Alexander Burgener had seen a woman on the Matterhorn. Years earlier he'd encountered Meta Brevoort there. Perhaps as a result of his familiarity with the abilities of both Le Blond and Brevoort, he later encouraged other women with the opinion that females "really can climb."[14]

Evidence of Elizabeth's expertise and reputation as a climber emerged again the following summer. She joined one of the preeminent guides of the time, Joseph Imboden, in climbing what they christened the Beishorn (and now called the Bishorn). Imboden considered the 13,625-foot mountain north of Zermatt one of the only great 4,000-meter Alpine peaks left unclimbed. It was his ambition to lead one of his clients to the top, and he chose Elizabeth to share his wish. The guidebooks, she noted, considered the ridge leading to the Beishorn impossible to climb, but she was thrilled at the chance for a first ascent. Despite Imboden losing his ice ax, the pair found their way up the knife-edge ridge to the summit. It was one of the few times Elizabeth had the pleasure of helping build the "stone man," or large cairn used to mark a summit, and leave her name first in the bottle tucked within.[15] This ascent was just one of many climbs during her fifteen-year, mutually rewarding relationship with Imboden. In addition to climbing many more Alpine peaks together, he later joined her on a trip to Norway, where they made a series of first ascents above the Arctic Circle.

In another illustration of how she led her sport, Elizabeth bucked convention by occasionally going without guides. In the 1880s guideless climbing by men was just gaining acceptance in summer; it was still extremely rare in winter. It would be another forty years before women habitually climbed without guides—or men. An incident one winter in the mid-1880s reveals Elizabeth's relationship with male climbers, as well as her careful judgment in the face of potentially hazardous conditions. Good judgment is always important in mountaineering, but in winter it is doubly so, for the consequences of miscalculation are vastly heightened by the short days, the tricky snow conditions, and the cold.[16]

She'd agreed to guide two friends up the Diavolezza Pass near St. Moritz, an area she knew from summer excursions. She didn't consider the pass particularly challenging but realized that winter snows could conceal treacherous crevasses. While the surface might appear solid, a climber could fall through the brittle snow and into a crevasse. Her companions, a German whom she identified as "Mr. H." and an Englishman, "Mr. S.," both had some mountaineering experience, and she figured they knew to look out for such conditions.

Mr. S. found the morning's climb unusually tiring, and it was midafternoon by the time they reached the top of the pass. Elizabeth advised returning the way they'd come. Fortified with a swallow of brandy, however, Mr. S. insisted they climb down the other side.

They roped up and started their descent through a snowfield littered with crevasses, some so deep they couldn't see the bottom. But at least they could see them.

When the snowfield broadened into a smooth, unbroken slope they unroped, leaned on their axes, and glissaded down, making much better time. Still, dusk had robbed the terrain of details by the time they reached the séracs guarding the glacier's lower reaches. Elizabeth considered maneuvering around these ice pinnacles easy enough in summer. But with snow hiding the crevasses between them, and no lantern for illuminating the way, she grew concerned. Both she and the men knew the correct path bordered a deep and treacherous whirlpool in the ice called the Grand Moulin. If in the dark one of them accidentally tumbled into this steep, smooth-sided chasm, getting out would be extremely difficult. But knowing they were on the right track meant finding the Moulin. They roped together again.

When Mr. S. claimed he knew the area well and offered to take the lead, Elizabeth gladly relinquished. Cautiously he led them forward, and within a few minutes they found the gaping Moulin. Relieved, they paused and listened to water gurgling from deep within. But an hour later they were still zigzagging around séracs, not making much downward progress. Mr. S.'s energy was flagging, and conditions were not improving. They inched along until they found another gaping crevasse. In the dark they could hardly discern the other side, but retracing their steps seemed just as precarious as going forward. Grimly, Elizabeth wrapped the rope around her ice ax and dug in as far as she could to hold Mr. S. in case he jumped short. He made it. She got up, took a deep breath, leaped, and scrambled to keep her footing on the other side. She held her breath again as Mr. H. joined them with an acrobatic tumble.

Finally, they thought, the rest of the way was clear. But before long Elizabeth realized they'd veered far off course. Anxiously she asked Mr. S. if he was sure of his bearings. He replied he was not and in fact felt "quite stupid." He was apparently suffering from what today would be recognized as hypothermia. Another swallow of brandy revived him a bit, and Elizabeth resumed the lead. But before long, the Englishman felt faint and had to stop. Brandy alone wasn't enough to power him over the remaining miles. Elizabeth reviewed their choices. She could continue on for help and leave the German with Mr. S. But even if she were fortunate enough not to fall into a crevasse on the way, it would still be at least six hours before a rescue party could get back. By that time Mr. S. might be frozen. The only choice was to lead him down.

Propping Mr. S. between them, she and Mr. H. slowly and carefully edged their way down, prodding the snow with their axes at every step to test for hidden crevasses. They proceeded this way for two exhausting hours. It was after 11:00 P.M. when they finally left the glacier and started on the path toward the village. They cheered when a search party met them in a horse-drawn wagon. At the hotel, while celebrating with their would-be rescuers, Elizabeth was astonished to hear Mr. H., whom she had trusted as understanding the risk of their nighttime descent, remark, "There was no danger, all the crevasses were covered with snow!"

Elizabeth's prolific and sometimes acid pen gives us a flavor of the Alpine social scene in the 1880s and 1890s. By this time tourism had become big business, and all sorts of people flocked to the mountain resorts and hotels. Her stories reveal the pleasure she derived from tweaking others' expectations and playing the role of the iconoclast. While no one escaped her wry eye, she especially enjoyed needling Americans. Among their irritating traits, she pointed out, was the habit of asking endless and detailed questions in butchered French. She also found them annoyingly self-confident and at the same time endlessly gullible.

One afternoon she was enjoying a hotel lunch when it became apparent that a tableful of American tourists were examining her. One of the women approached, and with a shaky voice inquired whether Elizabeth's reddened face was the result of "glazier" travel. "Because, if our faces are likely to get so blistered and burnt, I guess we won't go!" the questioner exclaimed. Elizabeth confirmed the cause of her condition, but helpfully suggested the woman and her friends might avoid sun damage if they each wore three gauze veils at one time. She figured "the temporary disfigurement" of all three veils (as well as the snickers they'd certainly elicit) would be "nothing when compared to the horror of having to appear at *table d'hôte* with a skin like mine." She then noted that many Americans fell victim to salesmen with "broken English and insinuating manners" who convinced them that wearing wool socks over their shoes would keep them from slipping on the ice and falling down precipitous glaciers. She described these tourists sitting all in a row pulling wool socks over their fancy, high-heeled boots and shoes, and then returning from their destination, the useless socks "hanging in draggled fringes" around their ankles.[17]

But most tourists, Americans included, usually ventured no farther than the Mer de Glace. She thought it notable, then, when she encountered a group of three young American men intent on climbing Mont Blanc.[18] Despite no previous climbing experience or even hard training walks, they were quite confident in their success, and had already instructed their hotel to fire the customary cannons upon their triumphant return. Even this practice of cannon firing got the Le Blond treatment. Each hotel, she informs us, "has two or three very diminutive cannons, which are fired by the respective porters, who give a prod with a long stick, and then turn and run, while a majestic puff, about the size of an egg, is seen to emerge from the mouth of these warlike machines, followed by a report resembling that of a pistol."

As it turned out, Elizabeth had her own ascent planned the following day. When she reached the Grand Mulets, the hutmistress told her three young men anxiously awaited her. They were the Americans. She found them lying prostrate on their mattresses, unable to move. One of them explained what happened. They'd left the hut that morning bound for the summit but had floundered up to their waists in soft snow. They struggled on for ten hours before finally deciding to turn back. Elizabeth related the conversation: " 'Madam,' he continued, feebly thumping the mattress with his fist; 'Madam, no woman can go up *Mount Blank* in all this fresh snow, or no man either, as far as that goes!' "

She commiserated with them while inwardly marveling at these youngsters' confidence in their own success as well as others' failure.

The next day she completed her climb, and "to avoid any well-meant salutations from the cannon," snuck back into Chamonix after dark.

Elizabeth also offered an interesting assessment of other "lady climbers," who were becoming much more numerous by the turn of the century. One class of these women ordinarily makes the summits and enjoys favorable weather, she tells us. But there is another "species against whom all the winds of heaven are arranged . . . who encounters a gale impossible to withstand, on one part of [a] ridge while another party is basking in hot sun and still air a little higher up." These ladies are forever "having their tents blown away, and [are] very critical as to the achievements of other lady climbers, by reason of the fact that they have failed to imitate them." Unsurprisingly, these ladies also have a hard time engaging the best guides. Whether she considered their "vinegary temperament" the cause or the effect of these climbers' experiences she didn't say.[19]

All the while she was building her skills as a climber, Elizabeth also worked on her techniques as a photographer and writer. After *The High Alps in Winter* she published a succession of other mountaineering titles, including a novel, and illustrated them with her own photos. The Alpine Club applauded her photographs as important contributions to the records of mountaineering, and her books earned her public acknowledgment as "an Alpinist of world-renowned fame."[20]

By the late 1890s Elizabeth gradually slowed the pace of her climbing, and by 1902 she retired completely. She was then forty-three, and other interests demanded her attention. She loved traveling, and for her journeys through Spain around this time wrote a small guidebook. A few years later, with her third husband, Aubrey Le Blond, she traveled through China, Russia, Korea, Turkey, and Japan, returning to England at the brink of World War I. During the war, when the British Red Cross deemed her too old to volunteer (she was fifty-three), she worked instead in a French army hospital. Later, she considered efforts to improve relations between postwar England and France her life's most important work, and her greatest honor the French Legion of Honor, awarded for her work restoring the Reims Cathedral.

But part of her heart was always in the Alps and with climbers. In 1907 she helped found the Ladies Alpine Club in London, the world's first climbing organization for women. During her term as its first president and for years afterward, she was known for encouraging younger and inexperienced climbers. In a move to honor her long career and contributions to the club, its members reelected her president in 1932, when she was seventy-one years old. She died of a heart attack two years later.

The Ladies Alpine Club devoted many pages in its *Yearbook* to memorializing her in 1934. "She was one of a small group of adventurous spirits . . . who did so much to pave the way for women climbers of a later day, by bearing the brunt of, and calmly ignoring, the criticisms heaped upon them for indulging in so 'unwomanly' a sport," the editor wrote. Men, too, recognized her achievements and contributed to the memoriam. Wrote Col. E. L. Strutt of the men's Alpine Club, "She was a highly skilful climber and, in her best days, was certainly rivalled in performance and form by Miss [Katherine] Richardson alone. Her chief characteristic was her extraordinary judgment. In this writer's opinion, as one who knew her well and made many ascents—both in summer and winter—in her company, this judgment has never been surpassed in any mountaineer, professional or amateur, of the so-called stronger sex."[21]

Elizabeth Le Blond dedicated her life to "meeting interesting people," and she certainly led a fascinating life herself. From starting out as a frail and sickly woman who couldn't tie her own shoes to becoming one of the champions of winter mountaineering, hers was the kind of life that few people witness, let alone experience. Her ascents, her writing and photography, and her work bringing the cause of female climbers to the forefront established her as one of the sport's great early ambassadors, as well as the first real leader in women's mountaineering.

"Moderation in All Things"

Vigorous climbing requires comfortable clothing, both on one's body and on one's feet. While styles of women's dress sparked debate, what they wore underneath was just as sensitive an issue.

As American tramper Mrs. William H. Nowell observed in the late 1870s, corsets "are positively hurtful at all times, and especially so on a long walk."[1] As an alternative, Mrs. Nowell enthusiastically touted the "emancipation waist," a new type of undergarment that, she explained, would exclude the use of a corset.

As was the case with dress generally, the evolution from corsets to more modern undergarments was slow and uneven. "Corsets may be worn or not, as one feels the need, but if worn should be loose enough to be no confinement to the lungs," lady trampers were advised in the 1870s.[2] Accordingly, some outdoorswomen abandoned corsets well before the turn of the century, but years later women were still being urged to drop the habit of wearing them, if only while engaged in recreation.

"The modern athletic girl does not need to be told that the ordinary corset is undesirable," admonished the president of the Scottish Ladies Alpine Club in 1920. "It is hardly necessary to say, in this enlightened age, that all garments must be loose." Nevertheless, Ruth Raeburn was careful not to let her readers assume it was acceptable "to go to the opposite extreme, and dispense with [corsets] altogether. There is moderation in all things," she advised, "and many women will find that a corset bodice of pliable material, and without bones, gives a certain amount of support to the body, and is quite suitable for climbing."[3]

Margaret Anne Jackson and her husband, E. P. Jackson. (ALPINE CLUB LIBRARY COLLECTION)

Chapter 7

An Easy Day for a Lady

The Teufelsgrat, Pennine Alps
August 1887

The guide shouted and Mary Mummery ducked. The rock whistled by— and instead of smashing her, hit her ice ax and sent it sailing over the precipice toward the glacier far below. *

Mary turned to her husband, her mouth open with alarm. "My ax . . ."

Fred Mummery simply gave her his enigmatic smile. "The Teufelsgrat is just earning its name. It isn't the 'Devil's Ridge' for nothing."

Mary supposed he was right. The Teufelsgrat was the jagged, exposed, breathtaking southwest ridge of the Täschhorn, a massive, nearly 15,000 foot peak north of Zermatt. Reaching the summit via the Teufelsgrat would be a major achievement—especially now that both guides were injured.

---

* Based on Mrs. A. F. [Mary] Mummery, "The Teufelsgrat," in A. F. Mummery, *My Climbs in the Alps and Caucasus*, pp. 45–65.

Mary ducked another spray of rocks kicked down from guide Alexander Burgener, who was still struggling up the cliff above them. Glancing at him, she could see the claret stain of blood darkening the white handkerchief binding his smashed hand. Sitting a few feet from her, head in his hands, guide Franz Andenmatten stifled another groan. He'd taken a nasty headfirst fall and was still badly shaken.

She shielded her eyes and looked up past Burgener. To her, the black cliff above him looked impassable. But she was confident that if there was a way up, Burgener would find it. It might require the contortions and balance of a gymnast, but she was equally confident she could handle it. For she wanted the summit as much as Fred did. Part of it was the simple joy of being there, of taking that last exhilarating step. But she also had something to prove: that she belonged.

Burgener himself had suggested her joining this climb. Fred then readily agreed, but she wasn't sure he'd have invited her himself. She knew he was proud of her performance on the Jungfrau and the Matterhorn earlier that summer, but those mountains had been done many times before. This was different. If they succeeded, it would be a first ascent by a route that had defeated every climber who'd ever tried it, including some of the Alpine Club elite. Could Fred resist the barbs of his A.C. friends if he included his wife in a first ascent? The club was dominated by men who thought that if members of the "weaker sex" had the audacity to climb at all, they should stick to the easy slopes. It seemed to Mary that the more women climbed, the more these men protested. Women simply aren't suited to steep ice or precipitous rock, they insisted. Stick to the easy slopes—for the rough stuff, they'd say, use a telescope and watch the climbing from the hotel porch, tea and crumpets set beside you! Their condescension and prejudice made her blood boil.

Burgener, however, had been with her on the Matterhorn. There he'd confided his admiration for Elizabeth Le Blond, a woman who'd come to the mountains to combat consumption and was now an expert winter mountaineer and author. She's smart, decisive, and never backs down from a challenge, he'd said. Burgener also told her about the ambitious American, Miss Brevoort, with her impressive list of ascents. "Women can climb," he'd pronounced, giving her a friendly poke in the ribs. "You must go up the Teufelsgrat."

THE LAST TWO DECADES of the nineteenth century produced a growing number of accomplished women mountaineers. Despite the antagonism from the male climbing establishment described by Mary Mummery, more and more men took along their wives to share their mountain adventures—and sometimes vice versa. As the strict Victorian moral code eased, women ventured out alone with their guides or with other female companions. And in some instances, men even partnered with women climbers for tough ascents. Three English women in particular stand out in the waning years of the Victorian era: Mary Mummery, her friend Lily Bristow, and Mrs. E. P. (Margaret Anne) Jackson. While there were other expert mountaineers, Katherine Richardson being perhaps the best of all, we can glimpse these three through their own writing. Unfortunately, they drifted off into history without leaving much trace of their lives outside mountaineering. In the case of Jackson and Bristow, even their birth and death dates are obscure. But the stories they left behind are wonderful mountaineering adventures.

Mary Mummery
(1859–1946)

Mary (Petherick) Mummery and Lily Bristow were old family friends, served as occasional rope mates, and were both associated with one of Britain's most famous alpinists, Albert F. (Fred) Mummery. Mary Petherick started climbing in the late 1880s after she married Mummery. She went on to establish an Alpine reputation in her own right. Lily Bristow joined Mummery and other Alpine Club members on some notable first ascents, and was considered one of the best rock climbers, male or female, of the last decades of the nineteenth century.

When she started climbing in 1887, Mary Mummery was the mother of a young daughter. She took to her new sport with exceptional quickness. Her first season saw her on the summits of the Jungfrau and the Matterhorn. But as impressive as these feats may have been, her crowning achievement that year was the ascent of the

The Immortal Miss Richardson

The French dubbed Englishwoman Katherine Richardson (1854–1927) "immortal" for her impressive list of peaks: nearly two hundred, starting when she was sixteen years old and visiting Zermatt for the first time. She posted six first ascents by any person and fourteen firsts by a woman. Elizabeth Le Blond, herself one of the greatest climbers of the century, stated that by the 1890s Richardson had "eclipsed all other women mountaineers."[1]

For a woman described as petite and delicate, Richardson climbed with remarkable speed, stamina, and efficiency. During a period of eight consecutive days during the summer of 1882, she climbed the Zinal Rothorn, Weisshorn, Monte Rosa, and the Matterhorn, all first-class peaks of more than 4,000 meters, or 13,123 feet. She was also creative and daring. In 1888 she and two guides climbed up the 13,294-foot Aiguille de Bionnassay and traversed its eastern arête to the 14,120-foot Dome du Goûter, both neighbors of Mont Blanc. Experienced mountaineers at the time considered this route an impossible feat because of its length and ruggedness. Two days later she traversed all five rocky spires of the Grand Charmoz, also near Mont Blanc, in another feat of climbing endurance and proficiency. The following year she returned to Chamonix and continued her speedy ascents of some of the region's most

Täschhorn by the route many considered beyond a woman's ability. In the tradition of all good mountaineering adventures, the climb took on epic proportions: accidents, injuries, blinding storms, an emergency bivouac, hunger, exhaustion, and a final, albeit less-than-stirring return. Mary wrote about it in a chapter in her husband's book, *My Climbs in the Alps and Caucasus*.[1]

difficult rock climbs. In one remarkably energetic five-day period, she climbed the Aiguille Verte (13,523 feet), Aiguille de Talèfre, and the Petit and Grand Dru (each more than 12,000 feet), all requiring deft balance and sure technique on their severe pinnacles. Fueling her on these strenuous climbs, according to those who knew her, was a diet of bread and butter with jam or honey and weak tea. And while by this time late in the century some female mountaineers had started wearing knickerbockers or bloomers, Richardson always climbed in a skirt.

For all her creative routes and first ascents, Richardson is best identified with the Meije (13,068 feet), the extremely steep, massive set of peaks in the Dauphiné region of the French Alps. Her career there started in 1888. In Chamonix after her Grand Charmoz climb, she noted an item in the local paper stating that an Englishwoman was about to attempt the first female ascent of the highest point of the Meije. Wondering who her enterprising rival might be, and anxious lest she should lose a first ascent she wanted for herself, Richardson quickly set out for the village of La Bérarde near the mountain's base. She got there to find out that the rumored "other" was actually herself, and that her own reputation had preceded her. She made the ascent, and it amused her for years later to think of her race with her shadow.[2]

The adventure started off on an exuberant note. Friends from Zermatt accompanied the climbing party, which included Fred, Mary, and the two guides, on their walk out of town to the highest hut on the route. Their lazy, sun-swept afternoon was interrupted by the appearance of a large, ill-tempered bull. He bellowed and charged, sending them all clambering onto the hut's roof. Flourishing hats and yelling wildly, they managed to drive the beast back down the mountain. Carefree once more, they toasted their conquest of the bull, picked at what Mary described as an "unwholesome and indigestible" supper, and then converted the tiny hut into a ball-room. All the hut occupants sang and danced, accompanied by reedy tunes piped by one of the guides.

The festivities ended fairly early, for the climbers wanted to start long before daybreak. But the floor was hard, the rug bedding scratchy, and sleep hard to come by. Then, just as everyone had finally settled down, a terrific roar and bang jolted them upright. The bull was back, apparently intent on knocking down the hut and reclaiming his territory. Brandishing ice axes, telescopes, sticks, and hobnailed boots, the occupants once again succeeded in driving him off, but any chance for sleep was gone. So the climbers packed up their gear, knocked the bottom out of two empty champagne bottles to hold candles, bade good-bye to their friends, and started on their way just after midnight.

It was a grumpy group. Little sleep, poor food, and hangovers made picking their way by candlelight through the moraine littering the mountainside all the more tricky. Only the men's occasional epithets broke the night's silence.

Dawn found them facing two steep, difficult-looking couloirs, or wide rocky gullies leading up the mountain. The problem of which one to take "did not arouse my enthusiasm," Mary admitted. Instead, she wrote, "turning my back to the cliffs, I watched the stately advance of the great red sun as it drove the last lingering darkness from the snowfields." But the climbing turned out easier than she expected, and her confidence grew even as guide Alexander Burgener regaled her with promises of "awful precipices" to come.

The route made them work hard for every inch. Rotten rock crumbled under their fingers and feet, making illusions of what seemed secure holds. Treacherous fangs of rock bristled from the ridge. Chasms with nothing but a thousand feet of air beneath their feet challenged them to leap across.

Burgener suffered the first injury. Just as he pulled himself over an overhanging slab, the rock shifted and crushed one of his powerful hands. A trail of blood followed him up the wall to the next ledge. "I no more strong in that hand," he muttered as they assessed the damage. Mary provided the first aid. "A somewhat mangled, swollen, and bleeding thumb offered an interesting problem to a student of the St. John's Ambulance Association," she observed. She bound it up with handkerchiefs and administered half a bottle of champagne along with a few bites from a chicken leg. These ministrations had the desired effect, for Burgener sneered at the suggestion of retreat and resumed the lead.

Then the second guide, Franz Andenmatten, lost his balance reaching for a difficult hold and fell head-downward over a cliff. Despite his hand injury, Burgener's iron grip on the rope saved the guide from possibly hurtling to his death. Instead, Andermatten dangled some 15 feet below. The others hauled him back to safety, but the experience had shattered his confidence. "The deathly silence was broken only by the sobs of the nerve-shattered bundle which lay at our feet," Mary recalled. "It was difficult to realize that this was the same active, sturdy, high-spirited man who had piped for us to dance—who had kept us merry by yodels, making echoes resound amongst the rocks, and whose cheerfulness had made even the stony moraine and endless screes lose something of their horror."

Thinking quickly, Fred hauled out another bottle of champagne. "How providential both bottles of Bouvier are not broken," he remarked as he offered a swig to the white-faced guide. Mary again took over as amateur nurse. Hoping the damage was more psychological than physical, she poked Andenmatten's ribs, bent his limbs, and "generally treat[ed] him in a reckless and unmerciful manner" before declaring him more frightened than hurt. Nonetheless, she wrapped his head "in a voluminous red handkerchief" for good measure. But the guide's enthusiasm was gone. As they went, they stopped occasionally to "apply a certain well-known remedy to his lips." After a while, as the climbing became more demanding and safe resting places less available, "a gentle hint was given that it was quite useless to develop pains of any sort . . . until a more favourable spot should present itself for their treatment," Mary wrote.

Meanwhile, Burgener's condition wasn't improving. The higher they got, the more ice and snow they encountered, finally forcing the guide to cut steps into the steep, icy slopes. "His hand was by this time bleeding afresh," Mary reported, "and a groan of pain escaped his lips as each stroke of the ax sent the brittle chips sliding and slithering down the glassy slope." Behind her, Andenmatten sobbed intermittently and looked as if he might faint. "The Teufelsgrat might have the best of the game," Mary worried.

But they kept climbing. Up the perilous rock they moved, until they faced an impossible-looking cliff, its dark rock ribs pockmarked with dense ice. Beyond it, snow and easy-looking rock led to the top of the ridge and then on to the summit. But now without her ice ax, Mary felt disarmed. She watched as Burgener tentatively fixed his ax in one of the ice-filled crevices dividing the cliff face. He pulled himself up and jammed his feet in the crack. He reached for another hold, and a shower of ice and shale splintered off beneath his ax. As he progressed higher almost every move unleashed an avalanche of sharp-edged chips. Mary finally heard him call for her to follow.

The cliff appeared to her like an assortment of thick black playing cards shuffled together by a careless hand, where one wrong move could bring the whole thing crashing down. She took a deep breath. With no ice ax, she relied completely on her own hands and feet. She reached into the crevice above her head. She cupped her fingers and locked her wrist and arm into place. She reached into the crack with her other hand and found a place to squeeze it tight. Then she wedged in her boot and lifted herself up. Painstakingly she edged her way up the face, using the crack and feeling for holds with her hands and feet. It was impossible not to send brittle rocks flying down. Every time she did, Burgener shrieked, "You kill your man if you not more careful are!"

But she didn't kill him, and once he'd made the top, Fred took over the lead. They used their hands, feet, ice axes, and occasionally a leg up on Burgener's shoulder to continue their advance. As the day stretched toward noon the wind came up, carrying an icy mist. Mary felt her feet and hands going numb. They made steady progress, but constantly feared falling rocks. "It was desirable to go as fast as possible, for the rock above us was constantly sending its superfluous icicles and stones across our track," Mary recalled. "We feared at every moment that larger missiles might follow, and sweep us with them in their mad flight of bounds and leaps to the gigantic blue crevasses far, far below."

Fred Mummery stayed in the lead, picking his way around the worst obstacles and over others. But then they faced a truly impossible obstacle: their ridge ended in a huge rock cornice that broke away into a yawning chasm. An impassable gulf separated them from the mountain's main spine. "There we four stood, absolutely powerless, our teeth chattering with the bitter cold, and the damp, cruel mist ever driving across, threatening to add obscurity to our other bewilderment," Mary wrote. After a few minutes, the shock of their predicament subsided as they assessed the "dull and narrow limits of actual fact." Even if they couldn't climb up, they decided, they could pick their way down the cornice and find another way to retake the ridge. More precarious climbing over crags, up steep buttresses, across hard ice, and they were back on track.

After more than twelve hours, they reached the summit. They hugged each other and toasted with champagne. But a clap of thunder cut their celebration short. All business now, Burgener grabbed the rope and hustled Mary back over the summit's edge. " 'You must go on, I could a cow hold here,' were the encouraging words I heard as I went helter-skelter over anything which happened to be in the way," she wrote. They descended by the easy ordinary route, following the footsteps of the previous day's party until new snow obliterated all signs. They ran as fast as they could through thick swirling snow. Thunder pounded their ears and the wind whipped around them, but they "laughed the tempest to scorn with jodels and triumphant shouts. The Teufelsgrat was ours!"

Hours later, the storm still blew and the four climbers grew increasingly exhausted, soaked, famished, and cold. With growing inattention they wound their way around open crevasses, managing to get off the glacier and onto the long sweep of moraine. After an hour on the stony slopes and still above treeline, they stopped to eat what little they had left for supper. It was now pitch black. The guides wanted to wait out the night and sleep, but the Mummerys favored reaching the forest, where they could find wood and make a fire. The guides agreed, but suddenly stopped in their tracks, pointing at a single weak light twinkling below them. Gleeful, Mary suggested it was a chalet. But the guides thought otherwise. "A ghost," Andenmatten whispered timidly, and Mary and Fred realized the guides' superstitions meant the forest was out of the question.

The guides squeezed under a large boulder and within minutes snored peacefully. But there was no rest for the Mummerys. Mary and Fred stamped their feet and clapped their gloved hands trying to stay warm and kept a weary watch on the horizon. At the first sign of dawn they roused the guides and the four of them stumbled down the rest of the way off the mountain. Just before sunrise they found an inn and plied the landlord for a hot breakfast. When they finally reached Zermatt a couple of hours later, their friends "were still peacefully slumbering in their beds."

Whether Mary continued climbing with her husband into the 1890s isn't clear, but their incomparable team ended when Fred died on Nanga Parbat in the Himalayas in 1895. Mary wrote a posthumous introduction to his book and included excerpts from some of his letters home from India. The last letter was written the day before he died. "On August 24th," she wrote, "my husband and the two Gurkhas were seen for the last time."

Mrs. E. P. Jackson
Pennine Alps
January 1888

Despite all her own accomplishments, Elizabeth Le Blond credited another woman, Mrs. E. P. Jackson, as being "one of the greatest climbers of her time."[2] Not much is known of Margaret Anne Jackson, but she made a series of pioneering climbs during the late 1870s and 1880s. Her husband, Edward Patten Jackson, was an Alpine Club member, and she became a Fellow of the Royal Geographic Society from 1892 until her death in 1906.

Mrs. Jackson started climbing with her husband, but which of the pair initiated their participation in the sport is unclear. Her first notable success was with him in 1876 when they and a guide made the first ascent of the ice-covered east face of the Weissmies, a 13,200-foot peak in the Pennine Alps northeast of Zermatt. In 1878 she began a long association with guide Alois Pollinger. Over the next nine years the pair collected an impressive list of peaks, including the 14,300-foot Dent Blanche near Zermatt (they pioneered a new route on the descent) and the soaring spires of the Grand Dru and Grand Charmoz in the Mont Blanc range.

Like Le Blond and Meta Brevoort, Mrs. Jackson became intrigued with exploring the Alps in winter. In January 1887 she set out on her first winter expeditions and, as it turned out, the last demanding climbs she'd ever make. She paid dearly, but she accomplished what no one had before—a winter traverse of the Jungfrau. Expert climbers considered this venture difficult enough in summer; the Jacksons themselves had tried and failed several times. Undeterred, Jackson mapped out a route she thought might work. In the days leading up to the climb she warmed up by making the first winter ascent of the Lauteraarhorn, a massive 13,261-foot peak.

So impressive were these feats that the stodgy *Alpine Journal* asked Mrs. Jackson for an account of her adventure—and published it without disguising its female authorship. The first essay the journal ever attributed to a woman, "A Winter Quartette," matter-of-factly reveals her courage and drive to succeed, her deep appreciation of the Alpine landscape, and her love of a good party and the company of friends.[3]

After celebrating the Christmas and New Year's holidays in high style at a Grindelwald hotel, Jackson and her party of three guides set out on January 4, 1888. The lead guide was Emil Boss, another outstanding climber with whom Mrs. Jackson shared a warm relationship. Also along was Ulrich Almer, who'd spent a chilly night in a snow cave with Meta Brevoort and William Coolidge more than a decade before. A procession of friends and acquaintances, plus dogs, walked with them part of the way. It was a glorious, sunny day, the mountains etched a brilliant white against the azure sky. Instead of the dusty, mule-filled dirt path of summer, the party had the snow-packed track to themselves. Their spirits soared as they stretched their legs on the "tolerably steep" hillside and reached the Schwarzegg hut in the shadow of the Lauteraarhorn and its close neighbor the Schreckhorn, both southeast of Grindelwald.

Well before dawn the next morning they set out for the massive Lauteraarhorn. "It was a keen, frosty morning, without a breath of wind," Jackson wrote. "The whole glacier glistening in the moon-light as if strewn with countless diamonds; it was just a fairy ball-room, and I much wonder whether we rough mortals had any right to trespass there and soil it."

The snow was hard and footing easy, and in the crisp air they kept a quick pace. By afternoon they reached the top of the Lauteraarhorn, where they could glimpse the Matterhorn and Weisshorn south across the Rhône valley. "Many smaller hills, too, almost unnoticed in summer, were changed by their winter garments into the most respectable snow-clad peaks," Jackson observed. It was the first time someone had stood on this mountain and admired the view in winter. They descended easily with a series of long glissades and made it back to the hut before dark.

The next day they planned to walk to the Bergli hut, from which they would start their attempt on the Jungfrau. Their route took them up a small unnamed peak, hardly worth a mention, except it was there they realized they could no longer ignore the thickening sky. With a light snow falling they turned back to Grindelwald, they spent the next three days tobogganing, attending parties, and other-wise waiting out a big snowstorm.

On January 10 they were back en route with "deepest laid schemes concerning the Jungfrau." They made the Bergli hut, but even the ambitious Mrs. Jackson showed she was only human. "We overslept ourselves," she admitted, and by the time they got going the next morning realized they'd better readjust their plans. Instead, they spent the day climbing what she identified as the Gross Viescherhorn, another peak never before scaled in winter. They whiled away a good part of the afternoon enjoying the view over the Oberland peaks all the way to Mont Blanc. The view "was more than worth the journey out from England to see," Jackson noted. They found a good slope for glissading down the mountain and made it back to the hut.

There was no oversleeping the next morning and the rising sun found them well on their way. But some of the peaks were "smoking," or wearing the wispy white clouds that signal high, cold winds. The weather was turning, and before long the wind forced them to their hands and knees. Nevertheless, the sun kept shining, so they continued on. But with the rocky Jungfrau summit in view, they admitted defeat. Three hours in the icy wind and they'd barely advanced on the hard ice slope. Bare rocks where Mrs. Jackson was sure they'd make quick progress to the top were still far away. They crept back down the mountain, half frozen, their clothes stiff as boards. Emil Boss produced a few shards of kindling, a kettle, and a tin cup "from some mysterious pocket" and brewed a pot of tea in the shelter of a small cave. Weary but somewhat warmed, they continued down and reached the hut by lantern light.

They returned to Grindelwald the next morning. Mrs. Jackson felt deeply discouraged. "It was certainly a black moment in my life when I was asked how we fared and had to answer that we failed," she recalled. The mountain obsessed her. "I could not rest. The disappointment of the Jungfrau was for ever in my mind," she admitted. But when she thought of the multiple attempts on the Matterhorn before it was conquered, she reached a simple conclusion. "I resolved to try again," she declared.

Her team was back on the mountain two days later. They made it without incident to the long ice slope and passed across easily. They reached the bare rocks, climbed a final snowy ridge, and soon stood on the cone of ice capping the Jungfrau summit. Only a bank of clouds in the north marred the lovely view. They allowed themselves just a few minutes before starting their descent. Winter days pass quickly, and they knew they still had a lot of work ahead of them.

Their problems started late in the afternoon. They had made excellent time, daring to "run a mild steeplechase" down a glacier. But there would be no quick descent of the steep rock face leading to an icefall and another steep glacier. In the fading light the tricky descent required even more care. Steep, shattered, snow-covered rock crumbled under their feet. Making matters worse, only one lantern stayed lit, forcing them to hand it back and forth as they picked their way through the icefall. This was uncharted territory in winter, and while they knew from summer experience that a route out led through this area, in the dim lantern light and covered with snow things looked very different from what they remembered.

They grew even colder as they searched for the route. They were also tired, hungry, and probably more than a little nervous. Wandering around the icefall in the dark was hazardous business. Boss finally called off the search and led them instead into a little ice cave. They would have to wait for morning with scarcely any food and just a few extra items for warmth. "It was not exactly the most cheerful prospect"; but even so, the perpetually optimistic Mrs. Jackson figured, "things might have been worse."

Even in these rather dire conditions, she found the ice cave a place of ethereal beauty. She described it as two long, narrow chambers hung with icicles of all shapes and sizes, divided by statuesque ice pillars. "The whole place glistened in the light of our faithful lanterns," she reported. They dug a hole in the snow, carpeted it with their empty knapsacks, and used their ice axes as seats. They divvied up the remains of their larder and "dined sumptuously" on a few raisins, a small piece of cheese, a slice of bread, a few drops of brandy—oh, and there may have been a chicken bone, she noted. Then they piled on a possum rug and "prepared to get through the night as pleasantly as we could and to make the best of a bad bargain."

In the first light of morning they found the route out of the icefall not twenty paces away. They were soon over the glacier and on their way home. "It is needless to say we did not linger," Mrs. Jackson remarked.

Reminiscing on her adventure a year later, she wrote: "It was a new experience, but to me a most enjoyable one. The cold was sometimes very severe, especially so directly after the sundown, but the pleasant and just sufficient warmth of the sun was most delightful, and when combined as it generally was with firm rocks and good hard snow more than compensated us for any of our earlier troubles."

Demonstrating mountaineers' traditional stoicism, Mrs. Jackson did not tell her readers that she suffered severe frostbite that night in the cave. She eventually lost several toes because of it, which effectively ended her climbing career.[4] Her triumph was also dampened with the death, just a few months later, of guide Emil Boss. His obituary appeared in the same *Alpine Journal* as her story, which she concluded by mourning his loss: ". . . there is just one little cloud to dim the brightness of it all—the thought that never again in any of my future wanderings will I meet the man, who by his experience in winter climbing, and his unceasing efforts to make things easy for me, contributed so much to all our success. I mean Mr. Emil Boss."

Lily Bristow
Swiss and French Alps
1893

It would be understandable if Lily Bristow found climbing with some of the premier members of the Alpine Club a bit intimidating. After all, in the 1890s the club was strictly men-only, and women's presence in the mountains was hardly welcomed by most members, as her friend Mary Mummery noted. Yet Lily had nothing but encouraging words about her male companions in describing a few exciting weeks of climbing in August 1893.[5] In fact, she had a remarkably close relationship with some of them, particularly A. F. Mummery, whom she credits for the success of her ventures. She relates that she was treated very nicely, even "coddled" by her partners, who saw to it that she was relatively warm and dry, sometimes at their expense. She occasionally shared a tent with the fellows (six of them in a six-by-four-foot tent on the Grépon, for instance), indicating they all must have felt fairly comfortable in each other's company. It also hints at how the strict Victorian moral code had loosened by century's end.

Nonetheless, it wouldn't be surprising if Lily had to be twice as competent as the next man to earn her place on the rope of Mummery, Ellis Carr, Norman Collie, William Slingsby, and other bright lights of the Alpine establishment. And she not only shared their rope, but sometimes led as well. Among her ascents with these men were a north-south traverse of the Grand Charmoz, a demanding 11,300-foot rock peak near Mont Blanc, the northern ridge of the 13,848-foot Zinal Rothorn in the Pennine Alps, and the Italian ridge of its neighbor, the Matterhorn.[6]

One of her greatest successes was on the 11,424-foot Grépon, one of the towering granite needles, or *aiguilles,* in the Mont Blanc massif near Chamonix. With a guideless party led by A. F. Mummery, she traversed the peak in 1893, making her the first woman ever to climb the Grépon. More than a decade before, Mummery achieved the first-ever ascent with Alexander Burgener and another guide. He described its "great towers, rising a hundred feet or more in single obelisks of unbroken granite, seeming to bar all possibility of progress. . . . Nowhere can the climber find bolder towers, wilder clefts, or more terrific precipices."[7] In the days before pitons, chocks, and other forms of modern climbing protection, the Grépon represented the outer limit of climbable rock. It became one of the classic climbs in the Alps.

Reaching the summit required a series of demanding moves up narrow chimneys and off-width fissures, including what came to be known as the notorious "Mummery Crack." This narrow 60-foot wedge promised catastrophe should a climber fall, for below its base nothing interrupted the view for another thousand feet. "It was more difficult than I could ever imagine," Bristow wrote enthusiastically of her experience. "A succession of problems, each one of which was a ripping good climb itself."

Ripping good and harrowing too. Five days of rain and snow had coated the rocks, and while the August sun left some spots comfortably dry, when the climbers moved into the shade, they raked snow from the cracks with their fingers and struggled to keep their footing on ice-glazed ledges. Nonetheless, Mummery applauded Lily's fluid style, remarking that she showed the other members of the party, all Alpine Club members, "how steep rocks should be climbed."[8] Lily also served as the expedition's photographer. Mummery noted that she'd shun the rope in order to get to just the right spot for snapping a few pictures, often while the men caught their breath. For her part, she credited her friend Fred with getting not only the first woman through the climb, but a camera too.

By the time they reached the Grépon summit in the late afternoon, the weather had turned. They made their descent through a "rampageous" wind pelting them with rain and hail. Soaking wet and cold, they piled into their tent shortly before midnight.

Lily's success on the Grépon inspired Mummery to offer up a remark that has been repeated ad infinitum since, usually to demonstrate the chauvinism of male climbers: "that all mountains appear doomed to pass through the three stages: An inaccessible peak—The most difficult ascent in the Alps—An easy day for a lady." But Mummery didn't come up with this gem; it appears to have been coined by another lion of nineteenth-century British mountaineering, Leslie Stephen. Nevertheless, Mummery revived it in *My Climbs in the Alps and Caucasus*. But his statement is not necessarily derogatory, and indeed may be tongue-in-cheek for the great climber goes on to admit, "The Grépon has not reached this final stage. . . . Indeed, owing to the great accumulation of ice and snow on the mountain, the ascent [with Bristow] will always rank as amongst the hardest I have made."[9]

Lily Bristow and Fred Mummery reunited a few days later. With several of the Grépon veterans, their goal was the 12,247-foot Petit Dru, another rock pillar with a formidable reputation. They planned to do it without guides, even though none of them had ever climbed it before. As they lay around camp in the evening, Lily carefully noted the route of a guided party descending from the peak. So despite a sprained ankle, she took the lead when they left the next morning well before dawn. She relinquished it several hours later, when the climbing got so difficult, she wrote, that "no one but Fred could lead up some of the places.

"The climbing was pretty stiff, I must say," Lily acknowledged, "though not nearly as difficult as the Grépon, which is a real snorker." At the summit she tucked in between some rocks and took a snooze. She reported that when she awoke, the "fellows gave me a lovely drink of lemons and half-melted snow."

The finale of that summer's Mummery-Bristow partnership was

in the Swiss Alps north of Zermatt. They took on the Zinal Rothorn, an extremely steep, sharp peak that had defeated even Lucy Walker. The climb very nearly didn't happen. The climbers wanted an extra-early start; 1:30 A.M. seemed sufficient. But the "natives" were slow to produce the ordered breakfast, so they didn't leave their hotel in the village of Zinal until 2:45. They had a "colossal distance" to cover before getting to the peak, and by 7:00 A.M. Mummery figured they'd already missed their chance. But Lily wasn't giving up. "I begged and prayed in my most artful manner," she admitted, and he agreed to go on. They set "little vows" for time and distance goals along the way, agreeing to turn back if they didn't make them. But Lily, the keeper of the clock, conveniently forgot to mention if they happened to fall behind schedule. Still, 2:00 P.M. was the agreed-upon cutoff; they'd turn back no matter where they were. At twenty-five minutes of two, they triumphantly stepped on the Rothorn summit. Then with no time to spare, "we scrambled down as fast as we could," Lily related. On the descent, she lost her hat and goggles over a cliff. So much for her "cherished complexion," she cheerfully reported, but admitted that by the end of the day her face had burned so badly it was difficult to smile.

Painful or not, Lily must have worn a triumphant grin when she and Mummery finally arrived back at their hotel at 9:00 P.M. "It was a great joke," she wrote. "None of the hotel people would believe we had been up the Rothorn: 'non, Mademoiselle, pas possible!' They are not used to non-guided parties here and the idea that Fred and I could calmly track up their most awesome and revered peak is quite beyond them—they think we must have mistaken some grassy knoll for the Rothorn."

With her superb rock-climbing abilities that had even men following in her footsteps, Lily Bristow showed the way for the finesse climbers of the next century, women who relied on technique, balance, and grace to take them up increasingly difficult routes. Her ascents show how far women had come in seventy-five years of Alpine mountaineering, from being hauled up Mont Blanc to leading men in guideless parties. Vestiges of the Victorian age held on after its official end in 1901, but World War I finally buried them.

The social, political, and economic world changed with the war, and women emerged with many more opportunities than before. A whole new generation of climbers, including many American women, took up mountaineering in the Alps and beyond.

No doubt, there were many women whose names are lost to history who were active Alpine climbers in the last decades of the 1800s. By the turn of the century "lady climbers" had become much more commonplace, though their general acceptance in the male-dominated sport was still questionable. At the time the only American woman known to have made a series of ascents in Europe was Meta Brevoort. But even as she was making her pioneering climbs, across the Atlantic women were taking to the hills. The White Mountains of New Hampshire were in a different league of difficulty from the Alps, but women there also considered themselves mountaineers. And they explored and built new trails into the uncharted mountains alongside men from the very start.

SECTION 3

The Lady Trampers

Accompanied by her new husband, Carolyn Morse Rea sports a new-style tramping outfit, 1904. (COURTESY EDWARD M. REA)

Chapter 8

Women of the White Mountains

1876–1895

I have reached a height found unattainable by stalwart men.

The Twin Mountain Range, New Hampshire
August 1882

A word that might have made most gentlemen blush escaped Charlotte Ricker's lips—and she didn't regret it one bit. Behind her, Martha Whitman chuckled.

"Miss Ricker!" Whitman said in mock alarm. "If they could hear you now in the dining room of the Maplewood!"

Turning toward her companion, Ricker pictured the surprised faces of the people staying at the grand hotel in town. "They would never imagine this. Ever. I can't believe it myself."

Both women began to laugh. They knew they were mirror images of each other—red-faced with sweat, black flies stuck on their skin, bits of leaves and spruce needles festooning their hair, their skirts streaked with mud.

A third woman, Dr. Laura Porter, joined them. "Where's Mr. Scott?" she asked after catching her breath. She too looked more than a little bedraggled. "I need his ax. I want to take a few cuts myself at these abominable trees—instead of them cutting me!" She lifted her sleeve and revealed a nasty scrape on her arm.

"Is tramping always like this?" Ricker asked, mopping her brow.

"Oh heavens, no," Whitman answered with a smile. "It's usually like a walk in the park—once the trails are made. They're marked, you see, with blazes cut on the trees. But we're really the lucky ones."

"The lucky ones?" Ricker sounded dubious. "How's that?"

"Because we're making our own way. We're not following someone else's trail."

"Yes," Porter joined in. "We're explorers—real mountaineers. No one has ever been here before—isn't that grand!"

"I heartily agree," Ricker answered. "But this abominable scrub—do you always encounter it near the top of a mountain?"

Whitman shook her head. "Twin Mountain scrub is the worst I've ever seen. It is awful, I admit. Oh—I think that's Mr. Scott."

Sure enough, they could hear the thwacking of an ax getting closer. The sound was punctuated a moment later by a bellowed epithet that made the ladies cover their mouths to suppress their giggles.

"We'd better see if he's all right," Porter said, regaining her composure.

She started off, squeezing sideways through the dense spruce scrub, fending away branches with one hand and gathering her long skirt close to her with the other. Whitman followed, and Ricker took a deep breath. "This is going to make a great story," she thought to herself as she seized a fist full of branches. "If I live to tell it."

WHILE THEIR EUROPEAN counterparts climbed snow-crested peaks in the Alps, American women of the nineteenth century also took to the mountains, though on a much different scale. In the northeastern United States, where much of this early outdoor recreation took place, the highest summits were also measured by 4,000—but feet, not meters. Climbing these mountains was a chore, though not because of avalanches, icefalls, or crevasses, as in the Alps, but rather because few of them had trails to the summits. The traditional paths used by Native Americans, traders, and trappers followed the valleys and the notches dividing the mountain ranges. To be accessible to hikers—or trampers, as they were then called—these mountains needed to be explored and mapped, and trails built. Women played a major role, alongside men, in opening up the White Mountains of New Hampshire for recreation. Women's concerns and sensibilities about the mountain environment also helped lead to a significant portion of the region being conserved as national forest early in the twentieth century. And in the Whites and beyond—especially in Colorado, California, and the Pacific Northwest, where women were climbing mountains more comparable to the Alps— women's outlook on nature and the outdoors helped shape an American sensibility about wilderness and its role in people's lives. The story of the women of the White Mountains, then, is one of exploration.

Like their European cousins, Americans started flocking to the countryside for recreation in the second half of the century and especially after the Civil War. Soon clubs began organizing around mountain exploration and recreation. The Appalachian Mountain Club (AMC), founded in Boston in 1876, was one of the very first.

The AMC attracted well-to-do professionals in the Boston area, and soon New York, New Haven, and Philadelphia. Unlike its mountaineering counterpart, the Alpine Club in London, the AMC —and other early outdoor recreation clubs such as the Mazamas in Portland, Oregon, and the Mountaineers in Seattle, Washington— quickly accepted female members, and enlisted their participation in a spirit of camaraderie.[1] The difference of attitude in the United States was well captured by Moses Sweetser, an early AMC member who also authored guidebooks to the White Mountains. "In these days of the advocacy of female suffrage and woman's rights," he declared in 1876, "it needs hardly to be stated that American ladies can accomplish nearly everything which is possible to their sturdier brethren."[2]

The AMC was organized during a time of tremendous public interest in leaving the cities and enjoying the fresh air and sublime landscape of the mountains. The Adirondacks, the woods of Maine, and the White Mountains of New Hampshire attracted trainloads of visitors every summer. Members of the AMC, which focused primarily on the Whites, traveled north to the guest houses and great hotels, places such as Glen House in Pinkham Notch and smaller establishments such as the Ravine House in Randolph, the latter of which catered to the tramping set and became the club's unofficial summer headquarters. They'd devote their summers to exploring and path building, and then spend cheery winter evenings regaling club meetings with tales of their discoveries and adventures. Many of these reports were then printed in the club's biennial journal, *Appalachia*, which is still published today.

Although women were not among the core group of founders, they appeared on the club roster at its second meeting, and rather rapidly gained both in numbers and, to a lesser degree, in stature. With a regime of committees rivaling any modern corporate organizational chart, the club assigned its various functions with men controlling most of the leadership, or "councillor," positions, while women organized and hosted outings, lectured at club meetings, contributed papers on botany, geology, and natural history, and led subgroups such as the "Section for Field Studies." By its second decade the club had attracted nearly seven hundred members, many of whom were female, and women served as councillors of art and natural history.

In the field women quickly proved they were as adventurous as the men. In 1882, for instance, a party of twenty-eight, "more than half of them ladies," ascended and spent the night near Mount Adams, a 5,800-foot peak in New Hampshire's Presidential Range. "The ladies proved themselves to be good campers, and were very enthusiastic in their admiration for forest life," reported the *White Mountain Echo*, a local newspaper that also served as a bulletin board for the AMC. Similar reports of women's participation were common in the "Appalachian Excursions" sprinkled through its pages. By the mid-1880s wagonloads of AMC members disembarked at the Summit House on Mount Washington and spent a week each summer exploring the Presidentials. Parties of ten or more members were often seen strung along the various paths above treeline on these mountains. In July 1886 it was reported that on Mount Washington "about two-thirds of the [approximately one hundred] members present were ladies, and they showed equal endurance and enthusiasm on the walks with the men." Women also outnumbered men on the club's first excursion up Maine's highest peak, Katahdin, in the summer of 1887. And showing they weren't just warm-weather adventurers, twenty women joined the club's forty-six-member "Snow Shoe Section," organized in 1886.[3]

That women were actively involved was noticed outside the AMC. A New York writer attributed the club's fast growth and increasing prominence to its "training of both men and women to climb and walk easily distances of a considerable number of miles at a stretch—an accomplishment that the Americans, especially American women, rarely possess." A writer, presumably English, found a broader appeal in the club's activities. "In the conservative masculine mind, particularly of Europe," wrote Miss Emily A. Thackray in 1889, "it has been a mooted point whether a woman could climb, camp out and 'rough it,' with any pleasure to herself or comfort to the 'lords of creation.' But to-day in America, things are greatly changed; mountain-tramping has become a 'fad' among ladies and they are encouraged by their brothers, their cousins and their uncles." Many of the club's lady mountain climbers "are well-known in artistic, scientific, and literary circles," she noted.[4]

Women eagerly participated in two of the club's main activities, deemed "exploration" and "improvements." Explorers investigated the largely uncharted valleys and hills, discovering broad vistas and stunning waterfalls, and enjoying the challenge of bushwhacking and finding their way with compass and rudimentary maps. Improvers cut and blazed new trails, built shelters, and helped fill in the maps that would allow more people access to the pleasures of the mountains.[5] Those early trails were the beginning of what is today one of the most extensive trail networks in the United States. Several women in particular were among the preeminent improvers and explorers of the time. These included the mother-daughter team of Lucia and Marian Pychowska, Lucia's sister Edith Cook, their friend Isabella Stone, and Martha Whitman.

Lucia Cook Pychowska, her husband John, her brother Eugene Cook, and her younger sister Edith all lived in a stately residence on the Hudson River in Hoboken, New Jersey. Lucia was described as "a most restless, agile, lovable little lady, whose flashing thought and rapier repartee found a match only in her daughter."[6]

A tireless walker, Lucia's mountain-climbing career spanned four decades and crossed Pennsylvania, New Jersey, New York, and New England. During one long summer day in 1887, she traversed Mounts Washington, Clay, Jefferson, Adams, and Madison, a rugged chain of 5,000-plus-foot peaks in the Presidential Range. Lucia's interest in the mountains went beyond peak-bagging, however. As a self-taught botanist, she meticulously observed wildflowers and alpine plants, and established herself as an expert on local ferns. Marian, her only child, was born in 1859. Marian literally followed in her mother's footsteps, developing her own interest in botany and becoming an avid tramper. She was described as "tall, graceful, light-footed and almost as much at home on the mountain peaks as an Alpine chamois."[7]

Marian's Uncle Eugene and Aunt Edith encouraged her interest in the mountains as well. Eugene Cook was one of the AMC's pre-eminent trail builders and served as one of its earliest Councillors of Exploration. While a dedicated tramper and trailblazer, Edith Cook was also known as a landscape painter. Many a summer's afternoon found her atop a summit, sketching the scene below. When she wasn't painting, she joined her brother on many of his trail-building forays. In 1883 she took part in the AMC's first traverse of the Carter Range in the north-central White Mountains. She and her companions walked up the existing path to Mount Moriah, just southeast of Gorham, New Hampshire. From there they bushwhacked south 10 miles through difficult terrain to Carter Dome, a massive, round-topped peak opposite Mount Washington. Edith's report on the excursion was published in *Appalachia*, and the club soon constructed a permanent path across the Carter Range.

The Stones, who came from Framingham, Massachusetts, started visiting the White Mountains after the end of the Civil War, while the Cooks and Pychowskas arrived about a decade later. Isabella Stone's friendship with them was forged in the summer of 1876 when the families met at a guest house in Sugar Hill, a village overlooking Franconia Notch. While not always in the best of health, Isabella became the chief promoter and architect of many trails in Franconia

Notch and around Mount Moosilauke in the western White Mountains, including the trail to Bridal Veil Falls, still a popular destination below Cannon Mountain.

Isabella Stone, Edith Cook, and the Pychowskas described themselves as mountaineers, and to them the mountains they knew were "old friends," and ones they hadn't seen or climbed before were "new acquaintances." They loved the sense of exploration and discovery still very possible in their day and proudly threw themselves into the work of trail building alongside Eugene Cook and other AMC men. Mounts Success, Ingalls, Wildcat, Madison, Adams, Waternomee, Lafayette, Royce, Baldface, the Caribou Range—they dutifully reported for the club on their excursions to these mountains and many others. They advocated within the club for new trails and helped maintain old ones. They joined search parties for lost walkers. And like many other visitors to the White Mountains, they bemoaned the loss of paths to logging and fretted when forest fires plagued the hills and "smokes" obliterated an otherwise fine view. For unlike today, when much of the land these women tramped through is publicly owned, then it was controlled by timber barons who cut vast swaths of forest for use in Boston, New York, and other cities. Concern about the forest fires and erosion left in the wake of aggressive logging helped spark the conservation movement in the Northeast, and eventually led to the creation of the White Mountain National Forest.

These women were always proud to make a summit, and frequently noted how easily they beat the walking time for ladies suggested by the guidebooks. But they also expressed an aesthetic interest in the mountain landscape that reflected that of some of their counterparts climbing in the Alps. As they walked they made careful notes of what they encountered and described in often eloquent terms the beauty they observed, whether it was an entire landscape, a new plant, or a mountain sunset. They saw virtue in contemplation as well as in action and reflected their era's appreciation of the sublime.

"I do indeed remember our climb of Cannon Mountain and our walk home through those thrush-haunted woods in the hollow of the

Ham Branch," Edith Cook reminisced in a letter to Isabella Stone. "It was a day to remember with the weird mists sailing up the notch and lightly enriching the crests of Cannon and then that ruby light on Lafayette as we gained the top of the steep hill above the mill, that trial for impatient feet at the close of the day's labor."[8]

"Black-flies aside, these June woods have a sociable charm that will be lost ere July is half over," Marian observed in *Appalachia* with melodramatic flourish. "Then the forest will be lonely and silent, with little more than the beguiling scream of a hawk or the sudden, loud shrilling of a locust, to break the stillness; but now it is full of many-voiced domestic warblings and twitterings that form a bourdon for the clear, ringing fife of the Swainson thrush."[9]

In the course of their explorations, the women adopted practical measures that were somewhat unusual for proper ladies of the day—and were probably unfamiliar even to the convention-breaking women of the Alps. In the densely wooded landscape of the White Mountains, it was often impossible to get a view of neighboring mountains or into the valleys—a problem if one was exploring new territory. So the trampers—male and female—would climb trees to try to get some perspective. This skill was often as necessary as using a compass, but for women, it seemed quite remarkable, given their attire.

Marian Pychowska gives a glimpse of how the lady trampers overcame the challenge of their dress. In September 1879 she, her Uncle Eugene Cook, and her Aunt Edith bushwhacked up a ridge on the "dark, wooded mass" of Mount Kineo in the central White Mountains. The AMC hierarchy had commissioned them to report on this largely uncharted area.

"By dint of climbing a small tree, we saw, through an opening, [Mount] Moosilauke, with its great gorge, looking very near and grand across the valleys in which Baker's River rises," Marian wrote to her friend Isabella Stone. Later, Isabella expressed some surprise at her climbing, so Marian explained: "You wonder how my aunt and I climb trees. Consider first that the middle sized spruces were conveniently branched down to the ground. The getting up is very easy as the skirts come naturally after. A graceful descent is more difficult, as the same

American Solutions: Bathing Suits and Bloomers

When Appalachian Mountain Club member and White Mountains tramper Mrs. William G. Nowell decried women's dress in 1877, she echoed a critique of dress already gaining strength in the United States.

The issue had percolated since at least 1837, when reformer Sarah Grimké argued that "as long as we submit to be dressed like dolls, we never can rise to the stations of duty and usefulness from which [men] desire to exclude us."[1] Thirteen years later, dress was among the issues discussed at the first national Woman's Rights Convention.

A year later in 1851, Elizabeth Smith Miller, a cousin of reformer and activist Elizabeth Cady Stanton, became so fed up with dragging her long skirt through the dirt as she gardened that she resolved "this shackle should no longer be endured." She looked about for an alternative and settled on wide-legged Turkish trousers, gathered at the ankles, and a full skirt reaching just below the knees. Amelia Bloomer, a friend and neighbor of Stanton's, adopted the outfit and publicized it, and the dress was christened with her name.[2]

"Bloomers" were also dubbed the "American" or "freedom costume" and came to symbolize the suffrage movement. Equal rights advocate Julia Archibald Holmes proudly donned a calico version of the outfit in 1858 when she became the first woman to climb Colorado's Pike's Peak. "I am the first woman," she wrote, "who has worn the 'American costume' across the prairie sea."[3]

But not every woman adopted bloomers. Mrs. Nowell and her cohorts considered the bloomer skirt still too long and full. Instead, they suggested that women wear a somewhat more rugged version of the common flannel bathing costume. Mrs. Nowell dubbed this outfit a "mountain suit for women." It included a sacklike, long-sleeved upper garment neatly buttoned at the knee and belted at the waist, and bloomerlike trousers underneath.

There's little evidence the mountain suit gained many converts, though one observer did report "beach costumed maidens" cavorting about trails on Mount Washington in the late 1870s.[4] More typically, women followed the advice spelled out by the Appalachian Mountain Club at that time: "Short skirts become a necessity, and even these need to be curtailed in rough mountain work." *Short,* for the AMC, meant a "scant skirt reaching the tops of the boots."[5]

Inexorably, the conventions of dress changed, and both hemlines and bloomers shortened. Bloomers and knickers, their more tailored cousins, started appearing with and without skirts covering them. The changing styles are illustrated in 1904 by a young Massachusetts couple who spent their honeymoon walking about the White Mountains and the Adirondacks. Carolyn Rea, proudly wearing her modern "tramping regalia," recorded this memorable encounter in her diary: "Halfway down met a woman in lead of party with alpenstocks, long skirts, etc. who sank on a log at my approach and in tones of longing, envy and despair, said to me—You're the first woman I've met in the mountains that I have envied. I shall have some myself next year, meaning my knee-length skirt and long boots."[6]

By the time World War I ended, skirts were the exception, rather than the rule, for mountain travel.

———

skirts are apt to remain above, but my uncle and [another man] con-siderately left us, so that grace did not have to be considered."[10]

Dedicated as they were to exploring the Whites, the Pychowskas considered Martha Whitman the best of the lady trampers. "Seeing Miss Whitman dispelled a very wrong impression I had received from reading some things in *Appalachia*," Marian Pychowska wrote in 1882. "She is a person of about 35, evidently very independent, but ladylike and unassuming. I think she is the most thoroughly good lady mountaineer I have ever seen, short and stout and therefore somewhat scant of breath, but energetic and untiring. She seems to go through exposure, fatigue and campfood with unimpaired diges-tion." Just days earlier, on meeting her for the first time, Marian came away thinking Whitman was "the sturdiest walker I have ever seen and withal unassuming."[11]

Whitman lived in Lexington, Massachusetts, and her first excur-sions to the White Mountains in the mid-1870s appear to have been with a small group of friends calling themselves the Lexington Botanical Club. She and others, including her friends Augustus E. Scott, Martha Knowles, and Dr. Laura Porter, joined the new AMC. Whitman and her friends tramped and camped through the Whites in an effort—ironic sounding today—to get away from the increas-ingly crowded scenic tourist spots.

Martha Knowles, who lived in Boston, was one of the first women to join the AMC. Little is known about her life, but she was active in the club, leading excursions as the leader of the section on Field Studies and then serving on the executive committee of *Appalachia* well into the 1900s. More is known of her friend Whitman, but Knowles performed a feat that should earn her per-manent acclaim in the annals of White Mountain hiking. She made what was surely the first traverse of the Presidential Range by a woman—a marathon covering approximately 24 miles and more than 8,800 feet of climbing. According to reporter Emily Thackray, in 1889 Knowles "covered all the Presidential peaks in one day, a feat that would stagger most men."[12] Little is known of Laura Porter, other than that she graduated from New York University Medical School, practiced medicine in Boston, and enjoyed visiting the Whites.

When Marian Pychowska first met her, Whitman was actually forty-two—not thirty-five—and was a first-year student at Boston University Medical School. She was also only days away from taking part in the first traverse of the Twin Mountain Range, an epic adventure that would earn great notoriety, and no doubt served as fodder for entertaining stories by AMC members for many years afterward. It also illustrated the primary role women played in one of the club's earliest and important explorations.

The Twin Mountain Range in the northern White Mountains rises along the Little River, just a few miles west of Mount Washington. The range stretches south into what today is labeled the Pemigewasett Wilderness. Its peaks, including North and South Twin, Bond, Bondcliff, and Guyot, offer some of the most spectacular views in the Whites. But the Twins were a nemesis to early trampers—not for any physical aspect of the mountains themselves, as they are not particularly high, steep, or remote. Rather, it was the confounding dwarf spruce—"unflankable bayonet-lines of shrubbery," as one observer put it—defending their summits.[13]

The 1881 guidebook The White Mountains: A Handbook for Travellers quoted New Hampshire state geologist Charles H. Hitchcock on the Twin Range: "Scarcely any mountains are more difficult to reach than these owing to the stunted growth near their tops." That same year, Appalachian Mountain Club founder and president Edward Pickering recommended the construction of a path across the range. The trail, he asserted, would provide a view "second to none in the White Mountains" and would provide a link between the great hotels and guest homes favored by AMC members in the villages of Twin Mountain in the north and Lincoln and Woodstock in the south.[14]

In August 1882 Augustus E. Scott took up Pickering's charge. As the AMC's Councillor of Improvements, he proposed surveying the range as the first step toward trail building. He put the word out but found no one willing to join what was sure to be an uncomfortable undertaking. Finally he decided to do it by himself. As he was making final preparations, however, a female AMC member, through a letter written by an intermediary, made the astonishing proposition that she accompany him. Quite taken aback, Scott politely admitted he hadn't thought of seeking female companionship for the endeavor. He wrote back, attempting to dissuade her by painting the journey in epic terms. Hunger, thirst, arduous labor, sleeping without shelter of any kind, rain, heat, cold, and "scrub of the most fearful kind, where the clothes may be torn to shreds"—all these "and even greater hardships" awaited them, he promised. But if she still wished to make the attempt, he would invite another companion: "the only lady I know for whom the undertaking is feasible, to accompany her."

Scott's gambit backfired. The first woman's interest was merely piqued, and then another woman signed on.[15] "I was fairly caught," Scott admitted in his version of the expedition, published in the AMC journal *Appalachia*. "I had painted the probable difficulties of the proposed exploration in glowing colors, and had rather disdainfully expressed a willingness to invite ladies to accompany me if they dared attempt it; and here were three ladies who not only dared, but were eager to go. I would not retract, although I had many misgivings, and some doubts of their reaching even the first summit."

Who were these adventurous women? Scott never identified them by name, but he described a journalist, a medical student, and an "M.D. who is very happy escaping for a few days a wearisome city practice." The journalist was Charlotte Ricker, who had a nose for a good story but no outdoor experience. She wrote a lengthy and colorful account of her ordeal in the *White Mountain Echo*.[16] The medical student was Martha Whitman, with whom Scott had already traveled many miles. The Pychowskas name Whitman as being part of this expedition in their correspondence of August 2, 1882. The third woman was Dr. Laura Porter, who was in residence at the Hillside House in Bethlehem, along with Whitman and Scott, in early August.[17]

Thus committed, Scott also enlisted a sixty-something guide and packman named Allen Thompson who "claim[ed] to know something about the region" and Thompson's young assistant, Odin, "whose chief recommendations are his pleasant face and broad shoulders."

The adventure started early on the morning of August 3, 1882. They were a festive bunch; the packmen sported new embroidered shirts, and the women wore perky hats in addition to their normal walking outfit of long skirt, tailored blouse, and jacket. In the company of ladies, Scott no doubt dressed in coat, tie, and hat. He also donned a pack he allowed was "huge." Most likely, each of the ladies carried a raincoat or duster wrapped within a blanket bedroll looped over her shoulder and across her back. Each probably also carried in the bedroll an extra skirt for wearing when she reached civilization, and hung from her belt a tin cup and pouch with personal items. They likely wore kid leather gloves, light wool stockings, and boots of leather or canvas and rubber.

As the temperature passed eighty degrees, the group followed loggers' paths up the Little River toward North Twin Mountain. When these ran out, they edged along the bank or resorted to the river itself. The experienced walkers hopped from boulder to boulder; the old guide, Ricker marveled, flew "like an ancient petrel skimming his native beaches." She, on the other hand, stumbled along and soon stepped in water over her boot tops.

After several miles the group left the river and angled up a tributary stream toward North Twin's shoulder. They found a level spot for their first night's camp and Ricker's first night in the wild. The men constructed a "somewhat elaborate" shelter "in the usual fashion," Scott reported. They cut two long "crotches" out of fir or spruce trees and drove them into the ground about twenty feet apart, hung a "lug pole" across them, and, using nails or spruce roots, attached more poles as rafters extending back to the ground. They laid the roof with spruce and birch bark, and built up the sides with a thick hedge of spruce and hemlock boughs.

Meanwhile, the journalist paid attention as Whitman and Porter made the beds, or, as they called it, "stirred the feathers." First they laid hemlock bough "feathers" on top of their rubber coats, larger ones first, and then added layers of smaller branches, or "down," on top, making sure the stems, or "quills," were covered by each succeeding row. Shelter construction and bed-making done, the group added to its already prodigious use of trees by building a roaring fire against a newly felled ash. (The following summer, the Pychowskas and Edith Cook, along with other AMC members, camped in this same spot and found the shelter still standing.)

Their sumptuous supper included fresh trout, fried pork, bread, butter, tea, and Scott's personal favorite, Scottish oatmeal. Ricker, though, could barely stomach oatmeal at home, and declined this campfire concoction served without milk. But when an "army of mosquitoes" descended after dark, she felt prepared. From a pocket she drew a bottle of pennyroyal oil labeled with the druggist's directions: *One drop to each mosquito as often as necessary.* She rubbed it on her face and neck. "It vanquishes my enemy—for the time at least," she noted with satisfaction.

It was a congenial group. As night deepened, they told stories, traded puns, "proposed conundrums," and doubled up with laughter induced by "rhyming fever," Ricker reported. Eventually everyone quieted down, but the journalist found herself still wide-eyed. "I doubt if one ever sleeps much the first night in camp," she wrote, describing a first-night phenomenon with which campers of all ages and times might sympathize. "Everything is novel, so exciting, that the imagination is kept in a frictionary state . . . and the mind goes out in a newer and grander sphere than any it has hitherto known."

Ricker's depiction of the next morning may also ring familiar with many present-day hikers. "Morning arouses the camper to a sense of increasing age; he feels stiff and lame in every joint," she lamented. A dip in the brook restored her, but she shared this story with her readers: "In connection with the feathers which made my bed last night, I am reminded of the Irish laborer, who, having heard of the luxury of sleeping on feathers, placed one on a rock and made it his resting place for the night. In the morning some one questioned him regarding his experiment. His reply was, *'Bejabers, if one feather is as hard as that, phat musht a whole bedfull be loike?'* "

It was another steamy day. By midmorning the group left the hardwood forest and reached the edge of North Twin's fearsome scrub. "We are soon floundering helplessly," Scott wrote. "Twin Mountain scrub is unique; it is indescribable. We walk upon the tree-tops, only to disappear at last; we crawl prone beneath the lowest branches; we cut our way through with the hatchet; we try first one way, then another and always feel that some other way must be better." Ricker wielded an even more lurid pen: "I have been coura-geous enough to test my powers of endurance with hand-to-hand conflict with this villainous undergrowth. It is an army of porcupines over and under and around you; it is a phalanx of broadswords by which you are surrounded."

Battling through, they eventually reached the wide, flat, but dis-appointingly scrub-covered summit. Only a rock outcropping on the northwest side allowed a view. Here they slumped down to rest and enjoy a cooling drink. That's when they realized they'd made a seri-ous mistake—not carrying enough water. Despite Scott's admoni-tions, the packmen had already drained their canteens, and appar-ently there was only one other, for Scott reported "almost a mutiny for the possession of the pint canteen of water which one of the ladies has brought safely through." Lack of water would plague them throughout their excursion. But for the moment, they were blissfully unaware of the hardships to follow and simply basked in the triumph of obtaining the hard-fought summit. Charlotte Ricker was posi-tively transported by her first view from on top of a mountain:

> The heat is almost unbearable and the cry of our parched lips is still for water, but self is forgotten as we behold the mar-velous mountains, the distant villages—some holding thoughts of us—the sparkling flow of the Ammonoosuc [River] as it winds through its native valley. . . . When we have reached the heights how quickly we forget the pain and toil and hardship which are the concomitants of all upward journeying, and revel in the pure air and sunlight of the upper life.

As the group relaxed, the sky darkened with the approach of an afternoon thunderstorm. Rather than being apprehensive, the tram-pers welcomed this as a possible relief from their thirst. But it didn't rain hard enough to collect even a swallow in their tin cups. The storm served only to drench the scrub and make the afternoon's bushwhack even more miserable. They thrashed through wet, cling-ing underbrush down the mountain's western side, the women's skirts sodden and heavy, their hats drooping, and kid gloves turned slippery and slimy. They eventually found a small spring. That night's camp was a far cry from the commodious accommodations of the prior evening. "We are in a wretched plight, wet and torn but all jolly,— and the journalist only showing slight symptoms of discouragement," Scott reported.

In truth, Ricker was feeling more dispirited than she let on. "The position and surroundings are wretched," she complained. "Our beds are in and between large rocks. We go into camp, drenched through, at 6 o'clock having been nine hours without food or water." Under these conditions, her culinary standards were beginning to dissolve. "Our supper consists of bread and butter and oatmeal, which latter I am at last persuaded to try and find very appetizing," she admitted.

The next morning, her conversion to camp diet continued. "For breakfast I eat fried bread and pork, the latter being an article of diet which I entirely eschew when within the range of civilization; here it seems a delicious morsel."

Retaking the ridge, the group continued bushwhacking toward South Twin Mountain. It was less than a 2-mile walk, but Ricker fell farther and farther behind. First she felt nauseous. Then her heart started palpitating. She noted these symptoms with growing alarm, but gamely struggled on. Meanwhile, the rest of the party reached the broad, prominent rock pile capping South Twin. Clambering to the highest point, Scott declared the 360-degree view "grand beyond description." When she finally joined her companions, Ricker's spirits once again rose with the satisfaction of her accomplishment:

> I am well-nigh exhausted, but the scene outspread before me is of such exceeding glory and magnitude, and there is such an exultation in the thought that I, a woman, unused to privation and fatigue, have reached a height found unattainable by stalwart men because of the difficulties to be encountered along the way. I forget for the moment that I am suffering from pain and thirst and weariness, and in the contemplation of the world below me I quite lose my individuality.

The party decided to split up for the next leg of the journey. "The packmen and our journalist bear evident signs of demoralization," Scott reported. "The new, embroidered shirts have ceased to be attractive, and the flannel dress of the latter is torn to shreds; but the other ladies are fresh, and the three of us decide to press on." He, Whitman, and Porter continued hacking a trail south, through "illimitable wilderness" toward Mount Guyot. Ricker, Thompson, and Odin promised to follow after a longer rest.

"Scrub worse than any we have yet seen" surrounded Guyot, Scott declared, but once they broke through to its wide bare summit, they were "thrilled with delight." Even a century ago it was relatively difficult to get away from all signs of the human hand, and the group drank in the scene. "We are surrounded on all sides by mountain peaks which shut out all signs of civilization, save the buildings on Mount Washington," Scott observed. They could see south past the Hancocks to the pointy profile of Chocorua, east across the Zealand Valley to Crawford Notch and into Maine, north to the Kilkennys, and west to Lafayette and the Franconia Range. But their delight faded along with the daylight. By dusk, Ricker and the packmen still hadn't appeared, and they carried the food. Thompson finally showed up, but he'd left the provisions behind. So he, Scott, and the two women descended the mountain in search of water. They found a trickle of a spring and again prepared to camp without shelter. Scott dug around in his pockets and came up with a couple of chocolate squares, and Thompson produced a kettle. The group sipped hot chocolate for supper.

Meanwhile, Ricker and young Odin were on their own desperate quest for water. They too headed down the mountainside, but became separated in the thick woods. Tired, increasingly apprehensive, hungry, and thirsty, Ricker started hallucinating. She thought she glimpsed a sparkling brook just ahead through the underbrush. With growing excitement, she approached the soft gurgling sound. But as she knelt down to taste its cool refreshment, the image dissolved. Instead she faced Odin, who was lying on his stomach and unmoving. Stunned, she feared the worst: he was dead and she was lost in untracked wilderness. As she reached out to touch him, he lifted his head and gave her a mud-streaked grin. He'd been sucking what water he could from a scant trickle among some rocks. Relieved but not amused, the journalist noted darkly, "I left laughter on the tip-top of South Twin."

With night approaching and no idea where they were, she and Odin decided to camp on the spot. Ricker now felt exhausted beyond hunger, but knew she needed something for her strength. The oatmeal! Odin helpfully offered to cook it, but somehow he melted the saucepan handle in the fire. The pair watched in dismay as oatmeal oozed into the embers. Ricker tried calming herself by reciting "Old Mother Hubbard" nursery rhymes. Well after dark they heard Thompson's calls, but despite their shouts the old packman couldn't find them. Adding insult to injury, Ricker realized she'd lost her precious pennyroyal oil. To fend off the mosquitoes she tied a damp handkerchief under her hat, as she'd seen the other women do. It provided a semblance of protection, as well as some relief for her bitten and bleeding ears. Then she wrapped herself in her blanket and tried not to worry about having a heart attack.

When morning finally came, Thompson located Ricker and Odin and led them back to the rest of the group. It was Sunday, and the famished crew celebrated the Sabbath with a breakfast of canned baked beans. Then it was back to bushwhacking their way through more dense forest to Mount Bond, the next peak in the chain. From there they descended a rocky ridge to the dramatic crags of what today is called Bondcliff (they lumped both mountains together as "Bond"). Scott marveled that the view down the valley of the Pemigewasset River "surpasses everything we have ever beheld."

Lack of water still plagued the group. "Our lips crack and the skin peels from the roof of our mouths," Scott reported. "The old man declares he never will attempt another trip like this, and the young man would give a thousand dollars (which he does not possess) to be at home, and the journalist begins to discuss the easiest way of emerging from the valley below; but the rest are unmindful of their discomforts." Leaving Bondcliff, they descended through more scrub into the river valley, thinking they must find water there. But only "extinct streams" greeted them. When they finally located a running brook, they stopped for the day and built a shelter, their first in three nights. They enjoyed a "luxurious camp close to the noisy stream," according to Scott, but their dwindling larder left them eating oatmeal and stale bread for supper and again for breakfast. At noon the next day, though, they found the East Branch of the Pemigewasett, and Thompson merrily reeled in thirty trout. They all ate heartily, though Ricker noted that Odin snuck more than his share from the fry pan.

After luncheon on this fifth day, they followed a branch of the river north back toward the Zealand Valley. That evening Thompson pulled in a whopping two hundred trout, and the trampers' good humor returned. They feasted on fish and told stories and tall tales well into the night. The next morning, though, Ricker decided she'd had enough. The group was approximately seven miles from Crawford Notch, and she wanted to walk out before dark. The explorers decided they'd stick together and follow the river upstream to Willey Pond (now called Ethan Pond). From there, Ricker and Odin would follow a footpath out to the Willey House, an inn just south of the notch. The rest of the group would continue exploring the Zealand Valley.

The day proceeded as planned—until Ricker sprained her ankle. She sent Odin back to find the others and then sat alone in the forest, hungry and discouraged, her ankle throbbing. Life looked bleak indeed. "After Odin is gone," she wrote, "I sit quite still and think of many things—the dead, the absent, the little carefully-cared-for self of childhood days come back to me. I take out my notebook and write. Thought makes me weep. I am so weary . . . I wonder if I am not dreaming, if I shall not presently awake and find myself back in my old place."

To her relief, Odin returned with the rest of the group later that afternoon. But the long-suffering journalist's trials were hardly over. The men started building another shelter only to have a thunderstorm drench them all before it was complete. Later, as they sat around a smoldering fire trying to dry out, Scott pressed her to eat more oatmeal.

The next morning Ricker felt well enough to continue. This time, both Thompson and Odin would accompany her. When she was ready to leave, she noted that Whitman and Porter looked "nearly as fresh and unwearied as at the starting." One of these women pressed a "strengthening potion" in her hand and the other gave her cold cream for her lips. Scott presented her with one of the last sticks of his coveted chocolate. "She has shown a wonderful perseverance under very adverse circumstances," Scott later wrote, "but is much pleased with the prospect of returning home."

By early afternoon Charlotte Ricker arrived at the Willey House. For the first time in a week she viewed herself in a mirror. "Can that be me, that bronzed, wan-faced, hollow-eyed, ragged tatterdemalion?" she asked. But appalled as she was at her appearance, she must have smiled with unabashed pride. "I find myself a mass of bruises, my feet swollen and covered with blisters, my neck, face, hands and wrists fly-bitten, and my lips blistered, but what care I? I have accomplished my undertaking and have not once whined 'I wish I had never come.' "

Late that same day Scott, Whitman, and Porter emerged on top of Mount Willard. There they encountered a crowd of tourists from the nearby Crawford House hotel who had ridden up by wagon to admire the sunset. The ragtag threesome escaped notice by quickly setting off down the carriage road to the hotel and the train that would take them back to Boston.

Not long after this, Scott returned to the Twin Range and started building his trail. The following summer Marian Pychowska reported that the way up North Twin was "a model path, of which all Apes* should be proud." In addition, she noted, "thanks to Mr. Scott, there is a broad avenue" connecting the summits of North and South Twin.[18]

The pristine views the Scott party enjoyed would not last long. Within a few years forest fires ignited by lightning and locomotive sparks would devastate much of the Zealand Valley and the area around the Twin Mountains. To find unblemished forest, logging companies would carve railroads deeper into the valley, and timber

---

* AMC members, in Pychowska parlance.

harvesting became widespread and intensive. By the end of the century, the hardy women of the 1870s and 1880s would have had a hard time recognizing some of their favorite spots.

But by that time, Marian Pychowska had given up tramping for the contemplative life of a cloistered nun. And after the heady days of the mid-1880s, it's unclear what happened to Edith Cook and Lucia Pychowska. In 1889 they were at the Ravine House and were likely among the four women and two men who inaugurated use of the club's new hut on Mount Adams.[19] But neither is listed at the Ravine House after 1894, and they disappeared from the AMC's membership rolls shortly thereafter. We do know that they lived out their lives in Hoboken; Edith died 1902 at age sixty-three, and Lucia Pychowska three years later at seventy-nine. Strangely, *Appalachia* never ran obituaries for these pioneer members, nor for their relative Eugene Cook. Isabella Stone remained an AMC member for forty-one years, but it appears her problematic health ended her tramping days in the mid-1880s.

Sadly, the Twin Range excursion was probably Martha Whitman's last great adventure. She earned her medical degree (writing a thesis on "Medical Expert Testimony and Its Reliability") but within months was afflicted with typhoid fever. She died on December 12, 1884, at the age of forty-four.

In the meantime, a new generation of American mountaineers was coming along. The White Mountains provided them with some of their first tastes of outdoor adventure and inspired them to even loftier goals.

SECTION 4

The High Mountaineers

Annie Smith Peck in her Matterhorn costume, c. 1895. (SOCIETY OF WOMAN GEOGRAPHERS COLLECTION)

Chapter 9

Annie Smith Peck

(1850–1935)

Doing what one woman might to show the equality of the sexes.

New York City
January 1909

Annie Smith Peck paused in the doorway and leaned against the baronial mahogany frame darkened by the years and the smoke of innumerable cigars. Inside, a swirl of dark-suited men and light-gowned women mixed and flirted and laughed together. The warmth of the room, its aroma of perfume and tobacco, beeswax and wood smoke, seemed to engulf her. For an instant she felt heady and reckless.

Taking a deep breath, she slid into the room, parting the crowd in short, purposeful steps, nodding at greetings, but not pausing. The gregarious men fell silent, and their wispy wives turned toward her, stopping in midsentence to examine her as she swept by.

Annie felt the eyes upon her. And for a moment she could see herself as they did, her image reflected in one of the big gilded mirrors. A bantam-sized woman, hair up in a proper bun, a necklace of Venetian glass beads dazzling at her neck, her well-fitted, ivory-colored floor-length dress, the sharp-toed formal shoes. She smiled to herself. She knew that through the mix of awe, curiosity, resentment, and respect, they were trying to picture her in a sealskin Eskimo suit, miles high on an icy mountaintop, her only companions two Swiss guides and a handful of Indians.

Her lips betrayed only the barest hint of a smile. At the lectern, she shook hands with the president of the American Geographic Society, who stepped forward to introduce her. As he read from his notes, she half listened and scanned the faces in the crowd.

". . . it is my pleasure to introduce to you the Queen of Climbers, Miss Annie Peck." After she'd thanked him and exchanged another firm handshake, she moved behind the lectern. A triumphant smile blossomed across her face.

"I have stood where no mortal has stood before."

ANNIE SMITH PECK, born in Rhode Island on October 19, 1850, was the first woman in history to make high-altitude mountaineering her profession, her claim to international fame, and her way of leaving a mark on the world. She pursued her goals with perseverance and determination rivaling those of any of the better-known male explorers of her age—or any age. Unlike many of the early alpinists, she was not from money. She worked for a living; no husband supported her. Her resolve came from within her small frame, from a source we can try to understand from her correspondence and many published works. Her accounts tend to be guileless descriptions of both her successes and defeats, written in spare, matter-of-fact language. Yet she loved the spotlight and had a penchant for self-promotion—not typically "ladylike" behavior in her time, but a necessary and important ability for someone who organized, outfitted, and led major expeditions a continent away.

Peck started her professional life as a classicist. In her early forties a volume on "Leading American Women" recognized her as an "educator, musician, profound classical scholar, and distinguished archeologist."[1] This was before her career took an abrupt midlife turn, when in the summer of 1895, at age forty-five, she became one of the few women to climb the Matterhorn. The notoriety earned by that feat launched her career as a lecturer on mountain climbing and inspired her quest for major peaks. First she sought mountains unclimbed by women. She found them in Mexico, where in 1897 she climbed Mount Orizaba (18,660 feet) and Mount Popocatépetl (17,883 feet). With Orizaba she claimed the world altitude record for women, only to lose it two years later when another feminist mountaineer from New England, Fanny Bullock Workman, climbed above 19,000 feet in the Himalayas. The relentlessly competitive Peck reached higher still. In Bolivia and then Peru she sought to reach the "apex of America," the highest point in the Western Hemisphere, and at the same time win back the world's altitude record for women.

She thought she'd accomplished all this in 1908, when she reached the summit of Peru's Mount Huascarán. Ultimately, however, her claim to the women's record was vanquished after a nasty battle with Fanny Bullock Workman, and geographers pinpointed the hemisphere's highest point elsewhere. Nonetheless, Peck remains triumphant as the only woman who has achieved a first ascent of one of the world's major peaks.[2]

Peck lived at a time of great crosscurrents in American political and social culture. Her climbing career reflected, as well as contributed to, the changes in the world around her and women's role in it. It was also a time of great exploration. The public eagerly followed the expeditions of Robert Peary, Robert Scott, Roald Amundsen, and others as they pushed toward the poles. At the same time, high-profile mountaineers such as Britain's Sir Martin Conway and Italy's Duke of the Abruzzi were making pioneer ascents in Asia, South America, and Alaska. Annie's adventures reached a wide audience through her dispatches published in popular magazines and newspapers. She was even offered as inspiration to women through one of the most traditional of gender-role sources: the sewing machine. The Singer Company included postcards of Peck in full mountaineering regalia with its new machines. As one presumably male writer put it, "Ladies pumping away at the treadle could sigh with admiration at one of their sex who had launched into the world's more daring occupation."[3]

Peck's resolve, fortitude, and iconoclasm are emblematic of the traits women before and after her have needed to achieve their goals

as mountaineers and outdoorswomen. Her disappointments—
tension with her male companions, especially over leadership; pressure to prove herself again and again; the frustration of constant
fund-raising; challenges to her credibility—were often shared by her
predecessors and successors as well.

One of the distinguishing characteristics of Annie Peck is that
she was the first woman mountaineer who framed her climbing with
overt aspirations of feminism. She also considered her work a way of
advancing scientific knowledge and promoting international relations. At the outset, she found mountain climbing exhilarating and
satisfying in its own right. She loved the physical challenge, the
intense focus it demanded, and the beauty of rugged terrain. But as
she became proficient, mountaineering evolved into a very personal
form of political action. Through it, she sought to offer indisputable
evidence of the strength, abilities, and courage of the "New Woman"
emerging from the stifling Victorian era. As she asserted, it was
"what one woman might do to show the equality of the sexes."[4]
Putting it another way, she wrote, "Being always from earliest years a
firm believer in the equality of the sexes, I felt that any great
achievement in any line of endeavour would be of great advantage to
my sex."[5]

She was also acutely aware of how unusual activities by women
can become marginalized and articulated this in a hauntingly modern way: "A woman who has done good work in the scholastic world
doesn't like to be called a good woman scholar," she told the New
York Times in 1911. "Call her a good scholar and let it go at that. I
have climbed 1,500 feet higher than any man in the United States.
Don't call me a woman climber."[6] She set her sights higher than any
woman before her and higher than all but a handful of men. She
wasn't bashful about declaring her ambition. As a mountaineer and
as an advocate for women, Annie aimed for the top.

But in her day, as far as altitude was concerned, no one really
knew where the "top" was. The confusion around this point helps
put Peck's career into context. When she started planning her first
South American expedition in 1898, the rudimentary methods of
measurement made figuring altitudes an inexact science at best.

Several of the great Andean peaks could have been highest on the continent. Bolivia's Mount Sorata (called *Illampu* in the country; Peck referred to it by both names) was a good bet, and that is where Annie first set her sights. It was tough business; Sorata had already defeated Sir Martin Conway, one of Britain's top-notch mountaineers. His failure left Peck with the opportunity she longed to seize, but time was of the essence. Not only was she not getting any younger—she was forty-eight—but the year before, another British climber had scaled Argentina's Aconcagua, itself possibly the highest peak in the hemisphere.

Her attempt on Sorata was unsuccessful, but during her travels a Peruvian engineer assured her that his country's Mount Huascarán was the premier peak, possibly rising as high as 25,000 feet. Once back in New York, Annie left nothing to chance. She set about raising the funds for a new expedition on which she would ascend *both* Sorata and Huascarán, plus Sahama, reputedly the world's loftiest volcano. If she succeeded, "the highest point on this hemisphere will be attained, and the *world's record in mountain climbing will have been broken*," she proclaimed in a brochure for potential backers.[7]

But attaining the summit was only part of the challenge. The financial costs of her ambitious expeditions far exceeded what she earned as a lecturer. So she spent years wooing sponsors, seeking cash, equipment, food, and other supplies, and trying to secure magazine and newspaper commitments. She lectured tirelessly, and solicited funds directly from every potential donor she could find. She formed the Andean Exploration Society and offered a host of reasons for joining. For instance, subscribers could share in "science and adventure" without having to leave the "comforts of civilization to participate." They could also support feminist goals: "Especially should those who desire the recognition of woman's ability in whatever direction be disposed to encourage one [who] in an unusual line had already achieved large success and shown capabilities far beyond those of most men," she rather ponderously declared. And if advancing science and women weren't incentive enough, she promised a portion of the profits from her lecture circuit, which, she vowed, would "be extremely popular."[8]

To allay the doubts of those who considered her at best a dreamer and at worst a preposterous risk taker, she tried putting her work in a utilitarian context: "Mountain climbing for itself alone, to many, nay, to nearly all of our people, might not seem worth while; worse, it might appear folly: but as a means of drawing attention to a section of the world famed for the splendour of its great mountains, no less for the mineral riches along their slopes, it seemed that my efforts might appeal in a practical way to practical men."[9]

Her travels instilled in Peck a deep and genuine affection for the people and cultures of South America. Though she was not above cutting observations about the character of some of her native acquaintances, she viewed her travels as a way of "awakening interest in our sister Republics beyond the Equator." She was an energetic proponent of "commerce, travel, and trade" between the United States and South American nations. She took a keen interest in the building of the Panama Canal and advocated a Pan-American railway. She hoped her work would "aid in a small degree the cause of Peace by increasing our knowledge of countries with which we have too little acquaintance, a bond of sympathy and union taking the place of crass conceit and narrow prejudice." Late in life, she said that she regarded her efforts "promoting friendly relations with South America as far more important" than her mountain climbing.[10] Annie's post–World War I sentiment was reminiscent of Elizabeth Le Blond, the great mountaineer who placed her work improving Franco-British relations above her alpine accomplishments.

Like her predecessors, Annie's early life gave little indication she would one day become a world-famous mountaineer. She was the fourth surviving child and first daughter in the distinguished Providence, Rhode Island, household of George Bacheler and Ann Power Smith Peck. According to biographer Elizabeth Fagg Olds, Annie's mother descended from Roger Williams, the state's founder and champion of religious freedom. Her paternal ancestors arrived from England in 1638. Her father was a graduate of Brown University, was a practicing lawyer, and served on the Providence City Council and in the state legislature.

Fagg Olds suggested that as the youngest child and only girl,

Annie was forced to compete against her brothers in sports and games, perhaps priming her for subsequent interest in mountain climbing and feminism. But Annie herself didn't believe so. "I do not think association with my brothers had any influence on me," she told a reporter in 1898. "They were bookworms, and not particularly athletic boys. . . . I can swim, row, and whistle a tune better than my brothers can now," she added, before discussing her tennis game and mentioning that she'd just learned to ride a bicycle. Ten years later, she reflected again on her choice of avocation and told another reporter, "My mother believed in bringing up her children in healthy surroundings, in giving us good plain food, in getting us to bed at early hours, and in not keeping us from healthy play. To that I owe much, I think." Her family's summer vacations in the Adirondacks and White Mountains also introduced her to the outdoors and mountain tramping. As an adult, Annie still recalled with pleasure a childhood excursion when an Adirondack guide declared that "where a chipmunk couldn't walk, she would go."[11]

As much as she loved being outdoors, Annie was also a dedicated student. She read history, philosophy, and literature, and had a natural affinity for languages. She breezed through Greek and Latin, and was fascinated by the sciences. After high school she attended Rhode Island State Normal School, then taught in public schools in Providence and Michigan. But she was intellectually restless, and eventually prevailed upon her father to support further study at the University of Michigan. By 1881 she'd earned her bachelor's and master's degrees, both specializing in Greek. She took an appointment at Purdue University teaching Latin and elocution, making her one of the earliest female college professors in the country—another significant "first."

A trip to the Continent was de rigueur for many young American scholars, and Annie's visits in 1884 and 1885 shaped the rest of life, though not in a way she could have anticipated. She started in Germany studying music and language and then went on to Athens as the first woman admitted to the American School of Classical Studies. On side trips through the Alps she climbed several passes and smaller mountains. This got her thinking about whether she could achieve the apex of Alpine glory, the Matterhorn. She went to Zermatt in 1885, and the effect of seeing the mountain for the first time was immediate and profound. "On beholding this majestic, awe-inspiring peak, I felt that I should never be happy until I, too, should scale those frowning walls which have beckoned so many upwards, a few to their own destruction."[12]

She likely knew that Englishwoman Lucy Walker and American Meta Brevoort had each made the summit in 1871.* Peck longed to follow them. "Other ladies have scaled its ramparts, so why not I?" she told skeptical friends.[13] But lacking the $50 needed for guides and provisions, she contented herself with some lesser peaks. She headed back to the United States to teach Latin at Smith College but determined that one day she'd return.

Over the next several years Annie taught and started offering parlor lectures on ancient archaeology. She convinced her oldest brother, George, to accompany her to the West for some high mountain climbing. George, who like Annie remained single, practiced medicine in Providence and was the only member of her family who encouraged her mountaineering. In 1888 they went to what would soon be designated Yosemite National Park in California and climbed 10,000-foot Cloud's Rest, and then Annie tackled her first major peak, 14,162-foot Mount Shasta in the Cascade Range. They completed their tour by tramping through Wyoming's Yellowstone National Park. During the summers of 1890 through 1894, Annie returned to New Hampshire and scrambled through the Presidentials. "I can recommend those mountains as very good practice for rock climbing in the Alps," she commented.[14]

In 1895, ten years after she'd first laid eyes on it, she was finally ready to take on the Matterhorn. Her friends and family were less than pleased. They fired off letters "full of explostulation and

---

* Peck is sometimes mistakenly named as the first American woman to climb the Matterhorn. That honor, of course, goes to Brevoort. She is also often called the third woman ever to make the ascent. According to Cicely Williams in *Women on the Rope*, sisters Anna and Ellen Pigeon traversed the Matterhorn from Breuil to Zermatt in 1873. If correct, this would make Peck's ascent the fifth.

entreaty," according to Annie. "If you are determined to commit sui-
cide why not come home and do so in a quiet, lady-like manner?"
read one such missive. We might wonder if, in the several weeks
spent waiting in Zermatt for the right conditions on the slopes,
Annie wondered if her friends might be right. Surely she was aware
that four men perished after reaching the top in 1865. She may also
have known that in 1879, the seventh American to climb it was
killed on his way down. But she had hired a highly recommended
guide, Jean Baptiste Aymonod, and his twenty-five-year-old assistant, Sylvain Pession. And while she was certain they could hold her
if she fell, she worried that a dislodged rock could crack her head, or
worse, that one of the guides would fall and send them all tumbling
off a cliff.[15]

Aymonod wanted at least four clear days after a storm before setting out, so that the rock would have time to clear of ice and snow.
Finally, on August 20, conditions were suitable. They walked out of
Zermatt at dawn. Annie's excitement grew as they started gaining
elevation, leaving the town and outlying farms far below. At about
six o'clock that evening they reached the small hut where they'd
spend the night. To her dismay, a crowd of climbers and guides were
already there. Before long still more showed up, including two other
women whom she never mentioned again in her account of the
climb. She and her two guides waited for the group before them to
finish cooking, then edged up to the diminutive woodstove and prepared their own supper. After eating she watched the sun go down in
a cloudless sky. She jotted in her journal that in the fading light, the
mountains were "distinct, solemn, and lovely."

By 8:00 P.M. climbers were arranging themselves to sleep on a
straw-covered shelf running along the hut wall. The guides climbed
up to the loft. Annie squeezed onto one end of the shelf between the
two other women. Five men lined up on the remainder of the shelf,
giving them all the look and feel of a can of sardines. The climbers
joked about it: do sardines lie on their backs or their sides? Backs
would be a luxury they decided; here, the rule was sides. Jokes and
commentary and laughter finally subsided, and Annie was on the
edge of sleep when yet another latecomer stomped through the door.

It was absolutely impossible for him to shoehorn into the row, so he stretched across their feet. At midnight those who had managed to drift off were prodded awake, and the rest of the bleary-eyed group pried themselves from the shelf as the guides started preparing breakfast.

As eager as she was to get going, Annie was relieved at Aymonod's dictate that they should go last. First on top and first to descend, he told her, and the better your chance of getting struck by a rock kicked off by a climber above you. Better to go last and end the procession on the way down. Also, he wanted to carry the candle lantern as short a time as possible. They left the hut at 3:15 A.M. Aymonod took the lead, Annie second, and Pession last, all roped together with braided 1-inch hemp.

She found the predawn walk by lantern light "novel and interesting." She later allowed that it was in the light of day on their return that sections of the route were truly hair-raising as just inches from her feet the mountain sheared off to yawning crevasses thousands of feet below.

At 4:30 A.M. Aymonod snuffed the lantern. They continued on, arriving an hour later at the abandoned upper hut where parties traditionally took a second breakfast. The going from here would get much tougher. They left extra gear behind, including the lantern, food pack, Annie's ice ax, and—radically—Annie's skirt. Imagine her moment of decision: looking up at the towering precipice as the guides busied themselves with the gear, her knowing that wearing only knickerbockers might shock other climbers, but deeming it crazier still to proceed encumbered with a skirt. So she stripped the skirt off, revealing the knickers underneath, and stowed the garment inside the tumbledown hut. With a nod, the guides slung their axes across their shoulders so they'd have both hands free for climbing. They roped up and continued on.

The climbing required full attention and a steady head, but Annie didn't find it especially taxing. Even the chimneys, the vertical chutes of rock she often found difficult, seemed to offer hand- and footholds at just the right points. And she had full confidence in Aymonod, who fixed himself firmly above her and kept her rope taut as she scrambled up the trickiest sections. Ropes and iron chains were fixed in place to aid the climbers at the steepest parts.

By nine-thirty that morning she stood on the summit. It was a clear, sparkling day, and she knew friends and the curious were peering through telescopes far below from the Hotel Mont Cervin. She waved exuberantly. She never felt it, but her friends told her later that at the moment they saw her, a small earthquake shook Zermatt.

On her return to the United States she was met by what she modestly called "unmerited notoriety," but she quickly seized the opportunity to expand her parlor circuit repertoire and reach larger audiences. "It occurred to me that people would rather hear about me climbing the Matterhorn than visiting ancient Olympia," she explained. She proved a popular lecturer. Her "pleasing personality, an unusually graceful manner, [and] charming voice" filled Boston lecture halls at least thirteen times. At the National Geographic Society in Washington, "even standing room was hard to find," according to the *Washington Post*. "At many points the speaker was interrupted by enthusiastic applause." In her home state of Rhode Island, the mayor of Providence introduced her to "a large audience gathered at Infantry Hall," the local paper reported. "Miss Peck is gifted with a pleasant personality, a fine delivery, and a magnetic manner, holding the interest of the audience to the last."[16]

But Annie knew she couldn't trade on the Matterhorn forever. "I began to think that, as I seemed to be posing as a mountain climber, I had better really do something in that line worthwhile," she admitted. Seeking "some deed which should render me worthy of the fame already acquired," she traveled to Mexico in 1897 and climbed Popocatépetl and Orizaba. But attaining the women's altitude record of approximately 18,600 feet on Orizaba proved an "easy goal." She adjusted her ambition accordingly. "My next thought," she wrote, "was to do a little genuine exploration, to conquer a virgin peak, and to attain some height where no *man* had previously stood."[17]

No man had yet stood on Bolivia's Mount Sorata. But it took her five frustrating years of fund-raising, scrimping, and saving before she could launch the venture. During that time she continued climbing mountains, albeit of the 5,000-foot variety. She went back to New Hampshire's White Mountains, showing up at the Ravine House in Randolph to the delight of some of the Appalachian Mountain Club (AMC) regulars. In the summer of 1897, after returning from Mexico, she completed a traverse of the Presidential Range in a single day—a feat of endurance that relatively few people have cared to repeat since.[18]

In June 1903 Annie finally had the funds for a Sorata expedition. Her goals were clear, as she later explained to a meeting of the AMC: "to verify the height of this great mountain and ascertain whether it were indeed superior to Aconcagua, to make meteorological, geological, and any other observations possible . . . seemed to promise a worthy contribution to science. At the same time, should the mountain rise to its greatest possibilities, to reach a higher point than anywhere man has previously stood seemed also worthy of a sportsman's efforts; in a small way, like [then-Commander Robert] Peary's getting a degree nearer to the North Pole."[19]

To achieve the mission, she equipped the party with the latest scientific apparatus and the best mountaineering gear she could afford. While her heart may have been set on reaching the apex of America, she took her scientific endeavor very seriously, as the equipment list she recited to the AMC members illustrates: "two mercurial barometers, one of them (made especially for me) reading down to ten inches; two hypsometers, or thermometers for boiling, as the temperature at which water boils indicates the pressure of atmosphere and the height above sea level; two aneroid barometers, designed for comparison with the others; three psychrometers to measure the humidity of the air, clinical thermometers to take our temperatures, a sphygmograph to ascertain the strength and character of the pulse, a sphygmomanometer to measure blood pressure, and a transit instrument also to measure the height of Sorata."[20]

She also carried some rudimentary equipment intended for manufacturing oxygen at high altitudes, but this was later abandoned. Mountaineering equipment included two tents, one canvas and one silk; sleeping bags made from two blankets tucked into a canvas cover, complete with face flap; an aluminum candle lantern; a Primus oil stove; smoked glasses; four cameras; compasses; a rifle and revolvers. Along the way she'd add rope, ice axes, and climbing irons, or crampons, which were just starting to come into use.

Never fond of cold, Annie paid particular attention to her clothing. She gathered three sets of wool underwear, tights, a sweater, a cardigan jacket, flannel shirts, her infamous knickerbockers, heavy nailed boots sized large enough to contain multiple pairs of socks, heavy wool mitts, and a face shield. Her most prized possession and ultimate defense against freezing was Robert Peary's Eskimo suit, worn at the North Pole and loaned by the American Museum of Natural History. She packed rolls of German sausage, canned meat, Grape-Nuts (touted in late-nineteenth-century advertisements as "for those who live by brain work"), and dry beans. Her larder also included Peter's Chocolate, the maker of which was one of her few sponsors, and brandy, which she considered an essential "to be used not as an aid in climbing, but in the case of exhaustion or collapse."[21] This remained her basic outfit for all her South American expeditions.

Though "half dead with the fatigue of hasty preparation," Annie was in a cheerful mood June 16, 1903, when she left New York aboard the ship Segurança bound for Peru. After five years of planning, she considered herself well prepared. In addition to copious gear, she had with her two Swiss guides and "a stalwart scientific man." The lead guide already had experience on Sorata as a veteran of Sir Martin Conway's expedition. The scientist, a man she called only "the Professor," was reputedly an expert photographer and skilled in geography and geology.

A photograph shows the group as they left New York. Ice ax planted firmly before her and the tube of one of her scientific instruments slung across her shoulder, a primly attired Annie looks sure and determined, even defiant. A guide and the scientist hold their own ice axes, and the other guide grips a rifle in one hand and revolver in the other.

"I felt no misgivings as to the result, especially as hitherto I had always been favored of fortune and my every undertaking of importance had been crowned with success," she wrote some years later.

"But we have heard that of too much success the gods are jealous. At all events, on this occasion they frowned."[22]

The gods must have been more than a little jealous. Not only this occasion, but also her next four expeditions would be overcome with difficulties. Standing on the deck of her ship, Annie Peck, scholar of ancient Greece and Rome, was blissfully ignorant that she was just beginning a five-year odyssey that would test her time and again. The natural elements—life-threatening cold, fierce wind, extreme slopes, high altitude, falling ice, hidden crevasses, avalanches—she handled with aplomb, her courage and resilience unshaken. Rather, her leadership skills and relations with men nearly proved her Achilles' heel. Like a mythic character, she brought many of these trials on herself. For all her intellectual power, she seems not to have been the most astute judge of men. She recruited for her expeditions a constantly changing cast of characters, none of whom she knew well, and some of whom were complete strangers. Some-times she put herself at the mercy of those whose loyalty to her, as well as their mountaineering capabilities, were suspect. Other times she relied on individuals who had bona fide skills, but questioned or outright refused her leadership. On both accounts she struggled against being undermined. But this is easy to see in retrospect. At the time she may not have had much choice. As a single woman, traveling alone and without the benefit of ample financial resources, but possessing tremendous single-mindedness about her goals, she had to work with what was offered. As she once wrote a friend, "When I cannot get what I want I sometimes take what I can get."[23]

In 1903 her "first prognostication of disaster," Annie later reflected, was the Professor's sudden desire to return home. He cited academic responsibilities, but he'd suffered headaches, sleeplessness, and nausea, all symptoms of *soroche*, or altitude sickness, and expressed alarm about the cold—all before the party had even reached the base of Mount Sorata. Annie browbeat him into honoring his obligation to at least try the ascent; after all, she'd paid for his trip. But the Professor never proved an eager climber. The first night camping he lost his appetite (another sign of *soroche*) and got mightily chilled. The next morning the Indian porters registered their own complaints. None had ever climbed a mountain before, and they feared going higher. On top of that, they had only sandals to wear in the snow, which unusually bad weather had left much deeper and at lower elevations than usual. Sensing the Professor's reluctance, and assuming he was the leader, the Indians refused to go on. Using hand signals and gestures, Annie appealed to them, even offering to pay double, but to no avail. As they started loading the mules to leave she implored the Swiss guides for assistance with the Indians. But they, too, disappointed her, going "limp as a rag" and exerting no "moral force or energy." She implored the guides to go on without the Indian porters or the Professor. "Impossible!" they replied, and informed her they wouldn't proceed without "a third man" on the ice.

"I have never before felt so helpless," Annie later wrote. "Rage and mortification filled my soul. To manage three men seemed beyond my power. Perhaps some of my more experienced married sisters would have done better."[24]

The group headed back to the Bolivian capital of La Paz, where Annie intended to find a replacement for the Professor and then try the mountain again. But once more the fates intervened. Bubonic plague closed the port town of Mollendo, and not wishing to get stuck in South America for the winter, her Swiss guides abandoned Annie and set off looking for another way out of the country.

Undaunted, she continued preparing for a second attempt, this time with no one but Indians. Bad weather foiled her plans, but still she wasn't done. She walked up a 19,000-foot volcano called El Misti, and then she set out by horseback with a group of new acquaintances across 100 miles of uncharted desert. Ostensibly the most direct and least expensive way to get to an open port, this trek also helped quench her desire for adventure. All she needed to hear was a previous traveler's promise that she could get lost, perish from hunger and thirst, get buried by sandstorms, either freeze to death at night or faint from heat during the day, and she was determined to go. "If his feat was so extraordinary, there was the more reason for my duplicating it," she declared. She made the desert crossing without incident, and finally left Peru in early November.

Returning to New York "without having set foot upon the mountain was sufficiently mortifying to make me seriously ill," Annie admitted. One consolation was that she'd camped out at least 15,350 feet—higher than Mont Blanc—and stayed warm while doing so. She'd also gained valuable alpine experience, and it wasn't long before she started thinking ahead. "As soon as might be, I rallied my drooping spirits and began cogitating upon the possibility of making that long journey once again and a genuine attack on this tremendous mountain. I could not leave it as it was, having merely confirmed in the opinion of those persons who had previously regarded me as insane." To would-be funders of a second expedition she attributed her failure to "an extraordinary combination of circumstances, including a lack of enthusiasm, inefficiency, and desertion on the part of those who should have rendered assistance, followed by a succession of snowstorms throughout the remainder of the season." The bad weather, she emphasized, was *absolutely unprecedented.*" To a female friend she wrote, "I hope you may wish to have a share in my next expedition. . . . Perhaps you would like to go along too. I am sure you would do better than my scientist last season."[25]

Her friends gave generously in support of a new expedition, and with newspaper assignments in hand as well, Annie tried again the very next summer. This time, though, there were no Swiss guides and no stalwart scientific man. In June 1904 she set forth, "if less confidently than before, with good hope that, though alone, I might accomplish more than the year previous. I could not do less." When she reached La Paz, she hired an Austrian she'd met the year before named Victor Sintich. He was, she declared, "the only discoverable man in the place who had done any snow climbing." She also hired Indian porters and a local "major domo" to manage them. This fellow, named Garcilaso, had been with Sir Martin Conway's expedition. To her outfit she added some specialized equipment: crampons (also called climbing irons at the time), ice axes, vicuña fur mittens, and coca leaves (from which cocaine is derived), which she discovered the year before were "an invaluable stimulant." She tucked in extra alcohol—both for her stove and "for the benefit of the Indians, who with a small draught night and morning may be kept in good humor."[26] And to allay the Indians' fears about the mountain, she procured a wooden cross. They'd carry it with them up the mountain and plant it on the summit.

The expedition started out well enough. The group easily reached a spot Garcilaso identified as Conway's first camp and spent the night. "Already higher than I had been before, I count this as a favorable omen," Annie jotted in her journal.[27] But her relations with Victor Sintich quickly soured. They squabbled about the route, where to camp, whether even to pitch a tent as they moved higher over the next several days. Sintich "dearly loves his own way," she dryly noted. Meanwhile, the slopes stiffened, the crevasses yawned, and the temperature plummeted. At 18,000 feet and twenty degrees below zero, Annie pulled on nearly every stitch of clothing she had—including her Eskimo suit—to stay warm at night. But despite the harsh conditions and the interpersonal tensions, they kept plodding along, and the fourth day out they advanced past the spot where Sir Conway had turned back. Now they were in wholly untracked territory.

The afternoon of that fourth day, Annie thought they were within striking distance of the summit. But to her "great astonishment," Sintich ordered the group to turn around. He predicted a snowstorm, and considered it too late in the day to proceed. But Annie would have none of it. She wanted at least to get to the top of a ridge where she could clearly see the way to the summit. Roped to Garcilaso and ice ax in hand, she went off without the rest of the group, carefully picking her way up between wide crevasses. The slope angled into a tough ice climb, and she dug in with her climbing irons. She poked tentatively with her ice ax, using it to test the firmness of the hard snow beneath her as she edged between the chasms. When a crack opened up just inches from her toes she realized she was on a perilously weak snow bridge. "How I wished now for the Swiss guide I had on the Jungfrau," she thought. She turned to ask for help, and was stunned by the scene below her. "I saw, to my horror and disgust, the rope trailing idly on the snow, the two men where I had left them. On a steep and dangerous slope, on the very brink of a crevasse into which a careless step would have plunged me, and no one on the rope! A little less caution and I should be in the bottom of that crevasse now!"

Knowing "even a Swiss guide would not proceed alone in such a place," she inched her way back toward the men. If she expected an apology or explanation she was disappointed. Sintich shrugged off her indignation, stating if she persisted in going contrary to his judgment, he couldn't be expected to follow. Later, he told her he'd have gladly made the ridgetop—but declined because he knew she'd only insist on going farther. True, she admitted, and why not? After all, she reminded him, going for the summit was what they came for. If darkness overcame them they could have descended by moonlight, or dug a snow cave for the night. "One must be prepared to take a little chance when undertaking the conquest of a great mountain," Annie asserted.

Not surprisingly, Sintich demanded they start back to La Paz the next day. Once again, Annie was left feeling terribly let down and disappointed by her second in command. "La Paz, indeed, and so near the goal!" she opined. "Oh, how I longed for a man with the pluck and determination to stand by me to the finish!"

Nevertheless, back in La Paz she dismissed her qualms about Sintich and begged him to make another attempt, even offering him all the money she had if he'd get her to the summit. At first he seemed agreeable but ultimately decided to attend to other commitments. For the present, Annie Peck's efforts on Sorata were over. But no matter. She'd surpassed Sir Martin Conway and had climbed higher than any American in the Western Hemisphere. And in the meantime, she'd learned that her efforts might be directed at a higher mountain. So now she turned her attention to an even worthier goal: Peru's mighty Huascarán.

We Said, "Why Not?"

Quaint as it may sound today, even a century ago people complained that their favorite country getaway spots were becoming overcrowded. "Getting away from it all" meant leaving the ordinary tourists behind—and in the 1870s that meant trying the relatively new type of recreation for city dwellers: camping out.

Martha Whitman, the indefatigable tramper in the White Mountains in the 1870s and 1880s, decided to try camping out when the burgeoning hotels started pouring more and more visitors onto the nearby trails and scenic areas she'd always enjoyed. These people cared far more for "which hotel sets the best table or where the finest dresses are made" than the real outdoors, Martha commented.[1]

But there was something more to this idea of going into the woods in a self-sufficient way. In broad terms, it helps explain why women chose the pastimes of mountain tramping and climbing. Martha and her female friends envied men's ability to leave the well-worn byways—and thought that freedom was something they ought to share.

On the West Coast, other women echoed Martha Whitman's sentiments. Too many tourists—as well as the desire to share in adventures previously enjoyed by men— inspired them to strike off into untracked territory, and then urge other women to try this for themselves. Mary Schäffer, one of the first female explorers in the Canadian Rockies, related the joys of getting away from civilization's ordinary constraints. There is a place, she wrote, "where hat-pins are not the mode, and where lingerie waist a dream; that there are vast stretches where the air is so pure, body and soul are purified by it, the sights so restful that the weariest heart finds repose."[2]

Schäffer, along with her friend Mary ("Mollie") Adams, explored the Canadian Rockies in the first years of the twentieth century. They set out on a four-month excursion into the Canadian wilderness, despite the great disapproval of their friends and relatives. Mary described how the plan fomented in their minds:

> There are times when the horizon seems restricted, and
> we seemed to have reached that horizon, and the limit of
> all endurance,—to sit with folded hands and listen calmly
> to the stories of the hills we longed to see, the hills which
> had lured and beckoned us for years before this long list of
> men had ever set foot in the country. Our cups splashed
> over. Then we looked into each other's eyes and said:
> "Why not? We can starve as well as they; the muskeg will
> be no softer for us than for them; the ground will be no
> harder to sleep upon; the waters no deeper to swim, nor
> the bath colder if we fall in,"—so—we planned a trip.[3]

In her 1916 book, *Woodcraft for Women*, American Kathrene Pinkerton enthusiastically expressed how outdoor experiences could open up new ways of thinking for women.

It will give her a strong body, controlled nerves, and a poise and calmness of mind. . . . It will arouse the adventurous, exploring spirit. . . . It will result in a growth and a development of her spiritual and her mental being. It will afford opportunity to tally her outlook on life with the big, inspiring forces of nature. The view can never but clear away much of the pettiness of life and give a saner idea of the true proportions . . . and will help her measure up to the conditions and the possibilities of the new era that lies before her.[4]

In poignant terms, Pinkerton described how the light of adventure dimmed in her own life. "I can remember vividly the flutter and death of the adventurous spirit in my little girlhood," she wrote. While she was playing with a bunch of boys one day, a group of girls came along and scornfully called her "rough." She bowed to peer pressure and joined them, however reluctantly. But years later, she rediscovered that spirit of adventure in the woods. She dedicated her book to rekindling that "adventurous, exploring spirit" in other women.

—

Annie Smith Peck, her Swiss guides and scientist, leaving New York for South America, 1903. (FROM A SEARCH FOR THE APEX OF AMERICA, ANNIE S. PECK.)

Chapter 10

The Apex of America

Mount Huascarán, Peru
August 1904

> When I first saw from Yungay magnificent Huascarán tower-
> ing far above the valley, I was filled with dismay at my own
> temerity in dreaming for a moment of its conquest. Many
> thousand feet rise the rocky slopes and the well rounded earth
> covered buttresses, supporting the broad ice-clad substructure
> of the twin peaks, which at a startling angle pierce the blue
> sky above. The immense glacier below the peaks was so visibly
> and terribly cut by a multitude of crevasses that it seemed
> impossible for the most skilful, much less for men wholly inex-
> perienced to find their way through such a maze.
>
> —Annie S. Peck, *A Search for the Apex of America*

*A fierce gust jolted Annie awake. She listened in the blackness. The
tent's single pole groaned under the stress, and its silk walls billowed and
luffed as the wind shifted and blew. Stuffed in her flannel and eiderdown
sleeping bag and wedged among Swiss guides and Indian porters, she*

tried to clear her mind. "Relax," she told herself. "Go back to sleep."
But each time she'd nearly drifted off some image of what was before her
popped into her head, and she'd begin reviewing the details, one by one,
of what she expected the next day. The crevasses, the ice walls, the tricky
séracs, the steep slopes, the wind, and, of course, the cold. She shivered
in spite of herself.

As she listened to the whistling wind, she worried—should they even
try in these conditions? She'd come so far; she longed dearly for the sum-
mit. Yet it was senseless to make another doomed attempt. But if they
didn't try tomorrow, how would they know that the next day would be
any better? Each passing day in this cramped, cold tent meant less food
and fuel, less determined porters, and more grumbling from the guides.
She knew the importance of maintaining momentum to keep the men
occupied. Still, the wind and cold were powerful enemies. Annie won-
dered at what cost her attempt at Huascarán's summit might be made.

WHEN ANNIE SMITH PECK set off from New York for Peru and Bolivia in June 1904, she had in mind climbing three mountains: Sorata, Sahama, and Huascarán. One of them, she was sure, would prove the highest in the hemisphere. Now two months later and recuperating in La Paz after her unsuccessful attempt on Sorata, she spent her time sleeping, eating well, smearing Pond's Extract on her sunburned face, and deliberating about what to do next. With the first snowfalls of the season already sifting into the valleys, she realized there was no time for both of the remaining peaks. Sahama, reputedly the world's tallest volcano, was closer to La Paz but in the middle of the desert, where the view was said to be "tame." Accordingly, she dismissed climbing it as "unworthy of the toil required to meet the goal." Huascarán, though a "rugged journey" away, promised grand scenery. It would be a much tougher climb, but it offered the best chance for the altitude record. The only problem was, Annie had no one to go with her.[1]

Without a companion, and still having only a "meager acquaintance" with Spanish, she admitted some trepidation about venturing into the roadless wilds of northern Peru. Friends in La Paz suggested a few possibilities for climbing partners, and she tried tracking down some fellows she'd met on her voyages south. But to no avail; even as she booked a berth on a steamer bound for the coast of Peru, she still didn't have an escort.

The evening before her departure, however, her luck turned. Entering her hotel lobby, she noticed a burly fellow talking with the desk clerk. Though speaking Spanish, he looked to her like an American, perhaps a miner seeking work. She was right about his profession, though wrong about his nationality. Peter (she never mentions his last name) turned out to be Italian and Mexican, with a reasonable command of English. We can only imagine Peter's first reaction as he was approached by a solitary, diminutive, blister-faced woman proposing he join her assault on what could be the continent's highest peak. But within minutes, Annie tells us, he expressed "a cordial desire to assist an American woman in accomplishing so great an achievement as the ascent of this lofty mountain."

Annie felt blessed with good fortune. Though Peter lacked mountain experience, he'd traveled the world as a seaman and miner. In contrast to her other, more sophisticated companions, she foresaw a perfectly agreeable relationship: "He was evidently muscular and used to hard work, and I thought possibly an ordinary man with no pretension to education and technical skill might show better courage and be more amenable to my wishes than some gentleman."

Bubonic plague still threatened Bolivia and Peru, so before they boarded ship their luggage was decontaminated. Some of it was fumigated with sulfur gas, some baked. Annie later complained that after this treatment her leather Tyrolean climbing boots cracked like parchment.

The new partners steamed north to the port town of Samanco and then made their way with horses and burros east over the dusty plain toward Huascarán and its nearest town, Yungay. Several days into the trip, familiar signs of trouble began emerging. Peter, like Victor Sintich and the other men she had known, had designs on "going his own way," Annie noted with dismay. And physique notwithstanding, Peter proved not to be the bold adventurer she'd expected. One evening during their march through the Andean foothills, Peter urged halting at an Indian settlement rather than continuing another thirty miles to their planned destination, the home of an English mine owner. Traveling the ribbon-thin, winding mountain paths after dark was too treacherous, he argued, and they had no idea if the English family was even in residence. Annie balked. "I assured him that that was my affair, that I was paying for this expedition and would do as I saw fit." When he pressed further, she put it with even more plainly: "I was going on, I declared, and in my dignified manner I requested him to say no more." Peter followed reluctantly, grumbling that even for $1,000 he wouldn't let his sister ride the route. Annie dismissed him as a pessimist. In her journal, though, she admitted that she'd have done nearly anything to reach an English-speaking home that night, rather than stay in a "dirty indian hovel."

In Yungay, Annie's planned venture proved an exciting diversion to the local population. A variety of the community elite offered to accompany her on Huascarán, even though the "gentlemen of the town . . . all believed the ascent of the mountain impossible," Annie noted. Of the potential recruits, "all were alike inexperienced, mountain climbing not yet having become a fashionable sport in South America." But given her perpetual search for companionship, "it seemed wise not to decline any proffered assistance." She assembled a motley climbing crew, plus Indian porters. As a precaution against "possible superstitious prejudice," she equipped the expedition with a wooden cross. Accompanied by an entourage of local officials, the party headed on horseback for the east side of the mountain. Annie had ample opportunity to consider her destination.

Huascarán loomed over the landscape, a giant even among its massive neighbors. It was composed of two peaks, north and south, separated by a saddle, or col. From a distance, Annie was unsure which was higher, but suspected the south. This close to the equator, the plains and foothills were hot and arid, but bitter cold awaited the climbers at high altitude. The snow line, somewhere around 18,000 feet, made a brilliant contrast to the mountain's dark lower flanks. Its vast rocky walls reminded Annie of Yosemite, only "more gloomy."

Their approach took them by deep gorges and sparkling glacial lakes, miles of moraine, and increasingly rugged rock.

By the afternoon of the expedition's second day the going got too rough and steep even for the surefooted horses, so they left the pack animals behind. They slowly picked their way higher through a labyrinth of chunky rock slabs and cottage-sized boulders. At 17,000 feet above the sea, they stopped for the day on a plateau just large enough for their tent. Through her field glasses, Annie examined the great rock ridges reaching toward the north peak. The rock ran several thousand feet higher until disappearing beneath heavily crevassed glaciers. Then a nearly perpendicular wall of snow, overhung with an immense cornice, guarded the last approach to the summit. That way didn't look feasible, so she continued scanning the slopes for other possibilities. She considered angling toward the saddle and from there deciding which summit seemed more doable. But this route crossed the paths of avalanches they'd watched crash down all day. The prospects, she admitted, seemed neither inviting nor encouraging. There was nothing to do but sleep on the problem. Crammed into her tiny silk tent with Peter and three other men, however, she lay awake most of the night.

By the next morning she'd made her decision. She led the group toward the col between the north and south summits—but as the climbers moved closer, the worse the conditions appeared. "All parts of the mountain under and around the saddle were so swept by immense avalanches that it would be foolhardy to attempt the ascent there," Annie determined. Instead, she proposed crossing a small glacier, hoping the other side might reveal safer route upward. The men declined. She could hardly blame them. The glacier, she admitted, "was so seamed with crevasses that it appeared to be more holes than ice."

Still undeterred, Annie continued searching for another route higher when a snowstorm sent them all retreating back to their tent for the rest of the day. The next morning the sun rose in a clear sky, melting the new snow and charging Annie with hope for her "final effort." Not even another squabble with Peter punctured her optimism. He refused her request to carry her climbing irons and heavy camera, saying he would only carry himself. Declaring him useless, Annie struck off with two other men in tow.

One of her Yungay companions later published an account of the morning's climb in the Peruvian press:

> To the right and left were impassable walls of snow. We began, therefore, to scale the perpendicular rocks in front. Three hundred feet above [the tent] an immense rock, sloping dangerously, obstructed our passage. The courageous American woman, notwithstanding that below her feet was a precipice reaching down to the glacier, took the cross . . . and resolutely traversed this dangerous place where at every step she was liable to go down to certain death. From the place where we were standing I heard the terrifying crackle of the snows above our heads. . . . We saw Miss Annie erect the cross at a height of 19,000 feet and then descend rapidly.

Though she shrugged off the idea of this imminent peril, Annie conceded that "under existing conditions further advance was impracticable." They'd just made it back to camp when a nearby avalanche threw chunks of snow and rocks over their tent. Shaken, the men quickly packed up and started their retreat. Minutes later, another avalanche swept across the very place the tent had stood.

This avalanche-prone eastern side of the mountain was too dangerous, Annie concluded. She was typically sanguine about the experience. "Though tired, and disappointed in not having gone higher, I rejoiced that I had had the privilege of beholding scenery more magnificent than any which had previously come within my vision either in Europe or America."

And as usual, Annie wasn't done yet. The western side of the mountain, she decided, shouldn't be as susceptible to avalanches. It might be full of treacherous icefalls and crevasses, but she was prepared to confront these. First, though, she had to get rid of Peter, whom she felt had become a liability with his negativity and intractability.

After dismissing Peter she cast her fortunes with a new set of five

Indian recruits. She tried finding leather boots to replace their sandals, but with no suitable footwear locally available she instead provided each man with animal skins to wrap around his feet. She had
climbing irons and ice axes made for them and recommended that
each bring his warmest poncho. Then she gathered them around
and, in her slowly improving Spanish, instructed them in the use of
the rope and the ax. So prepared, the group headed up the mountain
toward the col. "It seemed odd to enter upon this enormous glacier,
covering the entire west slope of the mountain, with five men none
of whom had ever been on the ice before," she admitted.

For once, the way turned out easier than it looked from a distance, and for a while the climbers made steady progress. But soon
the mountain exerted its power. They found themselves in what
Annie described as a "labyrinth of crevasses far worse than anything
I ever saw in Switzerland." For hours they twisted and turned among
pinnacles of ice, slipped along narrow ledges and skirted crevasses
that disappeared into blue-tinged depths. The Indians persevered
gallantly, but eventually, the "rear guard" rebelled. Rather than
retracing their steps through the treacherous maze, Annie convinced
the men to try another route out—which happened to take them
higher on the saddle. They camped at approximately 17,600 feet.
Huddled together in her tent that night, they waited through the
worst snowstorm Annie had ever experienced. "With two suits of all-
wool underwear, other garments, and my sleeping bag, I was chilly,"
she recorded. "It is not strange that the men, with their ponchos
only, suffered from the freezing temperatures." They climbed a few
hundred feet higher the next morning before beginning their descent
back to Yungay.

Now convinced that Huáscarán was loftier than Sorata and
likely higher than Aconcagua, Annie already looked forward to her
next attempt. Even the name of her homebound Panamanian
steamship seemed propitious: the *Advance*. She felt satisfied. "If I had
not accomplished all I desired, I had done enough to show that I was
not insane in believing that I was personally capable, with proper
assistance, of making the ascent of a great mountain. I should bring
to the attention of Alpinists a new and accessible territory, worth

visiting not merely to make a record, but to behold a glorious collection of mountain peaks, some of which will defy their would-be conquerors," she wrote. By the time she arrived in New York in November—still "bronzed and athletic-looking," one reporter noted —she'd formulated her next strategy.[2] She'd start earlier in the season, take the west side up the col, and if she hadn't the funds for Swiss guides, simply employ Indians.

Of course, the fates would not let her off so easily. As she recorded in hindsight, "I did not fully appreciate the difficulties that lay above," referring to the several thousand feet left to the summit. Nor could she guess it would be two years before she'd muster the backing for a return to Peru. Despite her having climbed "higher than any man or woman now residing in the United States,"* she found herself unable to attract financial assistance. She predicted bitterly that that even an "incompetent man" would enjoy more support.

Her goal for her next expedition was a $3,000 war chest. But as New York came into bloom in the spring of 1906 she had barely a fraction of that. One Monday morning, she decided to make another call on *Harper's Magazine*, which she'd been fruitlessly pursuing for nearly two years. This time the editors were willing to take a story of her trip. She signed a contract Tuesday, and just two days later, on May 25, boarded a ship bound for Peru. She had no Swiss guides and all of $700 in her pocket—once again, she took what she could get, not what she wanted.

Back in Lima, she apparently reconsidered conducting her expedition solely with native assistance, for she hustled about looking for a suitable American or European companion, someone with a "more adventuresome spirit than Peter." She visited area mines in search of another stalwart lad, but without success. She was already on her way to Yungay when a telegram came through: a gentleman only a town away wished to join her. Though her local acquaintances vouched

---

* Her stipulation of "residing" in the United States may have been a way of sidestepping American Fanny Bullock Workman, who in 1903 climbed to 22,500 feet in the Himalayas, but who resided much of the time in Europe.

for this fellow, she found his reputation somewhat alarming: " 'True,' said my friends, 'he is *loco*,' which the dictionary interprets as mad or crack-brained, 'but he is intelligent, gentlemanly, energetic, and courageous, the best companion you could possibly have.' Perhaps they thought, as some of my friends at home had declared, that I was *loco* too, and he was therefore a suitable escort."

She hired the man she referred to only as "E____," and unsurprisingly, the venture did not work out quite as she wished. In Yungay she learned that her Indian porters from two years before had all moved on, so she had to start over with an inexperienced team. This new crew did not exhibit the valor, energy, and loyalty she had so prized before. Her party made its way ponderously up the mountain, and Annie agitated at the Indians' late starts, early quitting times, and clumsiness. E____ puzzled her by performing admirably one moment and recklessnessly the next. He also grew increasingly boorish and intolerant of her leadership. He "was confident that two days on the snow supplied him with complete and superior knowledge" to her own, Annie fumed.

Meanwhile, the Indians began fearing that if they climbed much higher the mountains gods would turn them into stone. Only a quarter of the way to the saddle, the porters declared they'd go no farther. Desperate, Annie offered to double—then triple—their wages if they'd simply get to the top of the col. They refused—what good was money if they were turned to stone? At this, she knew there was no alternative but to return to Yungay. Once the order was given, the Indians packed up the camp with amazing speed—"the first and only time I that have ever seen the natives hurry in South America," she wryly noted.

She didn't fare much better on her fourth attempt on Huascarán several weeks later. E____ assured her he'd find a worthier group than the Indians, whom Annie by now had deemed "useless." The new recruits were *cholos*, or "half-breeds," but the results were the same. The men got sick and frightened, barely escaped injury, dropped baggage into crevasses, broke various scientific instruments, and drank up the stove alcohol. After she and E____ disagreed about the route, he heedlessly started making his own way up the mountain—not safe mountaineering practice on an unexplored and treacherous slope. Then he stayed out long after dark, and Annie figured he was indeed *loco* and that this attempt was over. "In view of this adventure," she concluded, "I felt more than ever the folly of trying to do anything with such assistants," and "resolved never again to go climbing with one who had been really mad."

Once again, she would leave Peru without conquering Huascarán. But before departing Lima, she spent what proved her most enjoyable interlude in South America. Inspired partly by her interest in science and international commerce, and partly because she still sought additional adventure, she traveled by rail to Cerro de Pasco, site of the world's highest copper mine. She soon met two young American miners, Pat and Ned, who at her invitation "thought a little mountain climbing might be considerable fun." They heartily agreed to join her for a 100-mile trip on horseback northwest into Peru's rugged and largely unexplored Ruara Range. They'd choose a mountain to climb and, while they were at it, try to find the source of the Amazon River.

Neither of these "stalwart young fellows" had any prior climbing experience, but their mining boss enjoined them to climb at least a thousand feet higher than Annie—who was not only twice their age but also nursing broken ribs after pitching off a balky mule. "I think they did expect," Annie remarked, "to leave me far behind when it came to mountain climbing."

Naturally, Annie had the last laugh. Ned and Pat proved great companions: solicitous, good natured, and strong. But the "boys," as she called them, lost their nerve climbing a glacier towering over Lake Santa Ana, the spot Annie figured was the source of the world's longest river. The boys screamed and cursed their way through a tricky and treacherous ice climb, and when they finally struggled back down, congratulated their leader on guiding them to safety. Ned, she reported, "enthusiastically declared that he never *dreamed* that a woman could have such discretion and prudence, which statement Pat heartily endorsed; though I did not myself agree that those qualities are so rare in my sex." Annie basked in their praise, doubly so since it was her fifty-sixth birthday.

A few days later she led them on another unnamed peak. Soon after Ned declared mountaineering an insane sport practiced by "fools and idiots" (he'd fallen), she left the boys behind and made her own way up the challenging rock climb. Finally, she stood atop a virgin Peruvian summit:

> Triumph at last! It was not by any means the loftiest peak in South America, but it was the first ascent of a mountain higher than Mont Blanc, the monarch of the Alps, and I had done it alone. Surely it was better than nothing. I drew a long breath and for a moment enjoyed my triumph.

It was December before Annie arrived back in New York, and she was buoyed to see *Harper's* on the newsstands with her account of the Huascarán attempts. The endorsement of one of the nation's premier magazines, she thought, would surely boost her fund-raising efforts. But the endless and wearisome course of disappointment continued. Neither the *Harper's* editors nor other sources would finance Swiss guides for another trip. Two more years of "blasted hopes" went by as she tried gathering funds.

By late June 1908 Annie faced the prospect of missing yet another climbing season. Reluctantly, she set a final deadline. If she didn't have enough money by that date, Huascarán would have to wait yet again. But "at the ultimate hour," on the afternoon of the final day, the fates finally turned a sunny face her way. A special-delivery letter arrived, in it a note promising the necessary funds.* For the first time since she was a little girl, Annie literally jumped up and down with delight. Then she collected herself and fired off a telegram to Switzerland directing that two guides join her immediately.

On June 29, after a whirlwind of preparations that included a quick trip to Washington to receive President Roosevelt's encouragement, she once again boarded ship. With her were Zermatt guides

---

* Annie dedicated *A Search for the Apex of America* to Mrs. Anna Woerishoffer, "who, by her generous aid at the ultimate hour, enabled me to carry to triumphant issue my ten years' effort for conquest of what I hoped would prove the highest mountain on this hemisphere."

Rudolf Taugwalder and Gabriel Zumtaugwald. Six weeks later she was back on the western slope of Mount Huascarán.

In a discouraging reprise of the familiar scenario, tensions with the men soon arose. Perhaps they were unavoidable. Annie now had five South American trips to her credit, so she had real knowledge to back up her plans for the ascent. But she'd hired the guides for their expertise, and naturally, they wanted to use it. The guides questioned her leadership and her decision making, and it irked her that to them, her experience "counted for nothing in comparison with their own judgment." They disagreed on the best line of ascent, where to camp, and what to carry. "One of the chief difficulties in a woman's undertaking an expedition of this nature," Annie reflected, "is that every man believes he knows better what should be done than she."

Superior judgment notwithstanding, Rudolf succumbed to altitude sickness only a couple of days into the climb. He returned to Yungay to recuperate, and Gabriel determined he would guide Annie to the summit by himself. But the "Spirit of the Mountain," as Annie called it, had other plans. It blasted the group with fierce icy winds, at night threatening to rip its silk tent to shreds. Huddled inside the tent, Annie had other problems too. Her stove, though the latest model, threw off barely any heat, so the climbers had to content themselves with half-cooked rice. Simply melting snow for tea or soup took hours, and she got stuck with the chore. At the end of the day, as well as before the others arose in the morning, she found herself hunched over the little stove, nursing the feeble flame and adding bits of snow to the pot. She found it exhausting. "My work, though less arduous than the men's, continuing through a greater number of hours, was a severe tax upon my strength, obviously much less than theirs to begin with," she wrote.

Maintaining her strength had been a concern on all her climbs. She considered traveling unencumbered nearly a necessity, for even a few pounds of baggage slowed her appreciably, especially at high altitude. But with Rudolf gone, Annie had no choice but to carry several items, including a mercurial barometer and a gallon of kerosene. Gabriel grumbled at her slow progress, but even he found the going tough without Rudolph to help break a path through the

snow and ice. After a few days of strenuous step cutting and leading the way through waist-deep snow, Gabriel announced he was
"almost finished." Touting their restorative powers, Annie pressed
coca leaves on him, but he declined.

Slowly and painfully, they reached the saddle between the north
and south peaks. At last Annie could examine the way to the top.
She estimated the col at 20,000 feet, and each summit several thousand feet higher. It was unclear which was higher, but "impossible ice
walls and yawning caverns" guarded the base of the south peak. The
north peak "appeared not quite so bad," she reported. "It was steep
enough and broken above into perpendicular or overhanging walls.
Yet we could make a start and perhaps by devious ways could reach
the summit."

At three-thirty the next morning Annie was ready to begin their
summit bid. For once she'd slept fairly well, thanks to the diminished
wind. Gabriel, however, stirred only enough to pronounce it too cold
to set out before light. Three hours later the climbing party started
toiling up the steep north slope, all roped together, pausing often to
catch their breath in the thin air. The snow was hard as concrete in
the bitter cold. Gabriel laboriously hacked away with his ice ax. He
played out the rope behind him, then waited while Annie and the
Indian porters slowly caught up. Annie became more and more
nervous as the incline steepened to fifty and then sixty degrees. She
feared that if she or one of the Indians fell, a single guide couldn't
hold the rope, and the entire group would get pulled down the icy
slopes.

At lunchtime they perched on a tiny ledge and nibbled at hunks
of chocolate and chewed a few malted milk tablets, but no one had
much appetite. On they worked into the afternoon, Annie reporting
she felt strong and tireless. But as the wind rose and the slope grew
extreme, the guide's energy flagged. When Gabriel estimated another
two hours to the summit, Annie assessed their situation. So close,
and yet the risks were mounting. Gabriel had been "almost finished"
days before, had eaten little since, and now performed the work of
two men. "If he collapsed, that would be the end," she thought.
"Should we reach the summit and then slide 4,000 or 10,000 feet

down, what profit? No one would know of our triumph, and of what value a triumph to a dead man, or woman either? Better to return to Yungay with almost, than be dead at the foot of the peak." She turned to Gabriel. "If you think it dangerous to continue, let us retreat."

They retreated. Annie found that the way down the precipitous slope was harrowing as the full view of the tortuous route stretched out below her boots. She slipped trying to reach steps cut too far apart for her comfort. "We shall all be killed!" she shrieked. With no choice but to trust her feet and her crampons, gradually her confidence rose and terror diminished. Soon they were making good progress zigzagging down the mountain. A timely swig of cognac also helped ease the way back to camp.

The next morning it was evident that Gabriel truly was finished. As much as Annie yearned for one more try at the summit, nine nights on the snow, heavy labor, and scant food had worn them all out. Their feet especially suffered in the cold. Annie later realized her tight-fitting crampons had cut circulation, prompting frostbite in two toes and the top of one foot. Gabriel, too, suffered minor frostbite on his toes. They packed up their gear, the Indians shouldered the heavy packs and bags, and they started back down.

At a nearly vertical wall of ice the porters decided to lower the bags down with ropes. But two of the bags came loose, hurtled down the slope, and plummeted into a crevasse. A "truly lamentable accident," Annie realized, for now both her stove and prized Eskimo suit rested somewhere deep within the glacier. There were no replacements for either readily available, and without a stove, "there could be no more climbing."

Back in Yungay she discovered that her friends, residents, and Rudolf had watched the ordeal through telescopes. They'd seen the climbers make it over the saddle, and then spent anxious days without a glimpse of them. Fearing they'd fallen off the other side of the mountain, the Peruvian government sent a search party around to the east to look for them. Meanwhile, a story headlined NO WORD FROM MISS PECK telegraphed around the world. But not only was Annie safe and sound, she was also committed to trying again.

A day's rest, and she started preparations for another attempt. Friends and acquaintances incredulously asked why. "I don't *want* to go," she answered. "I *must* go!" Word was sent out, and a Norwegian kerosene stove was found in another town.

With needle and thread, Annie crafted replacement pairs of what she modestly called *unmentionables*, or long underwear. She hired two additional porters and outfitted them with heavy shoes, wool stockings, and flannel shirts. On August 28, 1908, Annie, the Swiss guides, and four Indian porters left Yungay again.

The conditions looked promising. With days of bright sunshine following freezing nights, fresh snow packed firm on the glacier. The party made rapid progress, climbing easily over the now familiar route. A potentially devastating accident interrupted this otherwise uneventful climb up the saddle. One of the Indian porters broke through a snow bridge spanning a crevasse. Dangling headfirst by the rope wrapped around his waist, he shrugged off his pack, which fell farther into the icy depths. The guides threw him another rope and he pulled himself up, a bit shaken but none the worse for wear. His pack, however, contained the invaluable stove. Gabriel volunteered to retrieve it. He inched his way down into the crevasse, the other men taking a strong hold of his rope. They all waited in suspense until he reemerged, pack slung across his back. The expedition could go on.

In just two days the group reached the highest tent spot near the top of the saddle. Wrapped in her sleeping bag that night, Annie buzzed with anticipation that the next day could find her achieving her long-sought goal. But when she poked her head out early the next morning, the fierce wind and cold sent her burrowing back into her warm bag. She suggested a day of rest, thinking the wind would die down and they'd all feel restored. But the guides favored climbing. Maybe, they said, the wind would slacken higher up. Annie disagreed, arguing that if anything the wind would get worse. As she and the men argued, the morning wore on. Finally, "against my better judgment," she noted, she agreed to go. It was past 8:00 A.M.— late for starting a long, arduous climb. Only Annie and the guides would go; the Indians would stay safely behind. As a precaution against them drinking it, Gabriel buried the can of stove alcohol some distance from the tent. Annie was skeptical, but he assured her he'd find it again.

To fend off the bitter cold Annie bundled up in every stitch of clothing she had: three suits of wool underwear, two pairs of tights, canvas knickerbockers, two flannel shirts, a jacket, two sweaters, and four pairs of wool socks. It's a wonder she could move at all, but these layers still didn't block the icy wind. She sorely missed her Eskimo suit. Over her head she pulled a wool face mask with a "rather superfluous painted moustache."

She started the day with big vicuña mittens and would later hand these over to Rudolf for carrying as the sun rose higher. Gabriel agreed to carry a heavy wool poncho in case she really suffered from cold. But despite Annie's warning about the danger of frostbite, the guides seemed unconcerned about the cold. They each settled for just one pair of heavy socks and no extra mittens. Though seemingly insignificant at the time, these decisions to depart late, bury the fuel, and leave extra mitts and socks behind would have major consequences.

For an hour or more the three made good time, but as they gained altitude and exposure, the wind blasted even harder, as Annie had suspected. The windswept slopes became expanses of sheer, rock-hard ice. Gamely the guides hacked steps, and they crept higher. Annie's hands chilled, and she asked Rudolf for her vicuña mittens back. She opened her mouth to warn him not to lose them in the wind, but caught herself. "Like most men, the guides were rather impatient of what they considered unnecessary advice or suggestions from a woman, even an employer," she reasoned, and this was no time to cause irritation. But an instant later her fears were realized. Rudolf cried out that he'd dropped a mitt, and they both watched it sail down the mountain. Furious, Annie pulled the remaining mitten on her right hand and took up her ice ax again.

The wind, cold, and altitude ground away on the climbers' nerves and stamina. By 2:00 P.M. Rudolf announced he could go no farther. Ahead of them lay the final, very steep approach to the summit. Annie favored leaving Rudolf where he was, but Gabriel took the other guide's rucksack and the three continued up the last icy pitch.

At the top they stepped onto a broad, gently inclined snow ridge that ended in Huascarán's north summit. The wind blew stronger than ever, and as she plodded on, Annie realized she'd lost all feeling in her left hand. She yanked off her wool mitten and found the hand completely black. Frightened, she rubbed it vigorously with snow. Soon it ached terribly—a positive sign of the blood flowing.* But without a vicuña mitt she was sure the hand would freeze again. She thought of the poncho, and, retrieving it from Gabriel, pulled it over her head and kept her left arm inside. Later, she figured the poncho saved her hand.

Gabriel now suggested they take a hypsometer reading for altitude, for the wind might be even worse at the very top of the ridge. They were so close to the summit, he assured Annie, a few feet wouldn't make much difference for the reading. To make the device work, they had to light a flame under a tiny well of liquid, then measure the boiling point. That would tell them atmospheric pressure, which they could convert into altitude. Reading a mercurial barometer would have been easier and faster, but Annie had left hers back in Yungay, afraid she'd get stuck carrying the yard-long tool. Now she must have rued that choice, for in the wind match after match extinguished before Gabriel could light the flame.

They thought of Rudolf—if he held the poncho to deflect the wind they might get a flame. They looked around, but he'd disappeared. Seeing his footprints Annie realized what had happened. With Gabriel in her wake, she strode into the wind, following Rudolf's tracks to the end of the ridge and the true summit. When she saw the guide there she was beside herself. Not only did he prevent their taking an altitude reading, but he'd made the unconscionable step of taking the summit before she. "Of course it made no real difference to the honour to which I was entitled, but of a certain personal satisfaction, long looked forward to, I had been robbed," Annie lamented.

But finally, she stood on the summit she had dreamed of for so

---

* Obviously, knowledge about treatment of frostbite had not progressed much at that time. This is not accepted practice today.

many years. She looked out on the snowy crests stretched out beneath her—except for the south peak of Huascarán, which she now realized might be higher than the north peak.[3] She never imagined victory could be so bittersweet. "There was no pleasure here, hardly a feeling of triumph, in view of my disappointment over the observations, and my dread of the long and terrible descent," she reflected. It was too cold and too late in the day to linger over the hypsometer, so she'd never get evidence to substantiate her belief that she was at 24,000 feet, higher than any man or woman before. But she could get pictures. Wincing in the cold when she removed her wool mitts, she squeezed off a photograph in each direction, then snapped one of Gabriel. But the shutter didn't sound right, so, fearing the camera wasn't working at all, she quickly stowed it away. As it turned out, the camera was fine, and she forever regretted not having a photo of herself on the summit.

It had taken them seven hours to reach the top of Huascarán. Now, at three-thirty in the afternoon, the sun was already dipping and they were only starting their descent. Those wasted morning hours plagued at Annie, and as she started down the precipitous wall from the summit ridge her anxiety rose. She was tired, hungry, and cold, and her boots slipped on the icy slope, for after her bout of frostbite she'd left the crampons behind. Flapping around her, the big poncho impeded her vision and compounded her fear of falling. If she had both vicuña mittens, she thought bitterly, she wouldn't have to wear the poncho.

She trusted Gabriel, who was roped behind her, but out ahead Rudolf looked shaky. The altitude, it seemed, was rendering him stupid. Suddenly she saw a black object fly away from him and disappear, and realized he'd lost one of his own mittens. A while later he lost the other, making grasping his ice ax a terrible chore. Then one of his feet began freezing. In this condition they lurched down the mountain, Annie and Rudolf slipping and sliding, Gabriel making superhuman efforts on the rope to keep them all from hurtling to their deaths. "My recollection of the descent is as of a horrible nightmare," Annie wrote. "Several times I declared that we should never get down alive. I begged Gabriel to stop for the night and make a cave in the snow, but, saying this was impossible, he continued without a pause." When the guide told her that stopping meant freezing to death, Annie realized she was in a fight for survival. "I said to myself, for the first time in my life, I *must* keep cool and do my best, and so I did; but after several of those horrible slides—Well, there was nothing to do but to plod along."

Utterly spent, the three crawled into their tent at ten-thirty that night, more than fourteen hours after leaving. Gabriel later told Annie that he never lost faith in their making it back, but Rudolf confessed he never expected to come down alive. Indeed, huddled with the four Indians in the little tent, Rudolf was the worst off. Frostbite blackened both his hands, and though Annie and Gabriel watched him feebly rub them with snow, they were too exhausted to help. The Indians might have, but they'd gone back to sleep.

The wind was just as fierce the next morning, and no one favored fighting it again. Gabriel went searching but never found the hidden can of alcohol. Without fire, they couldn't melt snow—so no water, soup, or tea. The best they could do was mix snow and sugar, and sprinkle on a little grain. They spent the day dozing and shivering. When a calm breeze greeted them the next morning they started back down the mountain.

A week after leaving the summit, Annie rode back into Yungay. As she went, she reflected again how her longed-for moment of glory was tarnished: "The sad condition of Rudolf, then and always, greatly marred the satisfaction of my triumph. His misfortune seemed indeed to outweigh any benefit derived from the ascent, my only consolation being that it was his own fault and not a necessary consequence of the climb, as the soundness of myself and Gabriel attested." Later, she'd learn that Rudolf lost most of his left hand, a finger on his right, and half of one foot. His climbing days were through.

Later, too, Annie would find her claim to the world altitude record attacked by Fanny Bullock Workman, daughter of a Massachusetts governor, wife of a physician, and a world traveler who'd been mountaineering in Asia since 1898. She'd also be criticized for taking undue and self-serving risks that resulted in the grave injuries to Rudolf.

But all that was ahead of her. For now, she simply tried to savor some satisfaction from her journey. "As I rode along the valley and looked up at that great magnificent mountain conquered at last, after so many years of struggle, days and weeks of hardship, and now at such a cost, I felt almost like shaking my fist at it and saying, 'I have beaten you at last and I shall never have to go up there again,' but I didn't."

Annie did return to Peru. She enjoyed long and hospitable relations with the government there, which awarded her a gold medal for her achievements and named Huascarán's north peak "Cumbre Ana Peck" in her honor. In 1911 she climbed the country's second highest mountain, Nevado Coropuna, and planted the yellow banner VOTES FOR WOMEN of the Joan of Arc Suffrage League on its 21,000-foot summit.[4] She was sixty-one years old. Before and after World War I she traveled extensively through South America, investigating trade opportunities and lecturing in Spanish, which over the years she finally perfected. In the United States she kept a steady schedule of lectures as well, published A Search for the Apex of America describing her Sorata and Huascarán expeditions, and wrote several other books on South America. In 1917 she was elected a Fellow of London's Royal Geographic Society, and became a member of the Society of Woman Geographers in Washington, D.C., in 1928.

She kept her remarkably adventurous outlook on life into her ninth decade, when she embarked on a seven-month, 20,000-mile air tour through South America. Around this time, American aviator Amelia Earhart said that compared to Peck, "I felt an upstart." Her résumé of adventures, Earhart continued, "gives me the impression . . . I am just a 'softie.' However, I am somehow comforted by the fact that Miss Peck would make almost anyone appear soft."[5] Back home from her travels, Annie churned out a book about her flying tour and climbed her last mountain, 5,363-foot Mount Madison in New Hampshire's Presidential Range. In 1934 she went unaccompanied on a cruise to the West Indies and Trinidad and a few months later traveled with a friend to Newfoundland.[6] In October of that year the Society of Woman Geographers celebrated her birthday with a reception in New York. Eighty-four candles bristled on a white frosted cake shaped like a snowcapped mountain. Wearing her prized Peruvian gold medal pinned to her dress, she offered a few comments on her career.

"I always hoped Huascarán would prove to be the highest mountain in the western world, but now it seems that Aconcagua . . . is highest," she told the guests. "But anybody can climb that. It's just a walk. No cliffs. No glaciers."[7]

Annie died less than a year later, on July 18, 1935, in her New York apartment after a short illness. In reporting her passing, the *New York Times* quoted a statement about her issued years before by the *Athenaeum*, a New York magazine: "She has done all that a man could, if not more. She had sagacity, and with it 'nerve' and 'grit.' "[8]

Fanny Bullock Workman, her husband, and guides on the summit of Mount Bullock Workman, 19,450 feet, 1899. (FROM *IN THE ICE WORLD OF THE HIMÁLAYA.*)

Chapter 11

Fanny Bullock Workman
and Dora Keen

Somewhere in the Himalayan foothills
September 1908

"Nonsense! Sheer nonsense!"

William Hunter Workman awoke from a midafternoon snooze with his wife's voice ringing in his ears. "What is it, dear?" he called. He could see her imposing shadow on the tent wall.

"That Peck woman. She says she's climbed to 24,000 feet. Preposterous!"

Fanny Bullock Workman flung back the tent flap and stepped inside brandishing a newspaper. "Here!" She thrust it at him, jabbing her finger at the page. William found his eyeglasses and peered at the paper. It was one of the stack of newspapers and letters that occasionally found their way via runner to their remote camps. Amazingly, this paper was only a few weeks old.

" 'Miss Peck Reaches Summit of Mountain,' " he read aloud. " '. . . daring ascent . . . Swiss guide injured . . . premier American woman climber estimates altitude at 24,000 feet, making a new world's record. . . .'

"Well," he said, putting the paper down. "It's going a bit far to say she's the premier American woman climber. . . ."

"Balderdash!" Fanny roared. "She's not the premier climber and she did not get to 24,000 feet. The mountains in Peru can't be that high. My record will stand—I will see to it."

She sat down at their portable writing desk and started feeding a sheet into the Underwood.

"I'm writing Schrader and Vallot. I want them to go measure Huascarán," she said, the typewriter keys already clattering under her fingers.

William shook his head, still a little groggy. "Schrader?" he asked. "Vallot?"

"You remember," his wife said impatiently. "They head the Societé Genérale d'Etudes et de Travaux Topographiques. The Topographical Society—Paris. They'll know exactly what to do. They'll triangulate that Peruvian foothill and prove that Pinnacle Peak is higher—by several thousand feet, I should imagine."

William knew there was no stopping his wife, and really, he mused, why should there be? She'd worked so hard to get to the top of the one of the highest peaks in the Nun Kun massif of Kashmir—23,300 feet, they figured. It had been among the most arduous of their many difficult journeys together, but his wife never faltered. Through the bitter cold, the pounding headaches from that awful thin air, the nausea . . . but it had been worth it. He smiled picturing her on that fearsome snowbound mountain, scrambling up the ice, wielding her ice ax like any fellow, her skirts flapping about her legs and her veil pressed against her face in that relentless wind.

"Do you realize, Doctor Workman," Fanny said, still facing her desk but addressing him in the way he knew meant business, "this Peck woman isn't only trying to take away my altitude record. She's after yours as well."

WHILE ANNIE SMITH PECK chipped away at Mount Huascarán in Peru, her rival Fanny Bullock Workman was campaigning in remote and largely unexplored areas of northern India and Tibet. And another American, Dora Keen, was beginning an alpine career that would shortly place her among the world's elite explorers. These women shared many traits—unbounded, never-say-die resolve, an unshakable belief in the abilities of their sex, courage, and stamina were just a few. Their circumstances, however, provide striking contrasts.

While Peck scrimped and scraped together funds for her travels, Bullock Workman (as Fanny preferred being called) and Keen, like many of the early English and European mountaineers, enjoyed backgrounds of wealth and privilege. Like Peck, they started climbing in the Alps but made their names as mountaineers in far-flung regions. Keen was one of the earliest climbers in Alaska, and Bullock Workman made pioneer excursions in the western Himalayas, Hindu Kush, and Karakoram Ranges.

Perhaps their most profound difference from Peck is that each enjoyed rich relationships with men, partnering with them in the mountains in ways that Annie longed for, but rarely achieved. Each of the three approached leadership differently. Peck organized and led her own expeditions, even as she enlisted help from men with various levels of expertise. It's likely these men had never taken direction from any woman before, and certainly not one so determined and single-minded as she. They resented her authority, and it would not be surprising if the more they resisted her, the more officious and inflexible her manner became, which of course only compounded her difficulties. Bullock Workman, on the other hand, climbed as an equal partner with her husband. Together they experienced plenty of cultural differences with their native subordinates—and often found them infuriating—but they never had trouble with their professional European help. Keen, in a further contrast, hired the best local leader she could find, and with his guidance picked a loyal and capable crew. While she chose the goals for her expeditions, she entrusted her leaders with critical decisions. These men did not let her down.

Like Peck, Bullock Workman and Keen viewed their mountaineering as proof of what women could achieve. And like her, they exemplified the "New Woman" striding purposefully from the confining Victorian age into the twentieth century. While, like Peck, they occasionally interpreted their actions in feminist terms, their motivations were also broader. Keen reveled in the transcendent beauty and awesome power of nature, and believed that through mountaineering both men and women could test themselves and live life to the fullest. Bullock Workman was driven by a pure love of exploration; she too saw mountains and glaciers as awesome and breathtaking objects, but also as foes and obstacles for conquering in a contest of wills.

The three women certainly knew of each other, though it is unclear if they ever met. All were Fellows of the Royal Geographic Society in London, as well as members of the American Alpine Club. In fact, Peck and Bullock Workman were charter members of the latter, and their conflict over the women's altitude record led to the resignation of some who resented it when the club sided with the patrician Fanny.[1]

Fanny Bullock Workman
(1859–1925)

Winning step by step.

Fanny Bullock was born January 8, 1859, the second daughter and youngest of three children in a prosperous and respected Worcester, Massachusetts, family. Her father, Alexander Hamilton Bullock, served as a Republican governor of the state. She took her primary education with private tutors in Massachusetts, attended a finishing school in New York, and studied for two years in Paris and Dresden before returning to the United States in 1879. In 1881 she married a Harvard-trained physician, William Hunter Workman, who had also studied in Europe. He was twelve years her senior. When unspecified health problems drove him from his profession in 1889, the couple, plus their four-year-old daughter Rachel, set off for Germany. For

"The Thrill of Adventure in Every Step"

Why did women of means and education, who even in the restrictive Victorian era had some other choices for recreation, decide to forsake the comforts of civilization and climb mountains? It was tough, unforgiving business requiring arduous labor, often in harsh conditions. Of course, the same question has been posed to men. The Romantic appeal of the mountain landscapes certainly attracted many, though few of those visitors chose mountaineering as a pastime. Some interpreters see the Victorian craving for hard physical exercise and the thrill of risk taking as an antidote to confining, progressively mechanized workplaces and the increasingly impersonal cities. Harvard lecturer Arthur Davis traced mountaineering to the Western ethos, the "ceaseless drive to master the environment and to push dynamically beyond the existing order of things and ideas."[1]

Appalachian Mountain Club president Charles Fay explained that the "element of conquest gives to moutaineering its zest. There is in every active man conscious of the possession of powers that which longs for something on which to exercise them."[2]

Contemporary feminism often seeks to put the relationship of women and nature in less confrontational, more harmonious terms than these early advocates of mastery.[3] But the pioneer women mountaineers sounded the cry for battle and conquest with the same vigor as their male counterparts. In fact, their imagery and language are remarkably masculine—in part, no doubt, because of customary writing style but perhaps too because they did not see their actions as any different from men's.

"There is no manlier sport in the world than mountaineering," the great mountaineer Elizabeth Le Blond declared in 1903. "A mountaineer sets his skill and his strength against the difficulty of getting to the top of a steep peak. Either he conquers the mountain, or it conquers him."[4]

A generation later, Annie Smith Peck's description of the satisfaction she found in mountaineering reflected her competitive urge: "The chief joy is the varied and perfect exercise, in the midst of noble scenery and exhilarating atmosphere, for the attainment of an object, the conquest of the mountain. The peak utters a challenge. The climber responds by saying to himself, I can and I will conquer it."[5]

Alaskan mountaineer Dora Keen saw climbing mountains as a hard-fought battle, and a metaphor for life:

There was a zest in the combat, a challenge to willpower and tactics as well as to endurance and muscle in that seemingly inaccessible summit. There was the thrill of adventure in every step, and with every foot won a sense of accomplishment, a new consciousness of power, which brought confidence and strength for the fray. In the space of a few hours, more than in years before, I seemed to be acquiring all the qualities needed for the hard battles and decisions of life.[6]

several years they immersed themselves in European art, music, and literature. Later, with Rachel parked in boarding school, they traveled together throughout the Continent.

Traveling together meshed the two in a rare partnership that William described years later: "From this point their lives and activities were inseparably united and they shared equally all the excitements, hardships, and the dangers of the adventurous life that followed, in meeting which Mrs. Workman was by no means the less courageous and determined."[2] In photos, Fanny invariably gazes out at the camera and the rest of the world with the "composed counte-nance associated with the very rich," as one biographer artfully put it.[3] Her steely gaze conveys an assurance and solidity of one in com-mand, sure of her abilities and her place in the world. William is taller and also solidly built. In studio portraits William wears a gen-tle and slightly amused expression; in the field, face framed with a bushy beard, he looks the rugged mountain man. They seemed to complement each other perfectly, so much so that over the years they traded roles on successive mountaineering expeditions. One organ-ized and led the trip, and the other kept the copious scientific records and diaries. On the next trip they'd switch roles. Then together they'd produce lengthy, profusely detailed and illustrated accounts of their excursions.[4]

Early in their marriage William introduced Fanny to New Hampshire's White Mountains. Even after she'd gone on to much more dramatic and renowned alpine locales, she expressed the importance of these experiences to members of the Appalachian Mountain Club:

> The first love of the hills was aroused in me . . . when we passed several summers in the White Mountains and, linger-ing on the slopes of Clinton and Pleasant and among the crags of Mount Washington, I realized that there was no beauty like the beauty of the mountains, no atmosphere—whether in storm or fair weather—equal to that which enshrouds them, and no solitude so soul-satisfying as that which reigns on the arêtes and summits of the eternal hills.[5]

As for so many before her, the Alps provided her first experi-ences of extended mountaineering. Clad in the proper tweed skirt and jacket she'd stick with throughout her career, Fanny climbed the Jungfrau, Matterhorn, and Mont Blanc, among other peaks. "I am not a light weight and am a slow climber," she admitted, but her early successes indicate she was supremely suited to the physical and mental demands of mountaineering. Her sturdy legs and sheer doggedness carried her where many had tried and failed.[6]

In the 1890s the Workmans learned to ride the bicycle, recently evolved from a rickety contraption to the fat-tired, still-single-geared "safety" model. It was the beginning of a cycling craze that swept Europe, and Fanny, along with other women, enjoyed the newfound freedom of the breeze billowing through her skirt. The Workmans embraced cycling as they did other pursuits—with great vigor. Inspired by this new form of conveyance, they eventually left the comfort of the drawing rooms and concert halls and over the next decade wheeled all over Europe, Africa, and finally Ceylon, Java, and India, where they racked up 14,000 miles. From these excursions they wrote *Algerian Memories: A Bicycle Tour Over the Atlas Mountains to the Sahara*, the first of their many books together.

In the summers of 1898 and 1899 the Workmans escaped the swelter of the Indian plains by visiting the snowy Himalayas. They soon realized that mountaineering in these remote, vast, and lofty ranges made Alpine climbing seem more like a Sunday walk in the park. "In the Himalayas," they told their readers, "there are no villages and hotels within a few hours' distance of summits, no shelter huts, where a climber may break the journey and spend a fairly comfortable night, no corps of guides, who in case of need are ready to render assistance."[7]

While in the Alps a summit might take two days of climbing, including a stop at a hut or roughing it in a bivouac, Himalayan mountaineers had to carry with them everything they needed for weeks and even months. "The mountaineer must go, fully provided with mountain and camp outfit, many days' march beyond even semi-civilized villages, into savage and trackless wastes that surround giants he would conquer," the Workmans explained. "He must brave fatigue, wet, cold, wind and snow, and the effects of altitude, for the bases of many peaks rest upon buttresses that are higher then the summit of Mont Blanc."[8]

And unlike the Alps, in the Himalayas there was no corps of professional guides and porters to assist the traveler. If anything, the Workmans' experience with local hires was even more frustrating than Annie Peck's in South America. "Worst of all," they wrote imperiously, the mountaineer "must wrestle with the peccadilloes of the half barbarous coolies, on whom he must rely for transport, who care nothing for him or his object, and who are likely to refuse to go with him, as soon as any especial difficulty is encountered." But even with these logistical, physical, and cultural hardships, the exhilaration of Himalayan exploration hooked Fanny. "The lure of unexplored mountain wastes held me . . . in its grip," she admitted.[9]

Imagine her clad in uninsulated leather boots, heavy skirt, and cloth puttees, head and neck swaddled in a wool scarf and mask, and bent into the face of a fearsome gale. This is how she described the scene during one of her early Himalayan climbs before a gathering at the Appalachian Mountain Club in September 1900:

> By noon we had reached 20,000 feet, and the snow came to our knees,—snow dry and mealy, which so chilled and benumbed our feet that we expected frost-bite. The surface beneath the snow was of ice, making our footing on the sharp slants most insecure. Zurbriggen [their Italian guide] worked hard, treading out every step, and the waiting for him to do this in the snowstorm was more than bitter. The mere lifting of the feet from one deep step to another caused us to pant for breath. We needed food, but could not find the kola biscuits in our pockets with half-frozen fingers. I called to Zurbriggen that I must change my gloves, for I could no longer feel my ice-ax. He scarcely heard the loudest scream at the end of thirty feet of rope. We halted and he rubbed my hands and pounded my feet as well as he could. He changed my fur gloves and tied on some rubber mittens, that in time restored circulation. Perhaps we should have turned, but we did not.[10]

Between 1900 and 1912 the Workmans launched six great expeditions, each lasting several months, covering hundreds of miles, and employing an entourage that included dozens of local porters, cooks, servants, and interpreters, Italian porters, yaks for carrying baggage, chickens, and herds of goats and sheep for eating.[11] They also took with them Italian guides, not for choosing the route, but to assist with the safe passage through uncharted glaciers and peaks. Along the way they collected "geological specimens," photographed and surveyed uncharted territory, and scaled virgin peaks. In the tradition of some of the great women mountaineers before her, Fanny insisted in *In the Ice World of the Himálaya* that her accomplishments were not all that extraordinary: ". . . in starting out, I was in no especial train-ing for mountain work." She did admit, however, that her "powers of endurance" built up over thousands of miles astride her bicycle left her in good stead. She also implied that others might follow in her footsteps: "For the benefit of women who may not yet have ascended to altitudes above 16,000 feet but are thinking of attempting to do so," she offered observations on her physical experiences at high alti-tude. For the most part, she fared quite well, although she felt short of breath, suffered headaches, and slept fitfully in "the rarified air." In a companion chapter on his experiences, William reported much the same. The doctor noted that he and his wife discovered the best method for "relieving intense thirst from heavy exertion" was "to drink freely of very weak hot tea, with a teaspoonful of whisky in each cup."[12]

In the summer of 1899 Fanny christened a 19,450-foot peak with her name (Mount Bullock Workman) and then set the women's world altitude record with an ascent of the 21,000-foot Mount Koser Gunge, both peaks in the Shigar Valley of Baltistan in what is now northern Pakistan. The thin air left her gasping for breath and strug-gling ahead at a rate of only 300 feet per hour near the top of Koser Gunge. "I do not endure severe cold at any altitude, and this great height found the chill and numbness produced by the icy wind bet-ter to bear," she admitted.[13] But that didn't deter her from seeking even higher goals. Three years later she broke her own record by climbing above 22,500 feet to the summit of Mount Lungma in Baltistan. No slouch either, William at age fifty-six posted a men's altitude record on 23,392-foot Pyramid Peak during this same trip. In 1906 the pair explored the glaciers and peaks of the Nun Kun massif in Kashmir. There they pitched their tent at 21,300 feet—a record altitude for camping, they proudly noted. Then Fanny, who was now forty-seven, claimed 23,300 feet on Pinnacle Peak, the massif's second highest summit, the altitude record she defended so vociferously against Annie Peck's challenge.

When Fanny got word of Peck's declaration of 24,000 feet on Huascarán, she dispatched a team of French engineers to triangulate the Peruvian mountain. It cost her $13,000—a fortune to Peck—and she got what she wanted. Armed with the latest scientific measuring devices, the engineers figured Huascarán's north peak at 21,812 feet and the south at 375 feet higher. (Today's figures are 21,831 feet for the north peak and 22,205 for the south.) At nearly 23,000 feet, Argentina's Aconcagua beat them both as the highest peak in the hemisphere. Bullock Workman sent off a letter to *Scientific American* denouncing Peck and reasserting the supremacy of her own women's altitude record. Annie fired back, questioning the accuracy of triangulation and disputing that she'd ever professed anything but an estimate of height.[14] She also challenged Bullock Workman to substantiate her altitude claims—a request that Fanny never answered. In 1911 the Academy of Sciences in London settled the controversy in Fanny's favor. MRS. WORKMAN WINS proclaimed the *New York Times*.[15] The estimate of Fanny's Pinnacle Peak later dropped to about 22,800 feet, but it was still high enough to secure her the altitude record for nearly thirty years.

Through all their expeditions, the Workmans persevered through the extreme discomforts and dangers of high-altitude mountaineering in "an unknown, unexplored world of eternal snow," including subzero cold, minor bouts of altitude sickness, temporary snow blindness, howling storms, hidden crevasses, precipitous slopes, falling ice, and avalanches.[16] Fanny's Italian bag handler plunged to his death in an accident she herself narrowly avoided. Native porters mutinied and deserted. Unlike Annie Peck, who struggled alone with similar challenges, Fanny and William had each other, and also enjoyed the assistance of a cadre of professional surveyors and topographers.

The Workmans' final expedition in 1912 was also Fanny's finest. She organized and led their exploration of the 50-mile-long Siachen Glacier in what is now a disputed area on the Indian-Pakistan border. The Siachen is the longest glacier in the Himalayas. In their

book *Two Summers in the Ice-Wilds of the Eastern Karakoram*, Fanny
wrote her own section on the Siachen Glacier. Included in the volume's many photos is one of Fanny casually reading a newspaper at
21,000 feet. Its headline reads VOTES FOR WOMEN. (In an amusing
juxtaposition, next to this photo is one of Fanny being hauled across
a river on a porter's back.) In a note at the end of the book, she articulated the significance of her taking credit for the expedition:

> The object of placing my full name in connection with the
> expedition on the map, is not because I wish in any way to
> thrust myself forward, but solely that in the accomplishments
> of women, now and in the future, it should be known to them
> and stated in print that a woman was the initiator and special
> leader of this expedition. When, later, woman occupies her
> acknowledged position as an individual worker in all fields, as
> well as those of exploration, no such emphasis of her work
> will be needed; but that day has not fully arrived, and at pres-
> ent it behooves women, for the benefit of their sex, to put
> what they do, at least, on record.[17]

William later wrote a testimonial to his wife's "unbounded
enthusiasm" and "undaunted courage":

> She concentrated her attention on the end in view, often dis-
> regarding the difficulties and even the dangers that might lie
> in the way of accomplishment. She went forward with a deter-
> mination to succeed and a courage that won success where a
> less determined effort would have failed. She believed in tak-
> ing advantage of every opportunity. She was no quitter, and
> was never the first to suggest turning back in the face of dis-
> couraging circumstances. She frequently urged her Alpine
> guides on to renewed effort where they began to hesitate.[18]

Fanny's Himalayan altitude record stood for nearly three decades,
until 1934. It was not until well after World War I that other women
tried climbing in Tibet. By that time, as biographer Luree Miller has

pointed out, modern equipment coupled with team climbing enhanced the success and reduced the risks of such ventures.

Despite her undeniable courage, creativity as an explorer and mountaineer, and documented successes, Fanny found her reception in the male-dominated mountaineering establishment chilly, if not outright hostile. Her husband—an Alpine Club member—rallied in her defense. He "wielded a pretty blade, never so keen or so quick as in her support," as another club member quaintly put it. Fanny's dominating personality, combined with her vigorous arguments sustaining her opinions, over time soured her relations with some of the club's high and mighty.

"It is not to be expected that a woman of such determination and energy, when assailed or assailing, would be other than a very doughty fighter, as, indeed, became her pure New England ancestry," wrote Alpine Club member J. P. Farrar in an almost apologetic memoriam.

> She herself felt that she suffered from "sex-antagonism," and it is possible that some unconscious feeling, let us say of the novelty of a woman's intrusion into the domain of exploration so long reserved to man, may in some quarters have existed. . . . But those who got to know her well could not fail to recognize her warmness of heart, her enthusiasm, her humour, her buoyant delight in doing. The Workmans have written their names large in the annals of Himalayan exploration. They have criss-crossed the map of Kashmir from Srinagar to the Karakoram Pass, from Leh to Hunza. Their tenacity, enterprise, and contributions to the adventure and scientific results of exploration deserve warm feelings of respect.[19]

Between expeditions and then after her climbing days were through, Fanny continued traveling the world and lecturing to alpine clubs and geographic societies about her explorations. Her lecture before the Royal Geographic Society in November 1905 was only the second ever by a woman (the first was by world traveler Isabella Bird

Bishop in May 1897).[20] Afterward, society president Maj. Leonard Darwin remarked, "I believe I am right in saying that the feats accomplished by Mrs. Workman are more remarkable in the way of mountaineering than those which have been accomplished ever before by any of her sex. Whether I ought to make that limitation or not I am rather doubtful, but, at all events, with that limitation it will not be denied."[21]

By the time World War I ended, she and William had nine books to their credit, including five devoted to the Himalayas. An illness that William described only as "long and painful" finally slowed Fanny, and she died in England on January 22, 1925, at the age of sixty-six. William outlasted her by twelve years. In his memoriam to her, he noted that her commitment to advancing women's education and encouraging equality with men in social, literary, and scientific fields followed her to the end, as she left bequests to Radcliffe, Wellesley, Bryn Mawr, and Smith Colleges.

Dora Keen
(1871–1963)

I thirst for adventure.

Though she was twelve years younger, Dora Keen's life in certain respects paralleled Fanny Bullock Workman's. The patriarch of her Philadelphia family was pioneering brain surgeon W. W. Keen. Dora first toured the world in his company, and a yearning for travel and adventure stuck with her for the rest of her life. Her interest in mountains started with childhood visits to the White Mountains and the Adirondacks and was boosted with trips to the Selkirks, Norway, the Dolomites, and the Andes. As one admiring magazine writer described it, "Where others went to the seaside to dress and dance, she preferred an expedition to the Alps, a horseback trip across Paraguay, or a hunting trip in the wilds of Africa."

When Dora was at home, she took a businesslike approach to satisfying her sense of noblesse oblige. After graduating from Bryn Mawr, she served as the executive secretary to the reform-minded

Public School Association. "Where others filled their winters with dinner and cards, theatre and opera," the same magazine writer continued, "she was immersed in work for the Society for the Prevention for Cruelty to Children, or the American Society for Labor Legislation, or the Society for Organizing Charity, or in Suffragist circles. Serious and strenuous: those were the words to describe the five feet of womanhood of brisk, bright-eyed Dora Keen."[22]

Dora first climbed in the Alps in August 1909, when she was thirty-eight years old. Over the next two years she climbed twenty peaks, including Mont Blanc, Monte Rosa, the Weisshorn, and the Matterhorn. She wrote about the latter for *Outing*, the *Outside* magazine of its day. In gripping detail, she described one of the Alps' toughest climbs made even more challenging by an unusual amount of snow. She also articulated the joy she found in mountaineering, in answer to a variation of the perennial question, "Why climb?":

"Where does the pleasure come in?" I am constantly asked. It comes in the wonderful, awe-inspiring views, in the sense of grandeur, of isolation, of harmony, of mighty forces dominating our littleness, above all in an inspiration that is not to be gained elsewhere, and spiritual uplift seems to be as great as the physical elevation. To see the panorama unfold hour by hour is as if one got a new realization of the universe, a new perception of how great and how beautiful is nature, a stimulation to rise above the small things of life, and a glimpse of the sublime. It is as if our earthly longings had been rewarded, as if we had actually attained the heavens by our long effort, and as if we were being shown a new vision of life, inspired to new resolves of service, of worth, of high-mindedness. And this sense comes only as a reward for struggle.[23]

In an article she wrote for *National Geographic* describing her Alpine experiences, Dora noted that what she'd accomplished was "not to be compared with the brilliant achievements of such spirited and versatile explorers as the Duke of the Abruzzi and others in the Himalayas, in Alaska, in the Andes, and even in the Caucasus." But the following summer of 1910, she started an Alaskan adventure that would eventually earn her a place in such company.

She traveled to Alaska, she later insisted, only as a tourist on a "voyage of discovery," content to enjoy the sights by rail and boat. But her natural inclination for adventure soon won out. The Kenai peninsula proved too alluring to observe simply from a boat in Prince William Sound. Instead she embarked on her first "rough camping" trips, the better to find a big Kodiak bear, she explained. Ascending a few 5,000- and 6,000-foot mountains along the way also whetted her appetite for a higher peak, especially when she discovered that the ferocious Alaskan mosquitoes vanished above snow line. While tramping about, she happened on a prospector's cabin and there found a tantalizing bit of information. A report by the U.S. Geological Survey declared Mount Blackburn, at 16,140 feet second highest of the Wrangell Mountains, "never ascended" and "worthy of the hardiest mountaineer."[24]

Looking at the map, she calculated she could ride the newly completed Copper River Railway nearly 200 miles north to within 35 miles of Blackburn's base. From there she'd have to spend several days negotiating the Kennicott Glacier on her way to the mountains and then the going would get progressively tougher. Dora realized, as Fanny Bullock Workman had in the Himalayas, that Alaskan mountaineering is a far cry from the Alps, or South America, for that matter. In the Tropics the snow line may be at 16,000 or 18,000 feet, leaving just a few thousand feet to the summits. Even on Mont Blanc, the loftiest of the Alps, food, water, wood, and shelter are all found in the comfortable hut at 10,000 feet, and an established route leads to the top. But in Alaska, timber dwindles out by 2,500 or 3,000 feet, and even in that unusually hot season of 1911, the snow line was still as low as 6,000 feet. Reaching Mount Blackburn's summit would mean climbing another 10,000 feet of snow and ice. In the twilight that passed for the summer night, new snow and loose ice had little time for freezing to the underlying slopes, making avalanches a constant threat and limiting the hours for safe travel. Moreover, the mountain's rock ridges were more than likely soft, crumbly sandstone rather than hard granite, making firm hand- and footholds elusive, and increasing the chances of crashing rocks as the ice coating them melted.

All these difficulties meant that up to that time, of Alaska's great peaks only 18,100-foot Mount Saint Elias had been conquered, and it by an expertly outfitted party led by the duke of the Abruzzi, one of the world's preeminent climbers.* Debate was also ongoing about whether various parties had made it to the summit of Alaska's Mount McKinley, the highest peak in North America. Dora had only brought the most rudimentary of her personal climbing gear. Still, the idea of climbing Mount Blackburn was too much to resist. All she needed were companions.

As Annie Smith Peck had a decade before in Peru, Dora sought out a mining community to supply them. Whether it was through luck, her discerning eye, or a wealth of appropriate choices, Dora was able to find the kinds of men that so often eluded Annie. Indeed, one must wonder if she had Annie in mind when she penned her glowing descriptions. "For a woman to explore, requires not so much strength as a careful choice of companions, and none are better than the hardy pioneers of Alaska," she wrote enthusiastically. "Their resourcefulness, efficiency, courage, and uncomplaining cheerfulness are hard to equal. They think for themselves, yet not of themselves first, and none are more chivalrous to women." It's a wonder that after reading this in *Harper's* that Peck didn't rush to Alaska herself, especially when Dora added that she considered "the seasoned Alaska prospectors far superior to Swiss guides."[25]

In the town of Cordova, situated at the head of the new railway, she enlisted R. F. McClellan, a Californian and former mine superintendent, as the expedition organizer and leader. His decade-plus of Alaskan wilderness experience included leading a party through the rugged Dawson Pass. McClellan recruited three other ex-prospectors, two from Seattle and one from Philadelphia; together the four claimed more than half a century of living and traveling in the Alaskan wilderness. The only problem was, none knew any of the

---

* The 14,000-foot Mount Wrangell had also been climbed, but Dora hardly counted this, explaining that its slopes are so gradual that "a dog team may be driven almost to its summit."

techniques of mountain climbing. "No one ropes in Alaska, nor are ice axes known," Dora commented. "When a man perishes in a crevasse, the glacier it is named for him."[26] A German painter with Alpine experience also happened to be in Cordova, and he presented himself to Dora with the promise that he'd get her to the summit even if the others turned back. She signed him up. A seventh man for handling the packhorses completed the party. Meanwhile, she had ice axes and crampons banged out by local blacksmiths.

It was a rough and ready bunch. None of the men had been above 10,000 feet, but all knew what it was to travel in winter at sixty degrees below zero. "You can't freeze to death at this season," they assured Dora. "Why how cold do you suppose it's going to be up there? It ain't going to be more than ten degrees below." This explained their refusal to pack anything warmer than khaki, fur-trimmed shells called Alaskan parkas, and overalls. "The Alaskan prepares for a 'trip' by preparing his mind to do without every article of comfort," Dora concluded.[27]

In mid-August the men, horses, malamute sled dogs, and enough equipment and food for a twelve-day ascent were assembled at the far end of the railway. Eighteen hours of skirting the edge of the three-mile-wide Kennicott Glacier took them to 3,000 feet, where the last timber for fires was available, and about halfway to the base of the mountain. The next day they sent the packhorses back, and in drenching rain cooked 25 pounds of beans and fifteen pans of biscuits for the rest of the trip. The third day they strapped nearly half a ton of gear on the dogsled and divvied up the remainder in roughly 70-pound packs for the men's backs. So laden, they continued on. The unusually warm summer had stripped the glacier of its normal layer of hard snow, leaving it covered with rough ice and rubble and rent with innumerable crevasses. Dora scouted out ahead for the best way through the treacherous maze, while the men hoisted the sled and threw frightened dogs across the crevasses. After a day of this strenuous work, a cold night on the ice, and a close look at Mount Blackburn the next morning, the German alpinist called it quits.

Dora, however, embraced these challenges of Alaskan travel. Her self-confidence—and her standing with the men—both got a boost with an unusual excursion during the party's third day out. This particular afternoon, the group camped on the moraine short of Blackburn's base. Someone spotted a herd of notoriously fleet-footed and wary mountain goats grazing about a mile above them. The climbers were downwind of the animals—the right spot for stalking—so they decided to hunt them for meat for the dog team. Braving the crevasses again, Dora joined two of the men and started the steep climb toward the herd. Hard and fast they traveled, jumping crevasses, crawling up and down slippery ice ridges, climbing straight up shale slopes and across steep gullies. But as they closed in, the sound of sliding rocks alerted the goats, which sprang off in a flash. In the evening gloom Dora and the two men picked their way back to camp. No goat, but Dora noted with pride, "At least I had won the confidence of my men." Back at camp, they told her, "If you can follow them goats, I guess you can climb Mount Blackburn."[28]

By the fourth afternoon they reached the snow line. But here conditions were even more hazardous, for deep soft snow concealed the crevasses. Cautiously they pushed on, McClellan ahead on their one pair of snowshoes, Dora next, poking the snow with her ice ax to try to discern crevasses, and the men with the sled behind. It was tough work that demanded the utmost focus, but step by plodding step Dora's spirits soared:

A new feeling of confidence, new zest came over me each day as I realized what a woman might do in America. Sure of respect and of every assistance, in Alaska at least, her limitations need be only those within herself, her measure that of which she is capable, her development in her own hands to make or mar. I had come to Alaska on a voyage of discovery. Being alone had seemed to put every limitation in my way, and now, on the contrary, my love of adventure and sport could be satisfied as never before, because of the character of the men of Alaska. I was actually launched on an expedition of my own, the most adventurous and hazardous I could desire, yet sure of being cared for in safety with consideration and respect.[29]

Making their way higher in the mealy snow, at various times all of the climbers fell into crevasses up to their waists, and one of the dogs disappeared entirely before being pulled out by his harness. But the most formidable obstacles were the avalanches. In the hot, cloudless days and short nights McClellan called "balmy" (though Dora confessed it was plenty cold enough for her), the snow cover never had time to freeze up sufficiently to withstand the next day's sun. The "beautiful but terrible avalanches," Dora reported, began between eight and nine in the morning and sometimes lasted until three the next morning. During these hours, "it was necessary to be out from under them slides," as John Barrett, the Seattle dog team driver, put it. The scant time when travel was possible, combined with an inferno of towering ice walls, chasms, holes, broken masses of snow, and wedges of ice ready to crumble and fall, made progress excruciatingly difficult and slow. Gamely they tried other routes, though Dora thought each way looked hopelessly difficult and dangerous, especially for men burdened with heavy packs.

The tenth day seemed to offer a break. They were high enough now to see all the way to the top, and McClellan and Barrett investigated the way and declared it feasible. They estimated only a two- or three-day climb to the top, given good weather—just enough time to get up, down, and back to Cordova before all their food and fuel gave out. But the "glorious days" did not hold. They awoke the next morning to a change in the wind and the first bursts of snow heralding a three-day storm. If they waited it out they'd have no food for the return journey. Their only choice was to turn back.

On the long trip home to Philadelphia, Dora had time to assess her experience. Despite falling short of her goal, it was deeply satisfying:

> The actual climbing in Alaska is not hard, as in the Alps, but the obstacles to reaching a high altitude in Alaska are so much more serious than in Switzerland, and the views of ice and snow are so much vaster and more wonderful, that Alaska makes one almost forget the Alps. Not to flinch when the way is hard, not to dread the unknown—to lose

fear,—these things one can learn in the high Alps, but to travel in a country that knows none but human limitations, and to travel with Alaska prospectors, gives one a new spirit, a new optimism, a new standard of courage, and a new inspiration for life.[30]

It was understandable, then, that the following year Dora returned to Alaska resolving to try again for the top of Mount Blackburn. Some of her friends shook their heads in disbelief; the only sensible one on her first trip, they declared, was the German painter who'd turned back. But Dora was adamant. "I was going again," she explained, "because I had need of courage and inspiration and because on the high mountains I find them as nowhere else."[31]

This time she planned to beat the avalanches by going in late winter, when the snowpack was firm. But she was delayed from reaching Cordova until April 16, and once there got bad news: spring had come early, and avalanches had already rumbled across the Copper River Railway. The frozen river was breaking up as well, and any day ice-out could carry away the railroad bridge. There was no time to waste if she wanted to get back up to the Kennicott Glacier.

So three days later Dora was on her way, accompanied by another German-born prospector from Cordova named George Handy. Handy came highly recommended as a climber, and he knew the Blackburn region from seeking gold there. Still, she admitted, "it was with some mistrust of my own judgment" that she agreed to take him on. Waiting for them at the end of the railway were six other men, all of whom lived and prospected within view of Mount Blackburn. Among them was John Barrett, the only man available from the previous year's expedition. Dora named him leader of the expedition.

The nights were somewhat colder than Dora had experienced in August the previous year, but the routine was similarly arduous. This time, however, the gear and provisions weighed a full ton; not wishing to again get caught short of food and fuel, Dora had brought enough for five weeks. With temperatures anywhere from a few degrees below zero to the teens above, the climbers would wake up at one o'clock in the morning and pull on their stiff boots (though Dora slept in hers to keep them from freezing), stamp their feet, and make breakfast. They'd pack up and be ready to start at first light, about three-thirty. As soon as the sun shone they'd put on snowshoes (unlike the last expedition, Dora made sure all the men had them this time). By ten in the morning the temperature usually rose into the fifties or sixties, and the eight dogsleds bogged down so much that they'd have to stop for the day. Still, it took the party only four days to travel up the glacier and reach the foot of Mount Blackburn. None of the men turned back, though Doodles, the most capable sled dog, had had enough and escaped for home. The men passed off the loss, agreeing that Doodles was "an ornery dog and crooked anyhow."

From the head of the Kennicott Glacier, Blackburn's snowy cap hovered 11,000 feet above them. They were surrounded by a majestic amphitheater of lofty, snow-covered peaks, rocky ridges, and precipitous ice walls. Seven other massive glaciers reached toward them with jagged flows of snow and ice. Dora and Barrett knew from the year before the most likely path of the avalanches crashing down from the mountains, so they set up their tent on an elevated snow mound that seemed well away from them. They chose for their route the steepest glacier of them all, but the one that looked least susceptible to slides. Dora called it the Barrett Glacier, for the year before John had climbed to 8,700 feet there. Because the rest of the way would be too steep for dogs, they and their handler returned to their base camp several thousand feet below, and the remainder of the men prepared to continue the journey hefting huge packs.

Dora's crew found plenty of time to study avalanches each afternoon from their successively higher camps and soon figured they could anticipate the slides. "You could most generally always sidestep them in time after you heard the first crack overhead," they assured her. But as she gazed up at the route they proposed, her doubts grew. It was a steep gulch, its floor littered with a jumble of fallen ice shards and blocks of snow, its sides studded with bulging ice masses that threatened to sheer off at any moment.

Barrett tried to reassure her, as Dora later recalled: " 'It's all right if we go early,' he said. 'But I tell you,' he confided, his face growing sober, 'we'll have to go light and rush it, for that gulch is going to slide down sometime, and if we keep a-traveling up and down it till we get all the stuff up, somebody's going to get killed. Just take the food and what you have to, and we men can sleep in the sun.' "

Dora was still unconvinced. It was a three-day climb at least. What if there was a storm and they had no protection? That's why they must "rush it," the men urged. "Anyway," they told her, they'd "rather take a chance than to pack all that junk up and down again any further." The "junk," Dora noted with some alarm, included shelter, fuel, and the men's extra clothing and bedding. But the crew was unanimous. "Thus were my carefully laid plans to be altered, almost daily," she mused, "according to the conditions and humor of the men—men, who think women whimsical."

The climbers started up the gulch, digging in for footholds as the slopes sharpened to seventy degrees. Dora kept a nervous eye on the ice chunks lodged perilously overhead. They didn't dare pause, and after nearly five hours of tough climbing emerged at the top. Here was the source of many of those fearsome chunks lying at the bottom: a crumbling ice wall 150 feet high. Every path seemed blocked by leaning towers, massive pillars, and house-sized ice blocks. Cautiously prodding for holes and chasms, they ducked and squirmed and scrambled their way over the wall.

The dangerous passage had brought them to 12,400 feet, a clear view to the summit, and a spectacular scene of avalanches crashing off the ridges below. In the distance loomed mountains they'd never seen before. Dora was thrilled, especially when she estimated it was at most a seven-hour climb to the top. "The panorama was one to linger over, but a chill breeze decided us to dig 'igloos' or caves in the snow," she reported. "The shovel flew and soon I 'holed in' to mine, which reminded me of a sleeping car berth—if only it had been as warm."

She'd left her warmest sleeping garments in camp, and shivered trying to sleep in the twelve-degree cave. Hours later she woke up with a start. The men hadn't called her before dawn—were they frozen to death? She crawled out as fast as she could and found a raging snowstorm. The five men were in their little cave, cold, silent, and dreary, stamping their feet, clapping their hands, or huddled over candles trying to warm water for tea. They, of course, had brought only the clothes on their backs. Going back down the treacherous gully in these conditions seemed an even worse proposition than staying, and with luck, the weather would clear and they'd still have a chance for the top before the food ran out. During the day Dora lent them her sleeping bag, and each man took a turn in it. She gave them her extra sweaters and sat on her leather mitts and stamped her feet like the rest. The men passed the long hours telling stories of living in the wilderness, of big game they'd hunted and big trees they'd felled.

Outside, the snow piled up. Two feet fell in twenty-four hours, and the storm gave no sign of abating. By the end of the third day, with their food nearly gone, they all knew they could wait no longer. Through the howling storm they forced their way to the top of the gully. "It don't look good to me," Barrett grimly told Dora. Whether George Handy had turned Dora's head before this escapade is unclear. But she certainly noticed him now:

> Without a word Mr. Handy took the lead, tested the snow, and started down. It was too cold to discuss the question. The slope was so steep and the snow so deep as to keep us wet to the waist half the time. Over crevasses and on down a now trailless path of danger, we seemed always to be just on the brink of some precipice or crevasse. We could not see fifty feet ahead, sometimes not twenty—and yet they did not call it a blizzard. . . . On went Mr. Handy, through all the hours never hesitating . . . never afraid, merely shouting back occasional warnings of crevasses or of steep ice underneath. . . . It was as cool and brilliant a piece of leadership as I have ever seen.

Back at camp, they discovered that snow had piled up on the tent walls and soaked through to their bedding. That was the last straw for three of the men. The next day they departed for good, and

Barrett left with them to fetch supplies from the base camp. Remaining with Dora were Handy and another German, Bill Lang. She would learn that a few days later the Associated Press flashed this headline around the world: MAROONED NEAR THE TOP OF MT. BLACKBURN, FACING STARVATION. Three men and two dogs "staggered into Kennicott, telling a thrilling tale" of the expedition, the story read. As for Dora Keen and George Handy, it concluded, "Once more the Arctic silence closed around them."

It was now early May, the beginning of two "months of slides," as the prospectors put it. Barrett returned from the base camp with a tiny woodstove, empty hardtack boxes for fuel, and more provisions. The group was equipped for a longer stay, but would the mountain permit it? Nearby avalanches were beginning to spray their campsite with debris; they'd stand no chance if a slide hit them directly. With another storm brewing, Barrett decided to return to base camp. Dora, Lang, and Handy would take their chances. Abandoning their tents, they tunneled into the steepest part of the campsite's snow mound and dug a bathroom-sized cave. They'd wait out the storm and—as long as the roof held—let any slides roll over them.

And wait they did, for thirteen days. Despite perpetual damp and chill—they couldn't light their stoves for fear of weakening the roof, so their clothes never dried—Dora reported that they slept more, ate more, laughed more, and even washed more than all the rest of the time put together. The only thing she really minded, Dora admitted, were the days when there wasn't enough water to brush her teeth.

There was plenty of time for the three companions to learn more about each other. Lang already considered Alaska too crowded, and planned to move on. Handy was the son of a German army officer. He'd attended a technical school and done his military service in Africa, mined in South America, Mexico, and California, and had even worked as a cowboy in Texas. "He was adventurous and daring by nature," Dora wrote, "but a disciplined soldier and always the first to subordinate his own interests to the good of the whole. . . . For money he cared nothing, but he had enlisted for the summit of Mt. Blackburn and he always said, 'Don't worry. We shall get to the top.'"

When the sky finally cleared they started up the mountain once more. Handy and Lang moved faster without Dora, and they wanted to go on ahead, ferrying gear and testing the conditions. Before leaving they asked her, "If we don't come back, do you think you can get home alone?" She replied that she'd try. Moments after they'd disappeared, a great pinnacle of ice crashed down on the very path they'd taken. Dora watched anxiously until she spotted the two again.

With the hours of safe travel dwindled to the brief interlude between dusk and dawn, the climbers inched back up the mountain, wallowing in waist-deep snow by early morning. The climb up through the gulch was even more harrowing than before, and took days instead of hours. They found their campsite at 12,400 feet buried under new snow and spent the night digging out their igloo, now about twelve feet below the surface.

At nine-thirty the next evening, the conditions looked right for a try at the summit. Only 4,000 feet remained between them and the top, and at this height, the slope had eased enough that avalanches seemed less likely. Still wanting to keep their loads as light as possible, the men left their bedding in the cave. They all exchanged snowshoes for crampons, only to rue that choice a few hours later. Despite an icy wind, the snow at midnight wore only the barest crust, and the three crept along on all fours, futilely attempting to keep from breaking through to their waists. By three in the morning they'd advanced only 1,600 feet. Lang dug another snow cave, and they crawled in to wait for evening to come again.

At five that afternoon Lang resumed breaking trail while Dora and Handy followed. He plowed along knee deep, zigzagging higher as the slope steepened. At 15,000 feet all three began feeling the effects of altitude. At 9:00 P.M., when Dora saw Lang drop his pack, she assumed he wanted to dig another snow cave and take a rest. But moments later Lang plunged down the slope past them, pausing only to say he was unwell, and would see them back at the igloo. Dora was crestfallen. Twenty-seven days of misery and only 500 feet from the top, and he'd turned back. Of the seven men who'd started with her, only one remained.

George Handy dug out a cave and huddled inside, he and Dora

took turns thawing a can of salmon over two candles. After an hour, the fish was soft enough to eat. Outside at midnight, the thermometer read zero. At sunrise it was three degrees warmer. The pair left the cave at about 7:00 A.M. and climbed the last steep slope to the top. At 8:30 A.M. on May 19, four weeks after she'd started, Dora stood on the summit of Mount Blackburn. Despite the frigid temperature and icy gale, she reveled in her triumph:

> There was nothing to impair a view upon which our eyes were the first that had ever looked and the panorama seemed limited only by the haze of distance as we gazed a full 200 miles on every side. Probably nowhere except in Alaska, not even in the Himalayas, could mortal man attain to the centre of so vast and imposing a stretch of unbroken snow over great glaciers and high snow peaks. . . . With aching hands and in wind-hardened snow—for lack of any rock at all—we planted and guyed the bamboo flag-pole which we had dragged up, burying beneath it a brief record of the first ascent of this great 16,140-foot sub-arctic peak.

This time Dora returned to Philadelphia flush with the achievement of joining the ranks of the world's most intrepid explorers. She counted off her expedition's successes: the first to use dogs on a mountain, the first to succeed without Swiss guides, the first to have members live in snow caves, and the first to make a prolonged night ascent. And of course she was the first woman to make an Alaskan ascent. She gave full credit to her men, and Handy in particular. "We succeeded because one man cared to succeed," she professed.

Two years later Dora returned to Alaska to explore and study the Harvard Glacier, the central glacier feeding into the College Fiord near Prince William Sound. She was urged to make the expedition—which promised "plenty of adventure"—by Prof. Lawrence Martin of the University of Wisconsin, who had studied the region for the National Geographic Society in 1909. Along for the trip was George Handy.[32]

In 1916 Dora returned to Alaska again, this time to embark with

Handy on an adventure of a whole other type. On July 8 in the little mining town of McCarthy, in the shadow of Mount Blackburn, Dora Keen and George Handy were married. The couple traveled through Alaska for several months before moving to the small town of West Hartford, near Vermont's Green Mountains. They operated a farm there until 1930. Dora and George divorced in 1932, after which Dora started a new career selling insurance. Her home was a favorite spot for whitewater canoeists from the Appalachian Mountain Club, who'd stop in to warm up after running the nearby White River.

Dora never lost her zest for travel and exploration. In her eighties, when the Vermont winters became too much, she toured the Congo, South Africa, Australia, New Guinea, Kenya, and Java. She tried Florida, but gave it up, she explained, because it was "just filled with old people." At the age of ninety-one she embarked on yet another world tour. She flew to Anchorage, Alaska, and continued on to Tokyo and then Hong Kong. She collapsed in her hotel room there, and died on January 31, 1963. A letter home from her final trip ended, "I thirst for adventure."[33]

Dora Keen, Fanny Bullock Workman, and Annie Smith Peck belonged to the great, pre–World War I time when explorers opened up remote corners of the globe and the stirrings of a new era lay ahead for women. The war interrupted exploration and mountaineering for recreation, but when peace resumed, a new generation of women, both American and European, seized the torch passed by these three intrepid pioneers.

Miriam Underhill in the Swiss Alps, 1930. (ADOLF RUBI, ALPINE CLUB LIBRARY COLLECTION.)

The Next Generation: Miriam O'Brien Underhill

(1898–1976)

I like to be high.

FROM MARIE PARADIS' first tentative footsteps on Mont Blanc to Dora Keen's bold Alaskan explorations, the nineteenth and early twentieth centuries produced a small but vastly impressive group of women who looked to the mountains for inspiration, challenge, and adventure. Bucking the conventions of their time, they dared go where few, if any, had gone before. World War I marked a social and cultural as well as geopolitical watershed. Many of the vestiges of the Victorian age were buried, and women emerged with a new sense of freedom and opportunity in the new, faster-paced world. Mountaineering remained an unusual sport, but it started attracting more and more people outside the ranks of the very wealthy. Exploration of big, remote mountains accelerated with improved transportation, technique, and equipment. Technical rock climbing boomed in popularity, and opened up the sport to a whole new wave of participants who could return to the same cliffs again and again to climb increasingly difficult routes. As one writer put it in a popular magazine,

"Women have now not only entered the ranks of the foremost mountain climbers, but of those pioneers who are satisfied only with 'first ascents.' "[1]

By 1930 the Ladies Alpine Club scanned the scene and declared that given the "quite remarkable degree" to which the standards for women's climbing had been raised, it was "necessary to readjust our scale of values" with regard to what women could achieve, even if it clung to the idea that men were inherently superior:

> It is inconceivable that the average woman climber could ever compete with the average man, but the inequality is no longer so pronounced that any mountaineering feat by a woman should cause so much surprise. The time has come when a woman must no longer think it a matter of importance that she was the first or second of her sex to be taken up a difficult climb. In this respect the newspapers often give us a celebrity that is not of our seeking; nor is it our fault that well-meaning friends and relatives bore their hearers with tedious and incorrect accounts of our exploits. Can we hope that the day is not far off when our achievements will be judged on their own merits, rather than over-praised because we are women?[2]

Nonetheless, women continued to have to prove themselves again and again—as they still often do—and it was not as if the very masculine world of mountaineering suddenly welcomed them with open arms. But the ranks of women who far exceeded the abilities of the "average man" grew steadily. As one American newspaper quipped, "More and more, women alpinists are making molehills of men's mountains."[3] In Europe these climbers included Dorothy Pilley, Dorothy Thompson, Una Cameron, Alice Damesme, Micheline Morin, Nea Morin, and Winfred Marples. In the United States many were associated with the Appalachian Mountain Club and perfected their art in the Alps. Among these were Elizabeth Knowlton (who also climbed in the Himalayas), English-born Jessie Whitehead, Marjorie Hurd, and Margaret Helburn. The most accomplished of them all was Miriam O'Brien Underhill.

Grace, strength, balance, and determination—these were the qualities of Miriam Underhill, wrote her friend and accomplished climber Christopher Goetze.[4] While she negotiated snow and ice as well as anyone, her specialty was tricky, delicate rock climbing, finding and relying on tiny finger- and toeholds, sometimes just ripples or, as Miriam herself once said, "shadows" in the rock. "She was a beautiful climber, like an example from a climbing text," her friend and climbing partner Elizabeth Knowlton wrote. "Naturally graceful, she moved steadily and easily in rhythm, sort of flowing up the rocks. It was a pleasure to watch her."[5]

Like her great predecessors, Miriam started her career in the days before "protection," the removable hardware that today's climbers wedge into cracks to arrest a fall. Ropes themselves were still hemp; nylon was yet to be invented. Wool was the insulator of choice, and the warmth of goose down was still on a far-off horizon. Mountaineering boots were still nailed, although Europeans were starting to make innovations in shoes designed specifically for delicate rock-climbing maneuvers. Miriam herself preferred rubber (which eventually became the choice of all climbers), and sometimes wore tennis shoes to scramble up cliffs. Over the several decades of her most rigorous ascents, rock climbers also started experimenting with pitons—the steel spikes pounded into cracks that, when hung with an iron ring, and later a carabiner, would hold the rope and help arrest falls. These innovations made for a safer sport and also allowed climbers to reach places and try routes they would have avoided before.

In her breezy 1956 account of her climbing life, *Give Me the Hills*, Miriam acknowledged that times were changing, but she refused to cast aspersions at the new breed of climbers who mounted rocks with racks of hardware looped around their waists. "It is too easy to date yourself by things you disapprove of. Everybody uses 'artificial aids'; it is only a question of degree," she asserted. Why draw the line between pitons or expansion bolts and boots themselves, she asked rhetorically. "I don't think I regret, though, that I did my rock-climbing in those simpler days when it was still done pretty much with one's own arms and legs, fingers and toes."[6]

So armed with rope, shoes, and ice ax, she climbed the toughest "problems" in the Alps, including long, dangerous, technically tricky rock climbs like the Grépon; the Aiguilles du Diable, a crenellated ridge of five needlelike spires near Mont Blanc with a reputation as the "most difficult big ridge climb in the Alps"; and of course the Matterhorn, still the pinnacle of Alpine achievement.[7] Her reputation soared to new levels when she began leading the most difficult climbs. Then, as the ultimate challenge, she did them without men, or, as the French termed this new practice of having only women on the rope, *en cordee feminine*. Her style, daring, and dazzling list of ascents established her as one of the greatest American climbers of the century. Her success earned her honorary memberships in the Ladies Alpine Club, whose journals tracked her exploits with great but understated pride, the Alpine Club, the American Alpine Club, and the Appalachian Mountain Club (which she joined as an ordinary member in 1925). She was also a member of the Groupe de Haute Montagne (G.H.M.), a section of the French Alpine Club that accepted only the very best climbers. In 1957 Sir Arnold Lunn, a leading historian of Alpine mountaineering, called her "undoubtedly the greatest lady climber that America has produced."[8]

Miriam moved with equal poise among Boston society, Alpine huts, and ranch hands in the American West, where she participated in some pioneering climbs. But it was in New Hampshire's White Mountains that she first realized her calling.

Born in 1898 and raised in Dedham, a suburb of Boston, Miriam O'Brien came of age during World War I. Hers was a well-to-do and well-connected family. Her father, Robert Lincoln O'Brien, graduated from Harvard in 1891. He was an editor at the *Boston Transcript*, chaired the U.S. Tariff Commission, and eventually left the newspaper business to become a personal secretary to President Grover Cleveland. Her mother, Emily Young O'Brien, came from an old New Hampshire family whose ancestors fought in the Revolutionary War. Emily was one of the earliest female graduates of the Boston University Medical School and practiced medicine until she had children.[9] Miriam graduated from Bryn Mawr in 1920, the same year that American women won the right to vote.

Even as a child, Miriam was always looking for something to climb. "My feet just naturally took me uphill," she recalled.[10] Uphill, when she was a youngster, meant the White Mountains. She spent summers at her grandmother's home in Lisbon, New Hampshire, a small town not far from the Franconia Range, and her earliest outdoor memories involved family camping trips in the remote reaches of the state. In 1914 she saw the Alps for the first time when her mother took her and her younger brother Lincoln on a European tour. When the family returned to the Alps for several summers after the Great War, Miriam climbed a few smaller mountains. Though "slow in getting started," she later commented, from 1926 until the mid-1930s she climbed rocks with remarkable verve.

In 1926 her guide suggested climbing the Aiguille de Roc, a small but frighteningly steep pinnacle near Mount Blanc that had not yet been done. The ascent, accomplished in eighteen hours that featured lightning and a hailstorm, sparked in Miriam the drive that became a defining part of her subsequent career. "I felt a more stirring emotion just from being a part of this pioneer undertaking than I had felt on climbs where many others had succeeded before," she later wrote. "The most satisfying experience in all mountaineering, that of leading a first ascent without professional help, was in the future, but this did very well as a foretaste."[11]

In the following seasons she delighted in choosing peaks and routes with which her expert guides were unfamiliar, and she as well as they would have to figure out the problems presented. It was a natural step to begin leading climbs herself with the guide following. Among her accomplishments of this sort was the Grépon, which she traversed in 1928. Not every licensed Chamonix guide could lead that difficult climb, she noted. But even her most loyal guides deemed it extreme folly that she (or any other client) should dispense with their services altogether. Miriam was undeterred. She started with some smaller, familiar routes without guides, and as a partner for more ambitious climbs she enlisted an increasingly close friend, Harvard philosophy instructor and expert mountaineer Robert L. M. Underhill. But as well as she climbed with Robert and other men, Miriam determined that to really improve her skills, she needed to climb not only guideless but also solely with other women.

Miriam was not the first "manless" climber, as she and other women coined it, but she was the practice's most articulate advocate and chief innovator. She expressed the reasons behind it in a December 1932 *Appalachia* essay called "Without Men," and later in *Give Me the Hills*. The leader "tastes the supreme joys," she wrote. "The one who goes up first on the rope has even more fun, as he solves the immediate problems of technique, tactics and strategy as they occur." Mountaineering "is a sport which has a considerable intellectual component," she continued. For a woman to exercise her own judgment and skill, make the necessary decisions, and take responsibility for any unforeseen circumstances or emergencies, "she must climb manless." Even the man who agrees to take second place on the rope—and to do so he must be supremely self-confident and established in with his own reputation—will still "revert to type" and feel compelled to take over when difficulties arise, she explained. Not that she didn't enjoy climbing with men. "I take great pleasure in your society . . . and lots of you have let me walk in front and have given me a consulting voice in route-choosing. . . . But walking in front isn't leading."[12]

She first climbed manless on the Aiguille du Peigne, near Chamonix, in August 1929. Several days later she and Alice Damesme traversed the Grépon, the famously difficult rock tower where years before Lily Bristow had exhibited her prowess. On the way up, a crowd of male climbers gathered to watch the two women confront that famous rock-climbing problem, the Mummery Crack. Alice led the pitch, squirming up the narrow fissure while Miriam belayed, both knowing that if she fell, death was certain. No leader had ever fallen from near the top and lived, for beneath the 60-foot crack is nothing but thin air. "The key to an easy ascent of the Mummery Crack," according to Miriam, who had led it before, "is complete relaxation."[13]

Back in Chamonix that evening, as Miriam and Alice celebrated their success, a fellow climber and mystery writer named Etienne Bruhl cast a jaundiced eye their way. "The Grépon has disappeared," he intoned. "Of course, there are still some rocks standing there, but as a climb it no longer exists. Now that two women alone have done it, no self-respecting man can undertake it. A pity, too, because it used to be a very good climb."[14] There is no record of how Miriam responded to this comment, but we can imagine it was with characteristic aplomb. It certainly did nothing to diminish her sense of accomplishment or determination to continue with climbing *sans hommes*. The following year, she climbed manless with Marjorie Hurd, a Boston attorney she'd befriended on winter AMC expeditions. In 1931 she climbed the Jungfrau and the Mönch with Micheline Morin, who was also a member of the esteemed Groupe de Haute Montagne. After these successes, she turned to the most celebrated of all Alpine climbs, the Matterhorn. She, Alice Damesme (also in the G.H.M.), and Jessie Whitehead tried the ascent four times that summer, but bad weather always drove them back.

It was not until the following year, 1932, that she and Damesme climbed the Matterhorn—easily—on their first attempt. This time, a party in their honor by their G.H.M. friends was awaiting them back in Chamonix. But Miriam had other plans. She headed to the eastern Alps for some more guideless—but not manless—climbing. Her partner was Robert Underhill. They married later that year, and he would be her climbing companion for the next nineteen seasons. "Manless climbing is fun for awhile," she wrote, "but this other arrangement is better!"[15]

Within several years of these historic climbs, Miriam's attention turned to domestic matters. Son Robert was born in 1936, and Brian in 1939. World War II ended recreational trips to the Alps, and after the war her husband Robert was reluctant to return to a devastated Europe, so he and Miriam instead headed west to the Rocky Mountains. In Montana and Idaho they scaled numerous virgin peaks and explored territory little known by American climbers. In the early 1950s their sons were old enough to do some rock climbing themselves, and the family resumed its Alpine summers.

Even after the Alps had become a personal playground and she'd climbed extensively in the Rockies, the Whites remained Miriam's first love. In 1960 she, Robert, and their two sons eventually took up residence full time in Randolph, New Hampshire, with its tight-knit climbing community in the shadow of the Presidential Range. Miriam's larger-than-life presence made an unforgettable impression on Edith Tucker, an AMC member who was also acquainted with the Underhills when she was growing up. "Other women didn't behave like she did," Tucker recalled. "They were rather ordinary, but she wasn't ordinary at all. She went her own way at a time when people didn't often do that. She didn't worry about what other people thought of her at all."[16]

An active member of the AMC, Miriam helped build trails, led excursions, and as editor of the club's journal, *Appalachia*, brought to it some of the humor and liveliness that marked her own writing. She initiated the publication of a field guide to alpine flowers and contributed many of her own photos to the work, titled *Mountain Flowers of New England*.

She and Robert were charter members of the Four Thousand Footer Club, officially organized in 1957 and open to those who climbed all forty-eight of the highest White Mountain peaks. But the Underhills instigated a notable variation on this peak-bagging theme: making all of the summits in winter. And simply winter conditions wouldn't do; they insisted the climbs be done in the winter calendar months, when days are short and the weather most severe. This promised a "challenge suitably more sporting than ambling up the well-trodden paths in summer," Miriam asserted. They became the first to complete this rather arduous task by climbing Mount Jefferson on December 23, 1960. Temperatures ranged from a high of seven degrees below zero and a low of minus eighteen, with winds reaching 72 miles per hour—"cold weather," Miriam admitted. She was sixty-two years old and Robert, seventy-one.[17]

A sense of Miriam's character is related by George Hamilton, a former AMC hutmaster who accompanied the Underhills on many hikes, including the winter Jefferson climb. He recalls that she "had sparkling blue eyes, and when she spoke, she always looked you right in the eye. She spoke with firmness and authority, with that Beacon Hill accent. But she was a great story teller, and self-deprecating."[18]

Underhill friend Bill Nichols remembers Miriam, then in her sixties, during a winter AMC excursion up Mount Welch in New

Hampshire's Waterville Valley. The snow was many feet deep, and Miriam sternly instructed the participants they should on no account take off their snowshoes. When the group encountered a steep rock wall with a chimney crack up the middle, the young snowshoers were flummoxed. "Everybody was griping, but she went up it like a spider," Nichols recalled. "Now the trail goes around that spot."[19]

"The delight of climbing!" Miriam exclaimed in her later years. "It has been with me all my life. . . . When you have spent in the hills most of the time you have for recreation and pleasure, they come to mean so much more than just the fun of acrobatics. The most urgent desire, after an illness or an absence, is to climb a mountain again. And in occasional times of strain just to walk in the hills brings a strengthening of the spirit, a renewed courage and buoyancy."[20]

Miriam Underhill succumbed to cancer on January 7, 1976. Robert lived another seven years. The American Alpine Club still recognizes the tremendous influence of both of them with its Underhill Award, which annually recognizes a climber who demonstrates "the highest level of the mountaineering arts" through "skill, courage, and perseverance."

———

"I like to be high," Miriam Underhill once said in answer to that perennial question of why people climb mountains. She followed in the footsteps of many women, some known and others forgotten, who also liked the perspective of "life from on top," as the Canadian climber Mary Crawford put it in the early 1900s. Some sought mountain adventure as a way of expressing themselves in a world that was largely closed to assertive, creative women. Others found a sense of inner peace and a means of escape from the modernizing world. It is certain that all of them took great pride in what they did. From Henriette d'Angeville to Lily Bristow to Annie Smith Peck, these pioneers of mountaineering would likely all agree with the editor of the Ladies Alpine Club *Yearbook*, who in 1932 may have finally gotten the right response, as she put it, "to the oft-repeated question, 'Why do you do it?' " Her answer: "Because I like it."[21]

What better words for the next generation of women on high.

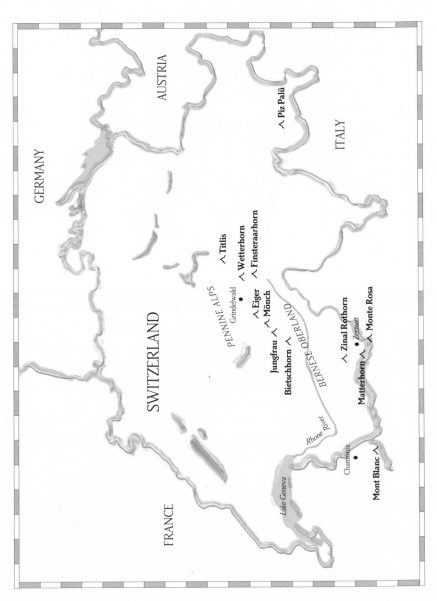

Switzerland

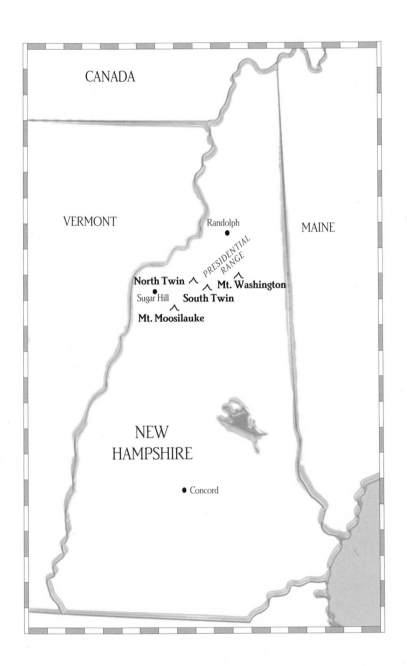

CANADA

VERMONT

Randolph

MAINE

PRESIDENTIAL RANGE

North Twin ⋏

⋏ Mt. Washington

⋏

Sugar Hill

South Twin

⋏

Mt. Moosilauke

NEW
HAMPSHIRE

● Concord

New Hampshire

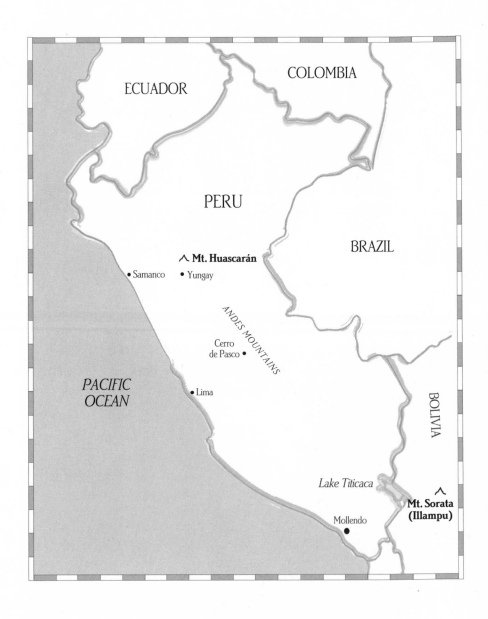

Peru

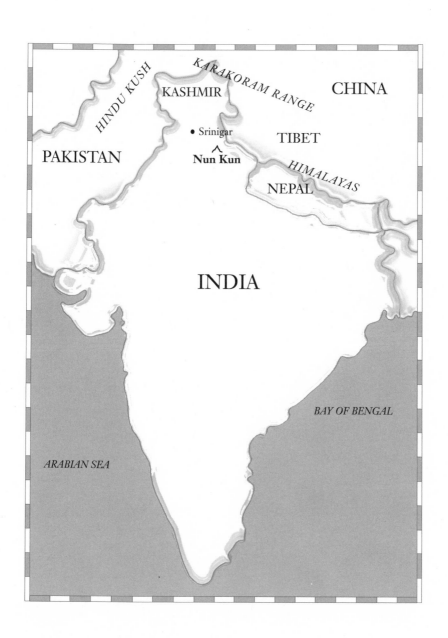

India

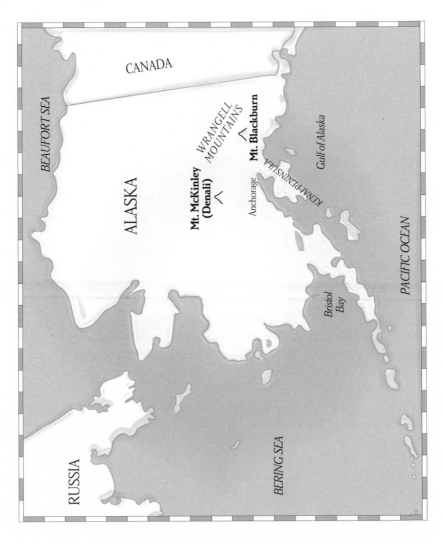

Alaska

Notes

Chapter 1: Maria Paradis

1. Accounts of Maria Paradis vary. Some have her ascent in 1808; some 1809. A few say she was thirty years old, but many peg her as eighteen. By her own account, she was thirty and made her ascent on July 14, 1808. Some interpretations describe her as a peasant, some as a maidservant, and others as the proprietor of a small tea shop. It's possible she was a combination of all three. Mrs. Aubrey Le Blond translated an account she says was written by Maria Paradis in *True Tales of Mountain Adventure* (New York: Dutton, 1903), pp. 203–4. Henriette d'Angeville met Paradis, and says she saw the certificate given Maria for climbing Mont Blanc with the date and the climber's age of thirty. D'Angeville described the encounter in *My Ascent of Mont Blanc* (London: HaperCollins, 1991), pp. 101–5. Francis Gribble quotes Maria's explanation, in French patois, in *The Early Mountaineers* (London: T. Fisher Union, 1899), pp. 239–41.
2. Le Blond, *True Tales*, pp. 203–4.
3. Gribble, *The Early Mountaineers*, pp. 240–1.
4. A. F. Mummery, *My Climbs in the Alps and Caucasus* (Oxford: Basil Blackwell, 1936), p. 96.
5. For a discussion of these themes see Ronald Clark, *The Victorian Mountaineers* (London: B. T. Batsford, 1953); J. A. Mangan and Roberta Park, eds., *From Fair Sex to Feminism* (London: Frank Cass, 1987); and Stephanie Twin, *Out of the Bleachers* (New York: Feminist Press, 1979).

6. William I. Thomas, *Sex and Society* (Chicago: University of Chicago Press, 1907), pp. 239–40.

7. Jules Michelet, *La Montagne* (1868), quoted in Claire Engel, *Mont Blanc: An Anthology* (New York: Rand McNally, 1965), pp. 59–60.

8. Sir Arnold Lunn, *A Century of Mountaineering* (London: George Allen & Unwin, 1957), pp. 26–31; W. A. B. Coolidge, *The Alps in Nature and History* (London: Methven & Co., 1908), pp. 207–8.

9. Coolidge, *The Alps in Nature and History*, pp. 210–11.

10. D'Angeville, *My Ascent of Mont Blanc*, p. 102.

11. Gribble, *The Early Mountaineers*, p. 240; Mary Crawford, "Mountain Climbing for Women," *Canadian Alpine Journal* 2, 1909, p. 85; Derula Murphy in introduction to d'Angeville, *My Ascent*, pp. xv, xxi.l; D'Angeville, *My Ascent*, p. xxi.

Chapter 2: Henriette d'Angeville

1. Gribble, *The Early Mountaineers*, p. 241, quoting a pamphlet by a Mr. Frederick Clissold, who encountered the Campbells. A variation of the story appears in Claire Engel, "Early Lady Climbers," *Alpine Journal* 54, 1943, p. 57.

2. D'Angeville, *My Ascent of Mont Blanc*, p. 3. Hereafter referred to as *My Ascent*.

3. Emile Gaillard's biography, *Une Ascension romantique en 1838: Henriette d'Angeville au Mont Blanc* (Chambéry, 1947), pp. 42ff, quoted in Simon Schama, *Landscape and Memory* (New York: Vintage Press, 1995), p. 497.

4. Engel, *A History of Mountaineering in the Alps*, p. 67–68; "Early Lady Climbers," p. 56. See also Cicely Williams, *Women on the Rope* (London: George Allen & Unwin, 1973), p. 21, and Engel, *Mont Blanc: An Anthology*, p. 223.

5. *My Ascent*, p. 38.

6. Letter to Markham Sherwill, Sept. 15, 1838, in Engel, *Mont Blanc: An Anthology*, p. 110.

7. *My Ascent*, p. xx.

8. Fay Fuller, "Historian's Report," *Mazamas* 1, no. 1 (1896), p. 15, quoting Murray's *Handbook of Switzerland* (1854).

9. *My Ascent*, p. xxi.

10. Quoted in Schama, *Landscape and Memory*, p. 496; cf. *My Ascent*, p. xxii.

11. My Ascent, p. xix. All quoted passages in the rest of this chapter are from this account, except as noted.
12. Sir Frederick Pollack, "The Early History of Mountaineering," in C. T. Dent, Mountaineering (London: Longmans, Green, 1892), p. 30.
13. Ibid.
14. Letter to Markham Sherwill, op. cit.
15. Williams, Women on the Rope, p. 26.

Sidebar: Romancing the Mountains
1. See for instance, E. Brooks Holifield, Era of Persuasion, p. 34, and Kenneth Clark, Civilization, "The Worship of Nature."
2. Quoted by Erica Goldman, "Why Climb Mountains," unpublished essay, 2000, Yale University, http://pantheon.cis.yale/edu~thomast/essays/Erica/eg1.html.
3. Charles E. Fay, "The Mountain as Influence in Modern Life," Appalachia 11, June 1905, p. 34.
4. "A Lady" [Jane Freshfield], Alpine Byways, p. 3.
5. Alfred Lunn, A Century of Mountaineering, p. 46.
6. Helen Hamilton, Mountain Madness (London: W. Collins Sons, 1922), p. 19.

Sidebar: The Dress Question: "It Is Time We Should Reform"
1. Mrs. W. G. Nowell, "A Mountain Suit for Women," Appalachia 1 (1876–8), pp 181–83.
2. Ibid, p. 183.

Chapter 3: Doing the Mountains Jolly

1. "A Lady" [Jane Freshfield], Alpine Byways (London: Longman, Green, Longman, & Roberts, 1861), p 1.
2. Ibid. For discussions of the "Golden Age," see for instance, Lunn, A Century of Mountaineering, and Coolidge, The Alps in Nature and History.
3. John H. Strong, "Swiss Mountaineering in 1859," letter printed in American Alpine Club Journal 5 (1943–5), pp. 389–93.
4. See Williams, Women on the Rope, pp. 33–35; David Mazel, Mountaineering Women: Stories by Early Climbers (College Station, Texas: Texas A&M University Press, 1994), p. 27.
5. Miss Jemima's Swiss Journal (London: Putnam, 1963), p. 30.

6. Ibid, p. 4.
7. This and all following direct quotations are from Freshfield, *Alpine Byways*, unless noted otherwise.
8. Coolidge, *The Alps in Nature and History*, p. 238.

Sidebar: Ladies Unattended

1. Mrs. Aubrey Le Blond, "Then and Now," *Ladies Alpine Club Yearbook*, 1932, pp. 5–6.
2. Williams, *Women on the Rope*, p. 31.
3. A. Barnicoat (Mrs. Julian Grande), "Women and Mountains," uncited magazine article copy, about 1912, Appalachian Mountain Club Library, Boston, Mass.
4. Quoted in Clark, *The Victorian Mountaineers*, p. 175.

Sidebar: Unfeminine Exploits

1. On American climbers' attitudes, see, for instance, John Cameron, "Shall American Climbers Adopt European Methods?" *Mazamas* 2 (Dec. 1905); John M. Gould, *How to Camp Out* (New York: Scribner, Armstrong, & Co., 1877), pp. 58–59.
2. Twin, *Out of the Bleachers*, p. xxiii; ibid., citing Carroll-Smith Rosenberg and Charles Rosenbergh, "The Female Animal: Medical and Biological Views of Woman and Her Role in Nineteenth-Century America," *Journal of American History* 60, no. 2 (Sept. 1973), p. 355; Karla Henderson, et al., *Both Gains and Gaps: Feminist Perspectives on Women's Leisure* (State College, Penn.: Venture Publishing, 1999), pp. 33–4.
3. Quoted in Mangan and Park, *From Fair Sex to Feminism*, p. 66.
4. Ibid., p. 67.
5. Mary Crawford, "Mountain Climbing for Women," *Canadian Alpine Journal* 2 (1909), pp. 86, 91.
6. Harold Raeburn, *Mountaineering Art* (New York: Frederick Stokes Co., 1920), pp. 119–20.

Chapter 4: Lucy Walker

1. Claire Engel describes Walker in *They Came to the Hills* (London: George Allen & Unwin, 1952), p. 102, and "Early Lady Climbers," p. 58.

2. For another good discussion of Walker and her family, see Bill Birkett and Bill Peascod, *Women Climbing: 200 Years of Achievement* (Seattle: The Mountaineers, 1989), pp. 18–22.

3. Engel relates this story in *Hills*, pp. 100–1.

4. Quoted in Lunn, *A Century of Mountaineering*, p. 72.

5. Engel translated this letter for "Early Lady Climbers," p. 58, and later used it in *Hills*, pp. 105–6.

6. Coolidge, *The Alps in Nature and History*, pp. 237–40.

7. Ronald Clark reports Horace's broken arm in *An Eccentric in the Alps* (London: Museum Press, 1959), p. 85. In describing Lucy's climb I've drawn on the early account by Melancthon M. Hurd, "Ascent of the Matterhorn," *Appalachia* 4 (Dec. 1886), pp. 285–94; Edward Whymper, *Scrambles Amongst the Alps* (London: John Murray, 1893); and Arnold Lunn, *Matterhorn Centenary* (New York: Rand McNally, 1965).

8. A. Barnicoat (Mrs. Julian Grande) says she has it "on good authority" that this was Walker's preferred mountain diet. From an uncited reprint of her essay, "Women and Mountains," date about 1912, p. 357, in the collection of the Appalachian Mountain Club Library.

9. Whymper, *Scrambles Amongst the Alps*, p. 155.

10. *Punch* (Aug. 26, 1871), quoted in Frederick Gardiner and Charles Pilkington, "Lucy Walker: Memoriam," *Alpine Journal* 31 (1917), pp. 97–102.

11. Gardiner and Pilkington, op. cit., p. 98.

12. Ibid., p. 102.

13. Quoted in ibid., p. 98.

Sidebar: The European Solution: "Slipping Off and On"

1. Quoted in Clark, *An Eccentric in the Alps*, p. 39, and *The Victorian Mountaineers*, p. 177.

2. Mrs. Aubrey Le Blond, "Then and Now," p. 6.

3. Mrs. Aubrey Le Blond and Katherine Richardson, "Equipment and Outfit, " in C. T. Dent, *Mountaineering*, pp. 50–52.

4. Ibid., pp. 50–52.

5. Editorial, Ladies Alpine Club *Yearbook* (1930), p. 3.

Chapter 5: Meta Brevoort

1. "A Survey of American Ascents in the Alps in the Nineteenth Century," pt. 1, *American Alpine Journal* 2 (1935), p. 360.

2. Clark, *An Eccentric in the Alps*, pp. 25–27. This biography of William Coolidge also gives many mentions of Meta Brevoort and the dog Tschingel, and informs my understanding of them all.
3. Clark, *An Eccentric in the Alps*, p. 20.
4. Alfred Lunn, *A Century of Mountaineering*, p. 105.
5. Clark, *An Eccentric in the Alps*, p. 85.
6. A. B. Coolidge [Marguerite Brevoort], "A Day and Night on the Bietschhorn," *Alpine Journal* 6 (1872), pp. 114–24. All subsequent direct quotes are from this essay.
7. Clark, *An Eccentric in the Alps*, p. 77.
8. A. B. Coolidge, "The Wetterhorn and Jungfrau in Winter," *Alpine Journal* 6 (1874), p. 405.
9. Clark, *An Eccentric in the Alps*, p. 81.
10. Coolidge, "Winter," p. 413.
11. Clark, *An Eccentric in the Alps*, p. 100.
12. Ibid., p. 98; see also Williams, *Women on the Rope*, p. 52.
13. Cf. W. A. B. Coolidge, *Alpine Studies* (London: Longmans, Green & Co., 1912), pp. 189–90; Williams, *Women on the Rope*, p. 54; Clark, *An Eccentric in the Alps*, p. 98.
14. A. B. Coolidge, "An Ascent of the Meije," *Alpine Journal* 9 (1879), p. 129.
15. Lunn, *A Century of Mountaineering*, p. 102.

Sidebar: Tschingel, the Climbing Dog
1. Coolidge, *Alpine Studies*, p. 170; Clark, *An Eccentric in the Alps*, pp. 155–57.
2. Ibid., p. 174; Clark, *An Eccentric in the Alps*, p. 54.
3. Ibid., *Alpine Studies*, p. 183.
4. Ibid., pp. 172–77.
5. Clark, *An Eccentric in the Alps*, p. 64.
6. Ibid., p. 161.

Chapter 6: Elizabeth Le Blond

1. Engel, *They Came to the Hills*, p. 221. Her chapter on Le Blond, "Meeting Interesting People," pp. 221–32, provides good information on Le Blond's life and travels. See also Williams, *Women on the Rope*, pp. 62–65.
2. Mrs. Aubrey [Elizabeth] Le Blond, *Day In, Day Out* (London: John

Lane, 1928), p. 17.

3. Engel, *They Came to the Hills*, p. 224, suggests Elizabeth divorced Fred Burnaby, but no other source mentions that; indeed, in *Day In, Day Out*, she devotes five chapters to him.

4. Mrs. Aubrey Le Blond, *The High Alps in Winter* (London: Sampson Low, Marston, Searle & Rivington, 1883), preface; ibid., *Day In, Day Out*, p. 87.

5. Mrs. Aubrey Le Blond, "Then and Now," Ladies Alpine Club *Yearbook* (1932), p. 5.

6. Le Blond, *Day In, Day Out*, p. 90; see also a variation in "Then and Now," p. 5.

7. Le Blond relates this story in *Day In, Day Out*, pp. 87–91.

8. Mrs. Aubrey Le Blond, *High Life and Towers of Silence* (London: Sampson Low, Marston, Searle & Rivington, 1883), pp. 64–68.

9. Le Blond, *Day In, Day Out*, p. 90.

10. The "red shawl" reference is from Mary D. Glynne, "I Remember," Ladies' Alpine Club *Yearbook* (1975), p. 16; other quotes are from Le Blond, *High Alps*, preface.

11. Le Blond, *Day In, Day Out*, p. 91.

12. Dorothy Pilley, *Climbing Days*, quoted in Bill Birkett and Bill Peascod, *Women Climbing*, p. 34.

13. Le Blond described this climb in *High Life*, pp. 115–23.

14. Mrs. A. F. [Mary] Mummery, "The Teufelsgrat," in A. F. Mummery, *My Climbs in the Alps and Caucasus*, p. 45.

15. Le Blond related this story in *High Life*, pp. 98–113.

16. Ibid., pp. 45–53.

17. Ibid., pp. 25–26.

18. Ibid., pp. 27–29.

19. Ibid., pp. 35–36.

20. Le Blond, *Day In, Day Out*, p. 92.

21. "In Memoriam: Mrs. Aubrey Le Blond," Ladies' Alpine Club *Yearbook* (1935), pp. 3–4.

Sidebar: "Moderation in All Things"

1. Mrs. W. G. Nowell, "A Mountain Suit for Women," *Appalachia* 1 (1876–8), p. 181.

2. "Reports of the Councillors," *Appalachia* 1 (1876–8), p. 193.

3. In Raeburn, *Mountaineering Art*, p. 127.

Chapter 7: An Easy Day for a Lady

1. All direct quotes are from Mrs. A. F. [Mary] Mummery, "The Teufelsgrat," in Mummery, *My Climbs in the Alps and Caucasus*, pp. 45–65. See also David Mazel's discussion of Mary Mummery in *Mountaineering Women*, pp. 59–60; Birkett and Peascod, *Women Climbing*, pp. 24–25; and Williams, *Women on the Rope*, pp. 71–75.

2. Williams, *Women on the Rope*, p. 65. Other information on Mrs. Jackson's climbing career is given on pp. 65–70. See also David Mazel, op. cit., pp. 69–71.

3. All quotes are from Mrs. E. P. Jackson, "A Winter Quartette," *Alpine Journal* 14 (1889), pp. 200–10.

4. Williams, op. cit., p. 70; Lunn, *A Century of Mountaineering*, p. 143; Mazel, op. cit., p. 71.

5. All quotes are from Lily Bristow, "An Easy Day for a Lady," *Alpine Journal* 53 (1941–42), pp. 370–74.

6. For a discussion of Briston's career, see Mazel, op. cit., p. 78; Birkett and Peascod, op. cit., pp. 24–25 and Williams, op. cit., pp. 75–76.

7. Mummery, *My Climbs in the Alps and Caucasus*, pp. 84, 98.

8. Ibid., p. 112.

9. Ibid., p. 113. Lunn, in *A Century of Mountaineering*, p. 174, states it was Leslie Stephen who first made the "easy day" remark.

Sidebar: The Immortal Miss Richardson

1. Bibliographical information on Richardson is found in Williams, *Women on the Rope*, pp. 58–62; Elizabeth Le Blond, "In Memoriam: Miss Katherine Richardson," *Alpine Journal* 40 (1928), p. 160.

2. Le Blond, "In Memoriam: Miss Katherine Richardson," op. cit.; "In Memoriam: Miss K. Richardson," *Ladies Alpine Club Yearbook* (1928), pp. 23–25.

Chapter 8: Women of the White Mountains

1. See Joshua Greenfield, " 'Good Fellowship and Camaraderie': Group Hiking Trips and the Growth of the Early American Conservation Movement," unpublished manuscript, Hunter College, in Appalachian Mountain Club Library collection.

2. Moses F. Sweetser, *The White Mountains, A Handbook for Travellers* (Boston: James Osgood, 1881), p. 35.

3. "Appalachian Excursions," *White Mountain Echo* (July 29, 1882), p. 6; "A Great Walking Club," *Outing* 9 (January 1887), p. 381; George C. Mann, "Excursions for the Season of 1887 and 1888," *Appalachia* 5 (Dec. 1888), p. 255.

4. "A Great Walking Club," op. cit.; Emily A. Thackray, "The Fair Mountaineers," *White Mountain Echo* (Aug. 3, 1889).

5. See Laura and Guy Waterman, *Forest and Crag* (Boston: Appalachian Mountain Club Books, 1989), pp. 199–200, for a discussion of these AMC activities.

6. George N. Cross, *Randolph Old and New*, (1924), p. 151; quoted by Waterman, *Forest and Crag*, p. 267, and Peter Rowan and June Hammond Rowan, *Mountain Summers* (Gorham, N.H.: Gulfside Press, 1995), p. 4. I am indebted to the Rowans for biographical information on Lucia and Marian Pychowska, Isabella Stone, and Edith Cook, whose correspondence they edited and presented in *Mountain Summers*. All direct quotes from the women's letters are from *Mountain Summers*, used with permission from the Rowans.

7. Thackray, "The Fair Mountaineers," op. cit.

8. July 4, 1881, *Mountain Summers*, p. 50.

9. M. Pychowska, "Two in the Alpine Pastures," *Appalachia* 8 (Dec. 1887), p. 186.

10. M. Pychowska, "Explorations Near West Campton," *Appalachia* 2 (July 1880), p. 103; Sept. 4, 1882, *Mountain Summers*, p. 103.

11. Sept. 3, 1882, p. 102; July 25, 1882, p. 80, both *Mountain Summers*.

12. Thackray, "The Fair Mountaineers," op. cit.

13. Sweetser, *The White Mountains, A Handbook for Travellers*, p. 162.

14. Ibid., pp. 161–62; "Proposed Twin Mountain Path," *White Mountain Echo* (Aug. 5, 1882), p. 7.

15. E. Scott, "The Twin Mountain Range," *Appalachia* 3 (April 1883), pp. 107–21. All Scott's direct quotes are taken from this source. See also Rebecca A. Brown, "Walking in their Footsteps," *AMC Outdoors* 67, (Sept. 2001) pp. 34–39.

16. Charlotte Ricker, "The Wilderness: Wild Places and Rugged Peaks First Visited by a Woman," *White Mountain Echo* (Aug. 26, Sept. 2, Sept. 9, 1882). All subsequent quotes by Ricker are from these articles.

17. *Mountain Summers*, p. 88; "Tourist Register," *White Mountain Echo* (Aug. 5, 1882).

18. July 27, 1883, *Mountain Summers*, p. 139.

19. *White Mountain Echo* (Aug. 3, 1889), p 14.

Sidebar: American Solutions: Bathing Suits and Bloomers

1. Sarah M. Grimké, "Letter XI: Dress of Women," *Letters on the Equality of the Sexes: Addressed to Mary S. Parker, President of the Boston Female Anti-Slavery Society* (Boston: Isaac Knapp, 1838). In a Web site by Melissa Karenty, State University of New York at Binghamton, fall 1999: http://womhist.binghamton.edu/dress/doc1.
2. Elizabeth Smith Miller, "Reflections on Woman's Dress and the Record of a Personal Experience," *Arena* (Sept. 1892), pp. 491–95. Available online in a Web site by Melissa Karenty, State University of New York at Binghamton, fall 1999: http://womhist.binghamton. edu/dress/doc28. Also in Elizabeth Smith Miller Collection, New York Public Library.
3. Weldon Heald, "Bloomer Girl of the Rockies," *Appalachia* 32 (June, 1959), pp. 349–51; see also Janet Robertson, *The Magnificent Mountain Women of Colorado* (Lincoln: University of Nebraska Press, 1990), p. 3.
4. Sweetser, *The White Mountains, A Handbook for Travellers*, p. 33.
5. "Reports of the Councillors," *Appalachia* 1 (June 1877), p. 194.
6. Paul Marshall Rea and Carolyn Louise Morse, "Packing Double, or Honeymoon in the Woods," unpublished diary, in the Edward M. Rea collection. June–July 1904.

Chapter 9: Annie Smith Peck

1. *A Woman of the Century: Leading American Women in All Walks of Life*, 1893, quoted in Elizabeth Fagg Olds, *Women of the Four Winds* (Boston: Houghton Mifflin, 1985), p. 10.
2. Laura and Guy Waterman make this point in "New England's Mountain Adventuress: Annie Smith Peck," *New England Outdoors* (May 1981), p. 15.
3. Fagg Olds, *Women of the Four Winds*, p. 12.
4. Quoted in Pam Cahn, "Ms. Annie Smith Peck," *Appalachia* (1975), p. 92. Cahn's essay, pp. 91–101, is an excellent source on Peck, as is Fagg Olds, *Women of the Four Winds*, pp. 7–70, and Dorcas Miller's *Adventurous Women* (Boulder, Colorado: Pruett Publishing, 2000), pp. 37–46. See, too, Watermans, "New England's Mountain Adventuress," op. cit., pp. 15–17, and pt. 2 of their article on Peck, "The Indomitable Annie Smith Peck: Conqueror of Mountains," *New England Outdoors* (June 1981), pp. 15–17, 46.

5. Annie Smith Peck, "Climbing Mt. Sorata," *Appalachia* 11 (1906), p. 95.
6. "Miss Peck Goes Out to Climb the Heights," *New York Times* (June 3, 1911), p. 11.
7. Flyer in the Peck Archives, Sophia Smith Collection, Smith College, Northampton, Mass. (italics in original).
8. Ibid.
9. Annie S. Peck, *A Search for the Apex of America* (New York: Dodd Mead, 1911), p. 217. Hereafter referred to as *Apex*.
10. Ibid., p. xi; "Annie Peck, 84, Lauded as First, Most Famous Woman Mountaineer," *Boston Transcript* (Oct. 20, 1935), in Peck Archives, Sophia Smith Collection, Smith College, Northampton, Mass.
11. Fagg Olds, *Women of the Four Winds*, pp. 8–9; "Climbing High Mountains," *New York Times* (Jan. 9, 1898), pt. 2, p. 2.; "Miss Peck's Story of Her Record Climb," *New York Times* (Dec. 23, 1908), p. 9.
12. *Apex*, p. ix.
13. S. Peck, "Up the Matterhorn," untitled newspaper clip from John Hay Library, Brown University (Aug. 23, 1895).
14. "Climbing High Mountains," op. cit.
15. "Up the Matterhorn," op. cit.; "A Survey of American Ascents in the Alps in the Nineteenth Century," pt. 2, *American Alpine Journal* 1 (1935), p. 510. All subsequent direct quotes about the Matterhorn climb are from "Up the Matterhorn."
16. *Apex*, p. x; *Boston Transcript*, op. cit.; flyer, op. cit.
17. "Climbing High Mountains," op. cit.; *Apex*, p. x; ibid. (italics in original).
18. Peck mentions this in "Climbing High Mountains," op. cit.; Julie Boardman also found a mention of this feat in the *White Mountain Echo* of July 1898. See Boardman's discussion of Peck in *When Women and Mountains Meet* (Etna, N.H.: Durand Press, 2001), pp. 120–25.
19. Peck, "Climbing Mt. Sorata," op. cit.
20. Ibid.
21. *Apex*, pp. 4–5.
22. Peck, "Climbing Mt. Sorata," op. cit., p. 97.
23. Letter, Oct. 9, 1892, in Peck Archives.
24. Ibid., p. 101; *Apex*, p. 51. Unless noted, subsequent direct quotes are from *Apex*.
25. Flyer, op. cit.; letter, April 14, 1904, Peck Archives, Sophia Smith Collection.

26. Peck, "Climbing Mt. Sorata," op. cit., p. 103.
27. Ibid., p. 104.

Sidebar: We Said, "Why Not?"
  1. Martha Whitman, "Camp Life for Ladies," *White Mountain Echo* (Aug. 2, 1879).
  2. Mary T. S. Schäffer, *A Hunter of Peace* (Banff, Alberta, Canada: The Whyte Foundation, 1980), p. 19. Prof. Deborah Bialeschki of the University of North Carolina—Chapel Hill discusses Schäffer in "We Said, 'Why Not?'—Historical Perspective on Women's Outdoor Pursuits," *Journal of Physical Education, Recreation, and Dance (JOP-ERD)* 62 (Feb. 1992), pp. 52–55. See, too, her article "The Feminist Movement and Women's Participation in Physical Recreation," *JOPERD* 60 (Jan. 1990), pp. 44–47, and Bialeschki et al., *Both Gains and Gaps: Feminist Perspectives on Women's Leisure* (State College, Penn.: Venture Publishing, 1999). These sources, as well as personal communication with Bialeschki, inform my thinking on Victorian-era women's recreation.
  3. Ibid., p. 17.
  4. Kathrene Pinkerton, *Woodcraft for Women*, (New York: Outing Publications, 1916) pp. 173–74.

Chapter 10. The Apex of America
  1. Annie S. Peck, *A Search for the Apex of America*. Unless noted otherwise, all subsequent direct quotes are from *Apex*.
  2. "Mountain Climber Back," *New York Times* (Nov. 17, 1904), p. 2.
  3. See Peck, "The First Ascent of Mount Huascaran," *Harper's* (Jan. 1909), p. 187.
  4. Pam Cahn, "Ms. Annie Smith Peck," *Appalachia* XX (June 1975), p. 100.
  5. Quoted in Daniel Buck, "Road Writers," *Americas* 50 (Jan. 11, 1998). Available at www.elibrary.com.
  6. Details of Peck's last years are offered in Fagg Olds, *Women of the Four Winds*, pp. 67–68; and Miller, *Adventurous Women*, pp. 45–46.
  7. *Boston Transcript* clipping, undated, Peck Archives, Sophia Smith Collection, Smith College, Northampton, Mass.
  8. "Annie Peck Dies, 84; Mountain Climber," *New York Times* (July 19, 1935).

Chapter 11. Fanny Bullock Workman and Dora Keen

1. Annals of the American Alpine Club, First Half Century, March 6, 1901, excerpts in Appalachian Club Library reading: "The smaller rash of resignations in 1913 is attributable to the apparent demeaning of Annie Peck Smith's [sic] Andean exploits by the well heeled and patrician Fanny Workman, an action supported by the Club."
2. William Hunter Workman, "In Memoriam: Mrs. Fanny Bullock Workman," *Appalachia* 16 (June 1925), p. 186.
3. Luree Miller, *On Top of the World: Five Women Explorers in Tibet* (Seattle: The Mountaineers, 1984), p. 103. Fanny is one of the five explorers on whom Miller focuses.
4. See H. S. H., Jr., William Hunter Workman, *American Alpine Journal* 3 (1938), p. 207.
5. Quoted in Lucille Daniel, "At Their Peak," *Appalachia* 50 (June 1995), p. 26.
6. Fanny Bullock Workman and William Hunter Workman, *In the Ice World of the Himálaya* (London: T. Fisher Unwin, 1900), p. 183.
7. Ibid., pp. 3–4.
8. Ibid.
9. Ibid.; Fanny Bullock Workman, "Recent First Ascents in the Himalaya," *Independent* 68 (June 2, 1910), p. 1203.
10. Ibid., "Pioneer Ascents in Balistan (Himalayas)," *Appalachia* 9 (1899–1901), pp. 251–56.
11. For a summary of the Workmans' expeditions, see William Hunter Workman's memoriam to Fanny, op. cit., pp. 186–90. In it, he identifies her altitude-setting peak as KUN. Lurea Miller, op. cit., identifies it as Pinnacle Peak.
12. Workman and Workman, *Ice World*, pp. 182–86, 188.
13. Ibid., p. 186.
14. "Miss Peck and Mrs. Workman," *Scientific American* (Feb. 12, 1910), p. 143; "Miss Peck Replies to Mrs. Workman," *Scientific American* (Feb 26, 1910), p. 183. See also Fanny Bullock Workman, "The Altitude of Mount Hauscaran," *Candian Alpine Journal* 2 (1910), pp. 197–98.
15. "Mrs. Workman Wins," *New York Times* (March 26, 1911), pt. 3, p. 3.
16. Fanny Bullock Workman, "First Ascents of the Hoh Lumba and Sosbon Glaciers in the North West Himalayas," *Independent* 55 (Dec. 31, 1903), p. 3111.

17. Fanny Bullock Workman and William Hunter Workman, *Two Summers in the Ice-Wilds of the Eastern Karakoram* (New York: Dutton, undated), p. 284.

18. William Hunter Workman, op. cit., pp. 186-88.

19. P. Farrar, "In Memoriam: Mrs. Fanny Bullock Workman," *Alpine Journal* 37 (1925), p. 182.

20. Dorothy Middleton, *Victorian Lady Travellers* (New York: Dutton, 1965), p. 81.

21. Fanny Bullock Workman, "Recent First Ascents in the Himilaya," *Independent* 68 (June 2, 1910), p. 1202, editor's note.

22. "The Romance of the Seventh Man," *New York World* (Aug. 6, 1916), Bryn Mawr Keen Papers, College Archives.

23. Dora Keen, "A Woman's Ascent of the Matterhorn," *Outlook* 95 (May 28, 1910), p. 210.

24. Keen, "A Woman's Climbs in the High Alps," *National Geographic* 22 (June 1911), p. 642; ibid., "Mountain Climbing in Alaska," *Appalachia* 12 (April 1912), p. 330.

25. Keen, "Exploring the Harvard Glacier," *Harper's Monthly* (Dec. 1915), p. 115; ibid., "Mountain Climbing in Alaska," op. cit., p. 331.

26. Keen, "Arctic Mountaineering by a Woman," *Scribner's Monthly* 52 (July 1912), p. 65.

27. Ibid.

28. Ibid., p. 68.

29. Ibid.

30. Keen, "Mountain Climbing in Alaska, " p. 339.

31. Keen, "First Up Mt. Blackburn," *The World's Work* 27 (Nov. 1913), p. 80. All subsequent direct quotes on this trip are from this source.

32. Keen, "Exploring the Harvard Glacier," p. 113; see also Lawrence Martin, "The National Geographic Society Researches in Alaska," *National Geographic* 22 (June 1911). Interestingly, Martin's report ran in the same issue as Dora's article on climbing in the Alps. Perhaps she was dreaming even at that time of someday joining the ranks of such explorers.

33. William W. K. Freeman, "In Memoriam: Dora Keen Handy," *Appalachia* 34 (June 1963), p. 540. For an account of Dora's last years, as well as a good description of her Alaskan travels, see Dorcas Miller's chapter, "A Thirst for Adventure," in *Adventurous Women*, pp. 55–64. Miller identifies Dora as making this statement to the *Anchorage Daily News*.

Sidebar: "The Thrill of Adventure in Every Step"

1. Arthur Davis, "The Profile of Mountaineering," *Appalachia* (Dec. 1946), pp. 166–68; and see Clark, *The Victorian Mountaineers*; Richard Mitchell, *Mountain Experience: The Psychology and Sociology of Adventure* (Chicago: University of Chicago Press, 1983), p. 41.
2. Charles E. Fay, "The Mountain as Influence in Modern Life," *Appalachia* 11 (June 1905), p. 37.
3. See, for instance, Lorraine Anderson, ed., *Sisters of the Earth* (New York: Vintage, 1991), and China Galland, *Women in the Wilderness* (New York: Harper & Row, 1980).
4. Elizabeth Le Blond, *The High Alps in Winter*, p. 4.
5. Annie S. Peck, "Practical Mountain Climbing," *Outing* 28 (Sept. 1901), p. 695.
6. Dora Keen, "Climbing the Giant's Tooth," *Scribner's Monthly* 60 (Oct. 1916), p. 434.

Afterword: The Next Generation: Miriam O'Brien Underhill

1. Esther Merriam, "Women Mountain-Climbers," *Harper's Bazar* 44 (Nov. 1910), p. 634.
2. Editorial, Ladies Alpine Club *Yearbook* (1930), p. 3.
3. *New Haven Journal-Courier*, undated newspaper clip, in Peck Archives, Sophia Smith Collection, Smith College, Northampton, Mass.
4. Christopher Goetze, "In Memoriam: Miriam Underhill," *Appalachia* 41 (June 1976), p. 125.
5. Ibid.
6. Miriam Underhill, *Give Me the Hills* (Riverside, Ct.: Chatham Press, 1956), p. 42. Hereafter referred to as *Hills*.
7. Ibid., p. 73, quoting a guidebook.
8. Lunn, *A Century of Mountaineering*, p. 173.
9. I am indebted to Julie Boardman for biographical information on Miriam Underhill. In addition to her section on Underhill in *When Women and Mountains Meet*, she also shared her correspondence with Miriam's son Robert and excerpts from an out-of-print book by Miriam's brother Lincoln. See also Goetze, op. cit, pp. 125–27.
10. *Hills*, p. 248.
11. Ibid., p. 54.

12. Ibid., p. 149; O'Brien, Miriam E., "Without Men," *Appalachia* 19 (Dec. 1932), pp. 187–8.
13. *Hills*, p. 154.
14. Ibid.
15. Ibid., p. 169.
16. Edith Tucker, personal communication, July 1999.
17. *Hills*, p. 249.
18. George Hamilton, personal communication, July 1999.
19. Bill Nichols, personal communication, July 1999.
20. *Hills*, p. 248.
21. Mrs. Herbert Dawson, editorial, Ladies Alpine Club *Yearbook* (1932), p. 1.

Bibliography

These are full citations for books cited in the text, as well as other sources used in the research but not specifically referenced. Journal articles and other publications, private conversations, and unpublished documents are fully cited in the endnotes.

A Lady [Jane Freshfield], *Alpine Byways*, London: Longman, Green, Longman, and Roberts, 1861.

Abraham, George, The Complete Mountaineer, London: Methuen & Co., 1907.

Anderson, Lorraine, ed., *Sisters of the Earth*, New York: Vintage, 1991.

Andrews, B. M., "Reminiscences, 1906–1936," Ladies Alpine Club *Yearbook* (1937).

Barrows, Samuel J., and Isabel C. Barrows, *The Shaybacks in Camp*, Boston: Houghton Mifflin, 1887.

Bialeschki, M. Deborah, "The Feminist Movement and Women's Participation in Recreation," *Journal of Physical Education, Recreation, and Dance* 60 (Jan. 1990), pp. 44–7.

————, "We Said, 'Why Not?'—A Historical Perspective on Women's Physical Outdoor Pursuits," *Journal of Physical Education, Recreation, and Dance* (Feb. 1992), pp. 52–5.

Birkett, Bill, and Bill Peascod, *Women Climbing: 200 Years of Achievement*, Seattle: The Mountaineers, 1989. A well-referenced overview of women's climbing.

Birkett, Dea, *Spinsters Abroad*, New York: Basil Blackwell, 1989. Looks at the social context of Victorian lady explorers.

Blakeney, T. S., "Some Notes on A. F. Mummery," *Alpine Journal* 60 (May 1955).

Boardman, Julie, *When Women and Mountains Meet*, Etna, N.H.: Durand Press, 2001. Well-researched look at women who explored and climbed in New Hampshire's White Mountains.

Brown, Rebecca A., "True Grit," AMC *Outdoors* 65 (Oct. 1999), pp. 28–34.

———, "Walking in Their Footsteps," AMC *Outdoors* 67 (Sept. 2001), pp. 34–39.

Cameron, John H., "Should American Climbers Adopt European Methods?" *Mazamas* 2 (1905), pp. 214–19.

Catalogue of Equipment for Mountaineers, exhibited at the Alpine Club, London, Dec. 1899. Booklet, collection of Appalachian Club Library.

Chamberlain, Alan, "Two Suggestions for Mountaineering Outfits," *Appalachia* (1906), pp. 287–89.

Clark, Sir Kenneth, *Civilization*, videotape, no. 11, "The Worship of Nature," BBC, 1969, Films, Inc., Chicago, Ill.

Clark, Ronald, *The Victorian Mountaineers*, London: B. T. Batsford, 1953. Breezy and informative overview of the times, with a chapter on "The Women."

———, *An Eccentric in the Alps*, London: Museum Press, 1959. Biography of William Coolidge includes much discussion of Meta Brevoort and Tschingel.

Cogan, Frances B., *All-American Girl*, Athens: University of Georgia Press, 1989. Historical perspectives on "real womanhood."

Connelly, Dolly, "Bloomers and Blouses Plus Waving Alpenstocks," magazine reprint, no citation, collection of Appalachian Club Library, Boston.

Cook, Edith, "A Reconnaissance on the Carter Range," *Appalachia* 3 (1884), pp. 299–314.

Coolidge, W. A. B., *The Alps in Nature and History*, London: Methuen & Co., 1908.

———, *Alpine Studies*, London: Longmans, Green & Co., 1912.

Cowles, Elizabeth S., "The East Ridge of the Grand Teton," Ladies Alpine Club *Yearbook* (1939), pp. 5–11. Refers to Mummery's "an easy day for a lady" without irony.

D'Angeville, Henriette, *My Ascent of Mont Blanc*, London: HarperCollins, 1991. Dervla Murphy wrote the introduction to this recent translation.

Dann, Christine, and Pip Lynch, *Wilderness Women: Stories of New Zealand Women at Home in the Wilderness*, Auckland: Penguin, 1989. Looks at the meaning of wilderness for women.

De Berard, Hazel, "Memories of Randolph," *Appalachia* (June 1956), pp. 190–98. Humorous account of the Ravine House and its occupants in the early days of the AMC, including a skit participated in by the "formidable Annie S. Peck, of mountaineering fame."

Dent, C. T., ed., *Mountaineering*, The Badminton Library, London: Longmans, Green & Co., 1892. Includes a chapter on "Equipment and Outfit" with a subsection on a "Climbing outfit for ladies."

Dickerman, Mike, and Steve Smith, *The 4,000-Footers of the White Mountains*, Littleton, N.H.: Bondcliff Books, 2001.

Douglass, A. E., "Effects of High-Mountain Climbing," *Appalachia* (1897), pp. 361–67.

Ehrenreich, Barbara, and Deirdre English, *For Her Own Good*, New York: AnchorPress/Doubleday, 1978. Historical advice to women, including on health and exercise.

Engel, Claire-Elaine, "Early Lady Climbers," *Alpine Journal* 54 (1943), pp. 51–59.

———, *A History of Mountaineering in the Alps*, London: George Allen & Unwin, 1950.

———, *They Came to the Hills*, London: George Allen & Unwin, 1952. Includes chapters on Lucy Walker and her family and Elizabeth Le Blond.

———, *Mont Blanc, An Anthology*, New York: Rand McNally, 1965.

———, *Mountaineering in the Alps: An Historical Survey*, London: George Allen & Unwin, 1970.

Fox, Charles E., "Description of a Model Tent and Camping Outfit," *Mazamas* 1 (1896), p. 267.

Galland, China, *Women in the Wilderness*, New York: Harper & Row, 1980.

Gould, John M., *How to Camp Out*, New York: Scribner, Armstrong, & Co., 1877.

Gove, Bill, *J. E. Henry's Logging Railroads*, Littleton, N.H.: Bondcliff Books, 1998.

Grant, Dr., "An Early American Attempt on Mont Blanc [1839]," *American Alpine Journal* 2 (1935), pp. 494–507.

Gribble, Francis, *The Early Mountaineers*, London: T. Fisher Unwin, 1899.

H. S. H. Jr., "William Hunter Workman," *American Alpine Club* 3 (1938), pp. 207–9.

Hall, Richard, *The Art of Mountain Tramping*, London: H. F. G. Witherby, 1932.

Hamilton, Helen, *Mountain Madness*, London: W. Collins Sons, 1922.

Hays, Samuel P., *Conservation and the Gospel of Efficiency*, Cambridge, Mass.: Harvard University Press, 1959.

Henderson, Karla, "Perspectives on Analyzing Gender, Women, and Leisure," *Journal of Leisure Research* 26 (1994), pp. 119–37.

Henderson, Karla A., M. Deborah Bialeschki, Susan M. Shaw, and Valeria J. Freysinger, *Both Gains and Gaps: Feminist Perspectives on Women's Leisure*, State College, Penn.: Venture Publishing, 1999.

Hickson, J. W. A., "Psychological Aspects of Mountaineering," *American Alpine Club Journal* 3 (1931), pp. 259–67.

Holifield, E. Brooks, *Era of Persuasion*, Boston: Twayne Publishers,1989. Early American thought on culture, wilderness, and landscape.

Hurd, Marjorie, "Fashion on the Peaks, 1876–1935," *Appalachia* (Nov. 1935), pp. 372–9.

"In Memoriam: Mary Vaux Walcott," *American Alpine Journal* 4 (1941), pp. 285–7.

Keen, Dora, Papers, Bryn Mawr College Archives.

———, "How I Climbed a 14,000-Foot Mountain," *Ladies Home Journal* 30 (Aug. 1913), pp. 7, 41.

LaBastille, Anne. *Women and Wilderness*, San Francisco: Sierra Club Books, 1980.

Ladies' Alpine Club Yearbook (1975). The last journal before the club merged with the Alpine Club. Reminiscences by many members and a list of major climbs.

Le Blond, Mrs. Aubrey, *The High Alps in Winter*, London: Sampson Low, Marston, Searle, & Rivington, 1883.

———, *High Life and Towers of Silence*, London: Sampson Low, Marston, Searle, & Rivington, 1886.

———, *True Tales of Mountain Adventure*, New York: Dutton, 1903.

———, *Day In, Day Out*, London: John Lane, 1928. Le Blond's reminiscences and autobiography.

Lerner, Gerda, *The Female Experience*, Indianapolis: Bobbs Merrill, 1977.

Lunn, Sir Arnold, *A Century of Mountaineering*, London: George Allen & Unwin, 1957.

————, *Matterhorn Centenary*, New York: Rand McNally, 1965.

Mangan, J. A., and Roberta J. Park, eds., *From 'Fair Sex' to Feminism*, London: Frank Cass, 1987. Scholarly essays on women and sports in the United States and Great Britain in the nineteenth and early twentieth centuries.

Mazel, David, *Mountaineering Women: Stories by Early Climbers*, College Station: Texas A&M University Press, 1994. Excerpts from women's own writing, with an extensive annotated bibliography.

McHenry, Robert, ed., "Annie Smith Peck," and "Fanny Bullock Workman," in *Her Heritage: A Biographical Encyclopedia of Famous American Women* (1995), online at www.elibrary.com. Brief biographical sketches.

Merchant, Carolyn, *The Death of Nature*, San Francisco: Harper & Row, 1980. Women, science, and culture through the ages.

Meredith, Jon, "Women in the Appalachian Mountain Club," unpublished manuscript, Dartmouth College (spring 1999). Appalachian Mountain Club Library collection.

Middleton, Dorothy, *Victorian Lady Travellers*, New York: Dutton, 1965. Social context of English explorers.

Miller, Dorcas, *Adventurous Women: Inspiring Lives of Early Outdoorswomen*, Boulder, Colo.: Pruett Publishing, 2000. Excerpts from women's writing and biographical introductions to women, including Annie Smith Peck, Martha Whitman, and Dora Keen.

Miller, Luree, *On Top of the World: Five Women Explorers in Tibet*, Seattle: The Mountaineers, 1984. Includes a chapter on Fanny Bullock Workman.

Miss Jemima's Swiss Journal, London: Putnam, 1963. Written in 1863 for private circulation.

Mitchell, Richard, *Mountain Experience: The Psychology and Sociology of Adventure*, Chicago: University of Chicago Press, 1983. A contemporary sociologist looks at why people climb.

Morin, Nea A., "Ladies Only," Ladies Alpine Club *Yearbook* (1935), pp. 30–38. Manless climbing by Miriam Underhill's contemporaries.

————, "Miriam Underhill," *Alpine Journal* 82 (1977), pp. 272–3.

Mummery, A. F. *My Climbs in the Alps and Caucasus*, Oxford: Basil Blackwell, 1936. Includes a chapter by Mary Mummery, "The Teufelsgrat."

Nash, Roderick, *Wilderness and the American Mind*, New Haven, Conn.: Yale University Press, 1982.

O'Brien, Miriam E., "A First Season in the Oberland," *American Alpine Journal* 1 (1929), pp. 151–59.

———, "First Steps in the Oberland," pp. 5–13, and "Finsteraarhorn (North-East Face)" and "Dreieckhorn," pp. 17–28, both in Ladies Alpine Club *Yearbook* (1931).

———, "On Some of Gertrude Bell's Routes in the Oberland," *American Alpine Journal* 3 (1931), pp. 282–89.

Olds, Elizabeth Fagg, *Women of the Four Winds*, Boston: Houghton Mifflin, 1985. Informative chapter on Annie Smith Peck.

Peck, Annie Smith, Papers, Sophia Smith Collection, Smith College, Northampton, Mass.

Peck, Annie S., "A Woman in the Andes," *Harper's* 114 (Dec. 1906), pp. 3–14.

———, *A Search for the Apex of America*, New York: Dodd, Mead, 1911.

Pinkerton, Kathrene, *Woodcraft for Women*, New York: Outing Publications, 1916.

Pope, Leyla, "Women Climbing," Cambridge University Mountaineering Club *Journal* (1996), from the Web site www.cam.ac.uk/societies/cumc/journals/96/leyla2.htm. A brief discussion of the meaning of Mummery's "easy day for a lady" quote.

"Proposed Twin Mountain Path," *White Mountain Echo* (Aug. 5, 1882), p. 7. Presumably written by A. E. Scott, asks for donations for trail construction.

Pychowska, Lucia D., "Loon Pond Mountain," *Appalachia* 2 (May 1881), pp. 284–86.

Pychowska, Marian, "Explorations Near West Compton," *Appalachia* 2 (July 1880), pp. 166–68. Climbing trees to get a better view.

"Queen of the Climbers," undated newspaper clip on Annie Smith Peck, Bentley Historical Library, University of Michigan. Used with permission.

Raeburn, Harold, *Mountaineering Art*, New York: Frederick Stokes Co., 1920.

Rahman, Shaista, "Annie Smith Peck" (1998), from the Web site www.anniesmithpeck.com.

Roberts, Tina, unpublished, untitled manuscript on outdoorswomen and dress from a feminist perspective, Appalachian Mountain Club archives.

Robertson, Janet, "Six Women Mountaineers," *The Climbing Art* 11 (June 1989), pp. 6–15.

————, *The Magnificent Mountain Women of Colorado*, Lincoln: University of Nebraska Press, 1990.

Rowan, Peter, and June Hammond Rowan, *Mountain Summers*, Gorham, N.H.: Gulfside Press, 1995.

Schäffer, Mary T. S., *A Hunter of Peace*, Banff, Alberta, Canada: The Whyte Foundation, 1980.

Schama, Simon, *Landscape and Memory*, New York: Vintage, 1995.

Sweeney, John P., "Food for Mountain Climbers," *Mazamas* 3 (March 1907), pp. 49–54. Cites Annie Smith Peck as recommending chewing coca leaves for high-altitude stimulation.

Sweetser, Moses F., *The White Mountains, A Handbook for Travellers*, Boston: James Osgood, 1881. First published in 1876.

Tarbell, Arthur Winslow, "Mrs. Fanny Bullock Workman," *New England Magazine* 42 (Dec. 1905), pp. 487–90.

Thomas, William I., *Sex and Society*, Chicago: University of Chicago Press, 1907.

Twin, Stephanie, *Out of the Bleachers*, New York: Feminist Press, 1979.

Underhill, Miriam, *Give Me the Hills*, Riverside, Conn.: Chatham Press, 1956.

Underhill, Mrs. Robert L. M. (Miriam O'Brien), "Climbing Notes from the American West," Ladies Alpine Club *Yearbook* (1935), pp. 21–30.

Wallach, Janet, *Desert Queen*, New York: Nan A. Talese/Doubleday, 1996.

Waterman, Laura, and Guy Waterman, "New England's Mountain Adventuress: Annie Smith Peck," *New England Outdoors* (May 1981), pp. 15–17.

————, "The Indomitable Annie Smith Peck: Conqueror of Mountains," *New England Outdoors* (June 1981), pp. 17, 46.

————, *Forest and Crag*, Boston: Appalachian Mountain Club, 1989. Comprehensive history of tramping and camping in New York and New England.

The White Mountains: Place and Perceptions, Durham: University of New Hampshire, 1980. Art exhibit catalog.

Whitman, M. F., "A Climb Through Tuckerman Ravine," *Appalachia* 1 (June 1877), pp. 131–37. The first story of a perilous mountain adventure published in AMC's journal.

————, "Camp Life for Ladies," *Appalachia* 2 (June 1879), pp. 44–48.

Whymper, Edward, *Scrambles Amongst the Alps*, London: John Murray, 1900. First published 1871.

Williams, Cicely, *Women on the Rope*, London: George Allen & Unwin Ltd., 1973.

———, "The Feminine Share in Mountain Adventure I," *Alpine Journal* 81 (1976), pp. 90–100.

Winthrop, Geoffrey, *Mountain Craft*, New York: Scribner, 1920.

Workman, Fanny Bullock, "Pioneer Ascents in Balistan (Himalayas)," *Appalachia* 9 (1900?), pp. 251–56.

———, "First Ascents of the Hoh Lumba and Sosbon Glaciers in the North West Himalayas," *Independent* 55 (Dec. 31, 1903), pp. 3108–12.

———, "A Woman in the Himalayas" *Putnam's* 7 (Jan. 1910), pp. 474–82.

———, "Recent First Ascents in the Himalaya," *Independent* 68 (June 2, 1910), pp. 1202–10.

———, "The Altitude of Mount Huascaran," *Canadian Alpine Journal* 2 (1910), pp. 197–98.

———, "Exploring the Rose," *Independent* 85 (Jan. 10, 1916), pp. 54–56.

Workman, Fanny Bullock, and William Hunter Workman, *In the Ice World of the Himálaya*, London: T. Fisher Unwin, 1900.

———, *Peaks and Glaciers of Nun Kun*, New York: Charles Scribner's Son, 1909.

———, *Two Summers in the Ice-Wilds of the Eastern Karakoram*, New York: Dutton, undated, probably around 1917, when English edition was published.

Index

Abruzzi, Duke of, 145, 201, 203
Adams, Mary, 162
Alaska, 189, 202–214
Algerian Memories (Workman and
    Workman), 194
Almer, Christian, 58, 63, 66, 68, 71,
    72, 73
Almer, Ulrich, 58, 66, 71, 107
Alpine Byways (Freshfield), 36
Alpine Club, 6, 34, 36, 49, 63
Alpine Journal, 66–68, 75, 87–88, 107
Andean Exploration Society, 147
Andenmatten, Franz, 98, 103, 104, 106
Anderegg, Melchior, 46, 47, 52, 53
Appalachia, 22, 122, 124, 129, 224
Appalachian Mountain Club (AMC),
    121–123, 124
Aymonod, Jean Baptiste, 151, 152

Bacheler, George, 148
Balmat, Jacques, 10–11
Barrett, John, 206, 207, 208, 209, 210,
    211
Bernese Oberland, 15
Bietschhorn, 67–72
Bishop, Isabella Bird, 200
Bishorn (Beishorn), 88–89
Bivouacking, 61, 73
Bloomer, Amelia, 127
Bolivia, 147, 153–160
Boss, Emil, 107, 109, 111
Brevoort, Marguerite "Meta," 37, 43,
    50, 53, 56, 58, 59–62, 65–76
Bristow, Lily, 99, 111–115
Brocken specter, 70
Bullock, Alexander Hamilton, 190
Burgener, Alexander, 88, 98, 102–103,
    104, 105, 112
Burnaby, Fred, 83
Burnaby, Arthur St. Vincent, 83

Cameron, Una, 218
Campbell, Miss and Mrs., 15
Canadian Rockies, 162
Cannon Mountain, 125–126
Carr, Ellis, 111
Carter Range, 124
Clark, Ronald, 62, 72–73
"Climbing Girl, A," 55
Clothing, 6, 18, 21–23, 49, 50–51, 65,
    80, 95, 118, 126–128, 155, 219
Cockerell, S. P., 66
Col du Géant, 15
Cole, Mrs. Henry Warwick, 35
Collie, Norman, 111
Conway, Martin, 145, 147
Cook, Edith, 123, 124, 125–126, 140
Cook, Eugene, 123, 124, 140
Coolidge, Frederick William, 62
Coolidge, W. A. B., 10, 43, 52–53, 56,
    58, 60, 61–62, 65, 66–68, 71–76
Couttet, Joseph-Marie, 14, 23
Couttet, Michael, 36, 42
Crawford, Mary, 41

Damesme, Alice, 218, 222, 223
d'Angeville, Henriette, 11, 12–15,
    18–30, 36, 39
Darwin, Leonard, 200
Dauphiné, 72, 74–75
Davis, Arthur, 191
Dent Blanche, 67, 107
Diavolezza Pass, 89–91
Dome du Goûter, 100
Dogs
    Diane (with d'Angeville), 25, 64
    sled, 204, 205, 206, 208, 213
    Tschingel (with Brevoort), 58, 60,
        62, 63–64, 66, 67, 69, 75

Eiger, 48, 60, 67